KU-634-572

The Business of Nature-Based Tourism

Bob McKercher

Hospitality Press
Melbourne

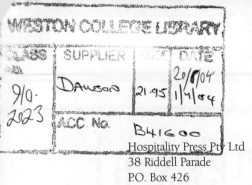

WESTON COLLEGE LIBRARY

CLASS	SUPPLIER	PRICE	DATE
910. 2023	DAWSON	21.95	20/8/04 1/4/54
ACC. No.	B41600		

Hospitality Press Pty Ltd
38 Riddell Parade
P.O. Box 426
Elsternwick Victoria 3185
Australia
Telephone (03) 9528 5021 Fax (03) 9528 2645

The Business of Nature-Based Tourism

First published 1998.

This book is copyright. Apart from any fair dealing for the purposes of private study, research, criticism or review as permitted under the Copyright Act, no part may be reproduced, stored in a retrieval system, or transmitted, in any form or by any means, electronic, mechanical, photocopying, recording, or otherwise without prior written permission. Inquiries should be made to Hospitality Press.

Copying for educational purposes
Where copies of part or the whole of a book are made under Sections 53B or 53D of the Copyright Act, the law requires that records of such copying be kept. In such cases the copyright owner is entitled to claim payment.

© Hospitality Press 1998.

National Library of Australia
Cataloguing-in-Publication data:

McKercher, Robert D. (Robert Douglas) 1954–
The business of nature-based tourism.

Bibliography.
Includes index.
ISBN 1 86250 475 X.

1. Small business - Australia - Marketing. 2. Tourist trade - Australia - Marketing. 3. Tourist trade - Environmental aspects - Australia. 4. Ecotourism - Australia. 5. Conservation of natural resources - Australia. 1. Title.

338.479194

Designed and typeset by John van Loon
Edited by Frances Wade (Wade's Distractions)
Printed in Australia by Sands Print Group
Published by Hospitality Press Pty Ltd (ACN 006 473 454)

WESTON COLLEGE

B41600

910·2023
FSS/ite

The Business of
Nature-Based Tourism

To Hilary

Contents

Preface

This book represents the culmination of a process that began in the early 1980s when I first saw the light, left the remote sensing game and embarked on my career in tourism. It began innocently enough when I started working as a guide and trip leader for Gary Watts and then for Dean Hammill, the owners of the Ottawa Outing Club, an adventure tourism business. Gary is no longer with us, having died in a skiing accident in the Canadian Rockies. That job piqued my interest in tourism and encouraged me to change my career path and pursue higher studies in tourism. Whilst doing my Masters degree at Carleton University with Duncan Anderson, I had an opportunity to become involved in a study of adventure tour operators throughout Canada. The study was most enlightening; among other things it revealed that, with few exceptions, most of the businesses studied were marginally viable and that the biggest factor inhibiting their viability was the lack of skills shown by the operators.

My experience in the industry resulted in my being offered a position as executive director of the Northern Ontario Tourist Outfitters Association, a trade association comprising over 1000 wilderness lodges and resorts in the Canadian Shield area of the province. Working with several presidents of the Association—Darrell Rogerson, Rod Munford and Bill Chambers—I again was struck by how many of the problems encountered by operators were due to their own lack of skills in operating and marketing their businesses. The successful operators, on the other hand, had these skills and knew how to use them to make their businesses grow. Indeed, it occurred to me that the greatest weakness of the tourism industry was the industry itself. Many people simply did not know what they were doing.

That revelation convinced me that the greatest contribution I could make to the betterment of tourism was to leave industry and enter the formal education system. And so, in early 1990, I emigrated to Australia to begin a new career in a new country. However, some things do not change. Here, too, I was struck by the disparity in knowledge, skills and abilities among tour operators. Australia has a world-class tourism product run by world-class tourism professionals. Of this it can be proud. Many tourism businesses are run at an extremely high level. Nevertheless, it is also evident that many struggling operators do not have the skills to perform the tasks needed to run a viable business.

And so, the idea of writing a book to help new and existing operators enhance their skill base was born. Over the last 18 months, I have had a great deal of assistance from a number of people in and associated with the tourism industry. In particular, I would like to thank Peter Shelley and the staff at the Victorian Tourism Operators Association for their co-operation and assistance. In addition, I would like to thank the literally hundreds of tour operators both here and overseas whom I have interviewed, surveyed and spoken to over the years for their ideas and suggestions. Megan Ritchie and Ross Dowling need to be singled out for special thanks for reading the manuscript. I would also like to thank Teresa Crowley for the artwork. And of course, this book would not have been written without the love and support of Hilary, Oscar, Lily and Poppy. While these people must all share in any success I have with the book, I alone must bear responsibility for any of its faults.

Introduction

Nature-based tourism, encompassing ecotourism, adventure tourism, out-door-oriented educational tourism and a whole host of other types of outdoor-oriented, non-mass tourism experiences, is arguably the fastest-growing segment of the Australian tourism industry. As a result, a wide variety of new business opportunities have emerged in recent years. However, a number of questions have been raised about the suitability of many new entrants to run professional and profitable nature-based tourism ventures. Typically, many of these entrants are under-capitalised, have no previous experience in tourism, lack relevant business skills, have no understanding of how to develop and market tourism products and lack a basic knowledge of the way tourism works. Moreover, many do not know where to go to learn the skills. As a result, the failure rate of nature-based tourism ventures is high, while many that survive operate well below optimal levels.

The text of this book has been written to address many of the problems that affect the viability of the nature-based tourism sector. Adopting an unashamedly marketing-oriented approach, it sets out to make the reader aware of a variety of research, business planning, financial, marketing and operational skills that are necessary to develop and operate successful nature-based tourism ventures. At its heart, it argues that any successful business begins by delivering products that satisfy the needs, wants and desires of its clients. This objective can only be achieved if the business knows who its clients are and understands their motives. In addition, the operator must be able to target his or her products at market segments that are large enough to be profitable, interested in the products on offer, easy to access in a cost-effective manner and willing to pay the price asked.

Chapter 1 sets the context for the book by presenting a review of the current literature on matters that concern the viability of many nature-based tour operators.

Chapters 2 and 3 examine a number of issues relating to business planning and the role that effective research plays in vetting ideas to identify potentially good business opportunities. The single greatest cause of business failures is the failure to identify a sound business opportunity from the outset. Too many people automatically think that, because they like to do something, it presents a workable business opportunity. These chapters outline how to use research and the business planning process to eliminate as much risk and uncertainty as possible before launching new products or ventures.

Chapters 4 to 6 discuss the legal and financial considerations involved in operating nature-based tourism businesses. Chapter 4 outlines possible legal structures for the venture and looks at licensing matters and other legal considerations, including obligations under the Trade Practices Act. Chapters 5 and 6 look at the vexing, but all important, issues of financial planning, budgeting, cash flow management and the costing and pricing of nature-based tourism ventures. Nature-based tour operators face a number of imposing financial challenges that are unique to their sector.

Chapters 7 through 11 discuss a variety of marketing issues that relate to the special needs of this sector. Chapter 7 begins with a discussion of the need to think strategically about positioning nature-based tourism products in the marketplace. The concept of sustainable competitive advantage is discussed as are a number of means available to define a product's unique attributes. Chapter 8 examines the nexus between nature-based tourism products and their markets. It begins by defining what a product is and explains that, at their core, products must satisfy a client's internal needs or wants. The chapter then proceeds to discuss the nature-based tourism market, its motives and its actions. Chapter 9 discusses pricing from a marketing perspective. While Chapter 6 looked at the financial considerations involved in pricing, in this chapter price is recognised as an important tactical tool that is a key step in the marketing process. Chapter 10 reviews the seemingly complex, but really quite simple, tourism distribution system. It explains how the various layers of the tourism distribution system (travel agents, wholesalers and inbound operators) work, sets out the benefits and risks involved in using different agents to sell one's product and discusses the costs involved in using intermediaries. Chapter 11 looks at the broad issue of tourism promotion. It begins by reviewing the buying process and then discusses a number of features of successful promotions. The chapter then studies the four major promotional methods used by the tourism industry: advertising, personal selling, sales promotions and publicity and public relations.

Chapter 12 examines the practicalities of developing and delivering tours. It begins by exploring the idea of packaging and discusses the importance of having demand generators or icons around which to build a tour. It then examines a number of factors involved in itinerary development, route selection and the component parts of a tour. This chapter also offers a number of practical suggestions that address the logistics of tour development.

Chapter 13 examines the subject of systems and, in particular, looks at on-site systems and self-management systems. It identifies the types of operational systems needed to ensure that a business runs efficiently, safely and in an ecologically sustainable manner. It also examines a number of issues relating to risk management and risk minimisation. Finally, the chapter looks at how individual operators must manage their own time effectively to ensure that they are not consumed by the business.

Lastly, Chapter 14 looks at some of the ethical concerns involved in running nature-based tourism businesses. It begins by discussing what an ethical business is and reviews some of the tenets of operating an ethical enterprise. The chapter then looks at the issue of ecologically sustainable development and examines how tourism can operate within ESD guidelines. As well, the relations between tourism and other users of public land, and between tourism and local residents, are examined.

A profile of the nature-based tourism sector

*n*ature-based tourism is one of the most exciting sectors in the tourism industry, growing by an estimated 10 to 30 per cent per annum.[1] The scope of nature-based tourism encompasses adventure tourism, ecotourism, alternative tourism, educational tourism, anti-tourism, sustainable tourism, responsible tourism and many other forms of outdoor-oriented, non-mass tourism.[2] It has been normal practice to put all these activities under the common label of 'ecotourism'. 'Nature-based tourism', however, is a more all-encompassing term and has suffered less from the marketing overkill that has damaged the credibility of 'ecotourism'.[3]

The sector is certainly diverse. The motives of participants and the experiences offered by various operators differ widely. Some 'ecotourism' operators feel superior to 'adventure' tourism operators. Yet, from the perspective of practical business planning, product development, product delivery, operations and ethics, these businesses have much in common. For this reason, the term 'nature-based tourism' will be used throughout the text to cover them all.

A number of factors have led to the rapid growth of this sector. Global interest in environmental matters has made more and more people want to experience our unique outdoor wonders. A desire for a healthier lifestyle has prompted many tourists to forsake traditional sun, sand and sea holidays for more active alternatives. Better-educated travellers are more interested in meaningful vacation activities; more sophisticated travellers expect their vacation experiences to meet higher-order personal needs.[4] Further, as society becomes more alienating, people are beginning to prefer personalised, small group holidays, rather than anonymous, mass tourism experiences.[5]

Nature-based tourism plays an important role in the delivery of a world-class tourism product. Firms operating in this field:

- help broaden a region's product base by providing ancillary services or experiences to complement mainstream accommodation and attractions
- provide special interest tourism experiences for niche markets
- provide low-cost business opportunities for people in regional centres
- can reduce adverse social and environmental impacts by providing a means of controlling tourists' activities
- provide a source of management funds for protected areas through licensing fees
- can better spread the message of environmental protection.

To a high degree, nature-based tourism ventures are typified by what have been described as micro businesses.[6] These tend to be small operations that lie outside the mainstream of the travel industry and may be 'bedevilled by inadequate marketing resources and an inability to forge links with the global tourism system'.[7] The businesses are run by owner-operators who have few or no full-time staff other than family members. Most have no formal business or tourism training. Many of the businesses are marginal, and many owners are forced to seek a second income to keep them operational. Too many operators say they are in the tourism game as a 'lifestyle' choice. Distressingly, the drop-out rate of failed businesses is extremely high. The sector needs help.

This text sets out to address many of the practical business planning, tour development and marketing needs of the nature-based tour operator. It has been written predominantly for small tourist operations—those businesses in which all management functions are performed by the principals. It is designed to give practical advice to people in the industry or those wishing to enter the industry who have no previous business training.

Features of small business

It is necessary to understand the features common to all small business before examining the unique aspects of nature-based tourism. As shown in Figure 1.1, small operations tend to be run by people with specialised but narrow skills who often have no prior experience in business. Management decisions are influenced by emotion rather than rational analysis. Many operators react to situations rather than lead them. As a result, too many small businesses are allowed to drift along, and too few are driven strategically.

Figure 1.1   Features of small business

- Small management team
- Strong owner influence
- Lack of specialist staff
- Multi-functional management roles
- Informal and inadequate planning and control systems
- Limited ability to obtain finance
- Labour-intensive nature of work
- Limited market share and heavy reliance on a few customers

Source: Reynolds, Savage & Williams (1994)[8]

Owning a small business can be either an extremely positive, self-affirming activity or, if the venture does not work out, one that takes a tremendous emotional toll. Small business owners often gain a strong sense of personal satisfaction and a feeling of achievement from developing a successful operation. Being one's own boss and being able to make decisions are other frequently identified benefits, as is the ability to use one's own skills and expertise. On the other hand, small business owners may work exceptionally long hours and receive a low income relative to those hours. There is also a real risk that the owner may become socially isolated, especially during heavy work periods.[9]

One feature of small business ownership that is hard for outsiders to appreciate is that the business becomes an extension of the owner's persona. The owner-operator lives the business 24 hours a day. Its success is his or her success; its failure represents a personal failure. In essence, the business becomes an avocation as well as a vocation. Employees, regardless of how committed they are to the organisation, can still quit a job. Owners who quit leave a part of themselves behind.

Unfortunately, small businesses are more likely to fail than to succeed. An Australian Bankers' Association study revealed that three-quarters of all small businesses fail within their first five years of operation.[10] Reasons cited included a lack of management skills and ability among principals; inadequate, inaccurate or non-existent books and records; a failure to operate with fluctuating costs and prices; excessive private drawings; and, arguably most importantly, a lack of start-up and ongoing capital. Reynolds, Savage and Williams, in their book *Your Own Business*, add that businesses collapse because of cash-flow problems, the failure to develop and implement adequate systems and an inability to identify appropriate markets and target them effectively.[11] Others have argued that the main reason why many a business fails in its first years is that the owner simply does not identify a good opportunity when it arises.[12]

In many ways, the tourism sector in general and the nature-based tourism sector in particular are no different from other sectors. Many of the problems facing the tourism industry are the same: a lack of business planning, inefficient operations, business and social isolation, under-capitalisation and a reliance on small numbers of clients. Nature-based businesses must also face the additional problems of highly seasonal and volatile operating conditions, lack of brand awareness, severe price competition and locations a great distance from main markets.[13] While no detailed study has been carried out on the entry and exit of tour operators, anecdotal evidence suggests that the drop-out rate among small tour operators is at least as high as the failure rate for small business in general.

Features of the nature-based tourism industry

How large is the nature-based tourism sector? No one knows for sure, but the best estimates suggest that Australia has about 600 ecotourism operators[14] and another 2000 or so adventure, outdoor or personalised tour businesses.[15] The largest concentrations are found in Queensland, New South Wales and Victoria. A recent study of the ecotourism sector reveals that ecotourism operators employ about 6500 full-time, part-time and casual employees, providing the equivalent of 4500 person-years of employment.[16] The collective payroll for the sector is about $115 million and its turnover is about $250 million. Overall, the ecotourism sector represents about one per cent of total employment and revenue generated from tourism. Its importance, however, lies in its export potential, in that ecotourism represents three per cent of total tourism export earnings. The general consensus is that nature-based tourism is growing at a rate faster than mainstream tourism, although Blamey questions this.[17] No figures are available on other aspects of the nature-based sector.

Nature-based tourism is typified by small, regionally displaced businesses. These businesses tend to have higher per capita fixed costs than mass tourism operations for a number of reasons: the need for minimal impact practices, the lack of scale economies, the requirement for a higher level of personal service and the need to provide more detailed information and interpretation. As a result, this sector faces a major challenge in managing its profitability.[18] Cotterill's nation-wide profile of larger ecotourism operators suggests that:

- the industry is typified by small operators with four or fewer staff
- the average life of enterprises is ten years
- each operator provides mainly day tours or extended tours to between one and three natural areas.[19]

There are three main categories of new ecotour operators. Some have a natural or physical sciences background and see ecotourism as a business that allows them to use their skills and knowledge to educate people about the environment. Others come from the mainstream tourism industry and see nature-based tourism as a logical product extension for their current suite of tours or accommodation packages. A third group consists of guides who set up their own businesses as a career progression. But one common element stands out: most of the people entering the sector have little practical business or business planning experience.[20] Many are also woefully under-capitalised. If they can survive their first three years, then they have a chance of learning the necessary skills to stay in business. Unfortunately, many do not or cannot survive as long as that.

Why many operators fail

Even though demand for nature-based tourism products is growing rapidly, the long-term viability of many businesses is not assured. Indeed, this sector is highly volatile. Literally hundreds of new operators enter the field each year and probably an equally large number leave. A variety of key business development issues confront the nature-based tourism industry.[21] Researchers writing about the Canadian ecotourism sector, for example, found that many tourism products were poorly marketed, that tour operators were wary of using the established travel trade and that many of the marketing activities undertaken were unsophisticated.[22] Other studies of the Canadian adventure tourism sector found that the sector was 'immature'.[23] Operators tended to enter for lifestyle reasons, had little business acumen, were isolated and fiercely independent, used unsophisticated marketing methods and often provided poor-quality products.

Lack of business planning

Developing better business planning skills is the overriding need of the Australian nature-based tourism sector. Tour operator surveys conducted by the Victorian Tourism Operators Association found that their greatest desire was a range of business planning seminars.[24] Topics that were identified included accounting and bookkeeping, accessing finance, pricing, booking and reservations procedures, taxation issues, cost control and developing new business. Operators also expressed a need to gain a better understanding of strategic planning.

The effect of seasonality heightens the need to run a business efficiently. In many instances, an operator has only a 20-to-25-week effective operating season. During that time, the business must make enough money to cover its annual costs, provide a 52-week income for the operator, produce sufficient cash to cover outgoings during non-revenue-generating periods and leave enough in reserve for the next season's promotional activities. If trips do not run, the effective operating season is reduced. As a result, the income-earning potential of the business, and thus its viability, may be threatened. Apart from the weather, the main reason why trips fail to run is simply because not enough clients have been attracted to make the trip economically feasible. What causes insufficient clientele? It is either the failure to identify a workable business opportunity or inappropriate marketing.

Small party sizes are one of the real attractions of this sector, but they also pose one of the greatest challenges, as few businesses achieve true economies of scale in their operations. This in turn has a number of implications for the successful running of the business. Most importantly, it means that the price charged for the product is usually higher than for mass tourism products. The pricing challenge is exacerbated by the reluctance of many accommodation houses to offer small tour operators the same discounts they would offer the major players, which means that sometimes operators must pay the full rate for accommodation.[25]

Gross revenues are surprisingly low for many operators. Cotterill's research suggests that the average gross revenue is about $400 000, but this figure is skewed by a small number of large operators.[26] Other research indicates that a median income of between $50 000 and $100 000 is closer to the norm for the sector.[27] As a result, most businesses operate on tight margins, limiting their ability to cope with unexpected expenses. Collectively, these four factors—seasonality, high fixed costs per client, small numbers of clients and low gross revenues—combine to pose a major challenge to the viability of the sector and emphasise an even greater need for effective business planning.

Poor marketing skills

As would be expected from a sector typified by players who have no previous business skills, the level of marketing expertise among new entrants is low. In particular, many operators do not understand how the travel trade works and are leery of paying up to 35 per cent commission to have someone else sell their products.[28] In many instances, their margins are so low that they cannot afford to pay commissions.

Overall, the sector has not been well served by the travel trade, which comprises retail travel agents, tour wholesalers and inbound tour operators. The mainstream travel system is geared to the mass market, in which large numbers of people purchase carefully packaged and standardised products. There is a perception that small tour operators do not have the capacity to process large numbers of visitors. Further, tour wholesalers often require up to 24 months' lead time to package a product. In addition, the low gross commissions paid, especially for relatively inexpensive day tours, make nature-based tourism unattractive to many in the travel trade. Finally, because the nature-based tourism sector has not traditionally used the travel trade, the travel sector is unfamiliar with their business practices. The effort required to educate operators is often not worth the meagre returns. This situation is changing, fortunately, with a number of specialist agencies emerging whose main business is nature, adventure and eco-travel experiences.

Inadequate market research

A request for marketing help can often mask a more fundamental problem with the business. Many successful tour operators lamented to the author that few of their colleagues carried out any market research to determine whether a real business opportunity existed before they started out. Instead, they assumed that there was an opportunity and invested in the business without looking further. Only when it was operational did they discover that no real opportunity existed in the first place. It is all too common for people in non-viable businesses to believe that 'if only I could market my product better', or 'if only I could access more marketing funds', then everything would be all right. Alas, earlier intervention in the form of a feasibility study would have shown them the truth—that no amount of advertising revenue would make the business viable.

Most tour operators appreciate the importance of market research, but few feel they have the skills or the financial wherewithal to conduct it effectively. Operators feel research would help them identify a business opportunity, find a lucrative target market, develop a product suitable for that market and service that market well. The lack of market research skills among tour operators is not unique to the nature-based tourism sector, however. A recent study in the UK revealed that the vast majority of British tour operators do not carry out any meaningful form of market research either.[29]

Operational issues

The need to develop and deliver tour products of a consistent quality is a key issue. Substandard accommodation for the quality and price of the experience offered will diminish the quality of the product.[30] Although many ecotourists are prepared to rough it, the facilities and services must still be of a suitable standard. A more strategic approach to planning the tour and a better understanding of client needs would address this weakness.

The lack of operating systems is seen as a key factor hindering the sector. In the case of family businesses, business and operational systems are often totally lacking. This does not mean that the business is necessarily a poor one. It simply means that it is probably running less efficiently than it could. As a result, the business is not able to respond quickly to changing operating conditions. The departure of a member of staff, the absence of another or the illness of one of the principals can mean that important knowledge is lost. Truly efficient small businesses develop operating systems that are every bit as rigorous as those developed by franchises.

Ethical and environmental issues

The tourism industry is unique in that it has to deal with a number of ethical and environmental operational issues faced by no other sector. As has been discussed in many forums, nature-based tourism is confronted by the dual and conflicting tasks of both using natural areas and ensuring that the environmental integrity of those areas is maintained. Indeed, it has been said that the greatest challenge of ecological sustainability for the tourism industry is to ensure the sustainability of access to its resource base.[31] Some of the ethical issues that ecotour operators must face involve the appropriateness of the commercial use of a protected area, the marketing of that area and the possible need to modify the region to accommodate visitors. In some cases, modifications may increase the robustness of the area visited, but may reduce the quality of the experience offered. In other cases, visible environmental or social degradation may result in a reduction of the operator's licence capacity. The failure to plan for any of these possibilities could have a serious outcome for the business.

Knowledge of local environment and the ability to effectively educate clients about the region is critical to the success of ecotourism operators. In most instances, the operator and his or her staff have excellent knowledge of the region, but they may not be particularly skilled at passing on that knowledge. In some cases, the knowledge is deficient. A failure to recognise a lack of knowledge or a failure to appreciate what sort of information clients are seeking will hinder the development of a business.

Personal issues

Finally, a range of personal issues can affect the individual's ability to deliver tourism products. As mentioned earlier, the ability of many operators to deliver quality products is hampered by their own lack of previous tourism industry experience. The first challenge they face, then, is to develop their own skills to a high enough level to operate a business. In addition, many new operators do not know how to conduct tours in a professional manner. While they may have a keen interest in the environment or a strong desire to serve their clients, they may be lacking in certain interpersonal skills.

Importantly, the greatest personal challenge facing all small business owners is the risk of burnout. This risk is especially high for operators who face the gruelling combination of a heavy workload, a lack of systems and a lack of financial resources to hire additional staff. Many nature-based tour operators conduct trips on weekends, yet have a full Monday-to-Friday schedule running the office, preparing for trips and being available to answer customer enquiries. They may work seven-day weeks for the entire season. As a result, many may find themselves doing the work of two people. Over time, such a relentless workload wears down many operators.

[1] P. Wight (1996b) North American ecotourism markets: Motivations, preferences and destinations, *Journal of Travel Research*, Summer, pp. 3–10; K. Lindberg (1991) *Policies for Maximising Nature Tourism's Ecological and Economic Benefits*, World Resources Institute, February.

[2] S. W. Litvin (1996) Ecotourism: A study of purchase proclivity, *Journal of Vacation Marketing*, 3(1), pp. 43–54.

[3] Tourism Victoria (1997) *Tourism Victoria: Strategic Business Plan 1997–2001: Building Partnerships*, TV, Melbourne.

[4] P. Pearce & G. Moscardo (1985). The relationship between travellers' career levels and the concept of authenticity, *Australian Journal of Psychology*, 37(2), pp. 157–74.

[5] R. C. Mill & A. M. Morrison (1985) *The Tourism System: An Introductory Text*, Prentice Hall International, London.

[6] G. Meredith (1995) *Small Business Management in Australia*, 5th edn, McGraw-Hill, Sydney.

[7] J. Clarke (1995) The effective marketing of small scale tourism enterprises through national structures: Lessons from a two way comparative study of farm tourist accommodation in the United Kingdom and New Zealand, *Journal of Vacation Marketing*, 1(2), pp. 137–53.

[8] W. Reynolds, W. Savage & A. Williams (1994) *Your Own Business: A Practical Guide to Success*, Thomas Nelson, Melbourne, pp. 29–35.

[9] R. Saxon & C. Allan-Kamil (1996) *A Woman's Guide to Starting a Small Business in Australia*, Allen & Unwin, St Leonards.

[10] Australia and New Zealand Banking Corporation (1990) *Summary of Small Business in Australia*.

[11] W. Reynolds, W. Savage & A. Williams pp. 29–35.

[12] S. C. Brandt (1982) *Entrepreneuring: The Ten Commandments for Building a Growth Company*, Mentor Books, Scarborough, Canada; J. W. English (1995) *How to Organise and Operate a Small Business in Australia,* 6th edn, Allen & Unwin, Sydney.

[13] P. Temple (1989) Prosperity without profit, *Accountancy*, 104(1151), pp. 86–90.

[14] D. Cotterill (1996) Developing a sustainable ecotourism business, in Richins, H., Richardson, J. & Crabtree, A. (eds), *Taking the Next Steps*, Ecotourism Association of Australia, Brisbane, pp. 135–40.

[15] Australian Tourism Operators Network, pers. comm.

[16] Cotterill, op. cit.

[17] R. Blamey (1995) The nature of ecotourism, Occasional Paper no. 21, Bureau of Tourism Research, Canberra; (1996a) *The Elusive Market Profile: Operationalising Ecotourism*, BTR, Canberra; (1996b) Profiling the ecotourism market, in Richins, Richardson & Crabtree, pp. 1–9.

[18] K. Donaghy & U. McMahon (1996) Managing yield: A marketing perspective, *Journal of Vacation Marketing*, 2(1), pp. 55–62.

[19] Cotterill, op. cit.

[20] Victorian Tourism Operators Association (1995a) 1995 Membership renewal survey, internal document, VTOA, Melbourne; (1996a) 1996 Member survey, internal document, VTOA, Melbourne.

[21] Cotterill, op. cit.

[22] C. Wild (1996) The North American ecotourism industry, in Richins, Richardson & Crabtree, pp. 93–6; D. Weaver, C. Glenn & R. Rounds (1996) Private ecotourism operations in Manitoba, Canada, *Journal of Sustainable Tourism*, 4(3), pp. 135–46.

[23] Tourism Canada (1988) *Adventure Travel in Western Canada*, MacLaren Plansearch, TC, Ottawa; (1990) *Adventure Travel in Eastern Canada*, Tourism Research Group, TC, Ottawa.

[24] VTOA (1995a) op. cit.; (1995b) New member survey, internal document, VTOA, Melbourne.

[25] L. Sorensen (1993) The special interest travel market, *Cornell Hotel and Restaurant Administration Quarterly*, 34(3), pp. 24–8.

[26] Cotterill, op. cit.

[27] B. McKercher & P. Davidson (1995) Women and commercial adventure tourism: Does the industry understand its dominant market? in Faulkner, B., Fagence, M., Davidson, M. & Craig-Smith, S. (eds), *Tourism Research and Education in Australia*, BTR, Canberra, pp. 129–40; McKercher (1996a) Attitudes to tourism in Victoria's Alpine National Park, PhD dissertation, University of Melbourne.

[28] Clarke, op. cit.; Wild, op. cit.

[29] G. E. Greenley & A. S. Matcham (1986) Marketing orientation in the service of incoming tourism, *European Journal of Marketing*, 20(7), pp. 64–73.

[30] Cotterill, op. cit.

[31] J. Herity (1990) Globe '90 policy making for tourism and sustainable development: The role of environmental impact assessment, paper presented at Globe '90, Vancouver.

Chapter 2

The role of research

*A*ll great businesses start from great ideas, but not all great ideas lead to great businesses. In reality, as few as one in seventy new ideas generated by major corporations may actually result in a successful new product. So how does one determine if an idea has the potential to become a viable tourism business? The answer lies initially in conducting rigorous market research. Appropriate research provides a structured process for screening ideas to see if real or potential opportunities exist. Research examines the market to see if it is interested in the product, whether sufficient numbers of people are willing to pay for the product, whether or not the product can be delivered in a cost-effective manner and whether the individual has the personal qualities necessary to operate a tourism enterprise.

In essence, then, market research is like a filtering process that is designed to distinguish business opportunities from ideas. This chapter explores the role that research plays and identifies where it needs to be conducted to ensure that ideas are vetted as thoroughly as possible before a new venture, product or service is launched. If it becomes evident at any point along the filtering or business plan preparation process that the idea will not work, the project can be abandoned. The cost of abandoning a project at an early stage is minimal compared to the personal and financial costs of proceeding with an unsound scheme and then watching the business fail.

Research is not infallible. Indeed, even when rigorous market research is conducted, the success rate for new businesses may be as low as one in six. Some ideas will be rejected that will later prove to be feasible; ideas that are shown by research to be impractical may work. Research will not eliminate uncertainties entirely; that is not its purpose. Its role is simply to reduce the risk to a level that is acceptable to the individual.

Distinguishing opportunities from ideas

The role of effective market research is well understood by large corporations. However, according to many tour businesses contacted during the research phase of this book, it is rarely used by new operators. Bill Avery from Federation Track Walkers in Pennant Hills felt that 'most people enter business without doing any market research to identify potential markets.'[1] Another bushwalking tour operator who wished to remain anonymous added: 'Many new entrants have not researched the field and have nothing to differentiate themselves from existing operators. They quickly go broke after hurting existing businesses.'

Much has been written about the reluctance of small businesses to conduct research. It is a common perception that research is too academic, too costly, too time-consuming and not really necessary for the needs of small businesses.[2] However, all business planners will declare that businesses cannot afford *not* to do research. Meredith feels that it is inconceivable, yet all too common, that businesses begin without having conducted feasibility studies to answer the one thousand and one questions that must arise.[3] Newell maintains that the personal and financial costs of business failures represent a sad loss of human potential and capital.[4] The challenge then becomes one of learning how to conduct cost-effective research that will achieve specific goals. It is not difficult, but it does require focus, dedication and discipline.

A number of simple rules should be followed to ensure that the research produces adequate results.

1 **Adopt a customer focus.** Research should always be conducted from the perspective of the consumer. The consumer's motives and desires are what is important. Why would someone want to buy the product or service? Why would they pay the price asked? Why would they switch from someone else's product? If these questions can be answered as honestly and dispassionately as possible, the prospective operator will gain valuable insights as to the potential viability of the business.

2 **Be conservative and sceptical.** It is important to appreciate that the filtering process is concerned more with rejecting ideas than with confirming that opportunities exist. All it takes is one fatal flaw to render a business possibility unsound. It is important to search for that flaw. If it appears, the project must be revised or abandoned.

3 **Remain focused on key issues.** Research is a lot of fun, but it has to be focused on specific outcomes if it is to have meaningful results. One of the risks of embarking on a research project is that it is easy to get lost following up a variety of irrelevant issues. It is necessary to identify the key pieces of

information needed and answer those questions first. Issues about the size and profile of the market, the overall trends in the sector, legal and licensing considerations and financial needs are a good place to start.

4 If the results of the research are unfavourable, modify or reject the idea. If at any point in the research process a fatal flaw appears, or a major obstacle that cannot be overcome, the business should not proceed. It may be possible to revise the concept, or it may be that the idea will have to be rejected.

The filtering process: points to examine
1 Personal and business goals

The best place to begin is with the individual's own aspirations and goals. The potential operator must ask: 'Why am I interested in running a small tourism business?' People enter business for a variety of personal reasons, some positive and some negative. Taking the step to enter the tourism business world is a major life decision. If it is successful, it will be an incredible personal growth experience. If it does not succeed, the personal toll may be high.

It is crucial to understand one's own motives for entering tourism. If it is from a genuine desire to grow, to be independent, to have a better standard of living, to have an improved quality of life[5] or to achieve a long-identified personal goal,[6] then the chances of success are enhanced. If, on the other hand, it is because tourism is the default option—perhaps because the current job is frustrating, or because there is no other work—then it is necessary to be cautious. Anyone who thinks of it as a form of semi-retirement is also in for a rude shock. It is important to determine whether one is buying a job or an investment. Many successful owners of small businesses admit that they would not have started if they had known from the outset all the problems they would have to solve.[7]

Bransgrove in the *Tour Operators' Business Guidebook* illustrates the pitfalls that beset many new tour operators.[8] He argues that many enter the tourism industry because of their love for certain non-commercial recreational activities. Their motives are often driven by a desire to get paid for playing, rather than to develop a quality tourism product. These new operators often find it difficult to adjust from the casual, low-pressure activity of leading friends on a tour to coping with the greater demands and expectations of paying clients who may be from different socio-economic or cultural backgrounds.

Above all else, the identification of financial goals must drive the entire research process. If, for example, a taxable income of $50 000 is desired from the business, then the likelihood of achieving this target will underscore the rest of the research process. Is the goal realistic? Is there a large enough market to generate that income? Is the public willing to pay the necessary prices? Is the product sufficiently differentiated? Can the product compete with those of other operators and still achieve the goal? Is the location suitable for achieving the goal? Do the financial figures suggest that the goal can be reached? If research indicates that the goal cannot be reached, then the project should be abandoned.

Different dynamics must be considered, depending on whether the business is going to provide a full-time income or be a secondary source of income. Before embarking on a full-time business, the potential tour operator must clearly determine the desired income, how long he or she is prepared to wait until that target is attained and how much time will be invested in the business. For a part-time operator, while financial objectives may be less important, they must still be plainly set out.

Many people in the tourism industry insist that they are in it for 'lifestyle' reasons—that income is really only a secondary goal. Unfortunately, 'lifestyle' is more often a euphemism for remaining in a non-viable business. What many full-time 'lifestyle' tour operators are really saying is that the business earns an insufficient income to provide a suitable standard of living. To make ends meet they often have to seek outside employment. Nobody should get into the tourism industry for a lifestyle. Poverty is not an attractive lifestyle! If the business does not have the potential to earn a reasonable living for the principals, then it is a non-viable business.

2   Generating ideas and seeking opportunities

Once the decision has been made to enter the nature-based tourism industry, the next step is to identify the core idea. Idea generation is both an intuitive and an inductive process. Almost any book on entrepreneurship will contain a list of possible sources of ideas. Among the most common sources are:

- existing businesses located elsewhere
- franchises
- patents
- professional contacts
- social gatherings

- friends or family
- existing businesses in the immediate area
- one's own interests.

Generating ideas is a relatively easy exercise. Within half an hour a typical group of people could develop a list of 30 or 40 possible tourism ventures. Confirming that a business opportunity exists from the germ of an idea, however, is a much more challenging task. Opportunities are different from ideas in that they have a real business prospect tied to them, have durable and attractive qualities, are timely and are anchored in products or services that create or add value for the buyer or end user.[9]

Opportunities are most likely to occur when prevailing business conditions result in vacuums or gaps in the delivery of existing products. Some examples are:

- chaos and confusion in the marketplace: an instance of this is the rapid growth of Microsoft brought about by chaos in the personal computing sector
- changing circumstances: the opening of Cairns as the northern gateway to Australia has created a number of ecotourism opportunities in far north Queensland
- inconsistencies or gaps in the delivery of products: this has created an opportunity for the development of a number of specialist ecotour wholesalers and retailers
- lags, leads or other information gaps: the proliferation of Internet providers is a direct result of just such gaps.[10]

The most attractive opportunities present themselves during the introductory and growth stages of the product category's life cycle, when the absolute number of consumers is growing. During this stage, new ventures can attract a portion of an expanding market without affecting existing operators. As a result, new players face fewer barriers to entry. At present it is still possible to enter the ecotourism sector with as little as $10 000.

On the other hand, during the maturity and decline phases of the product category life cycle, the absolute number of users has stabilised or may be in decline. Substantial barriers to entry may exist, be they through the establishment of major national players or an oversupply of operators. New ventures entering in these market conditions can only survive by taking clients (or share) away from existing operators. The cost of enticing clients away from established businesses is substantially more than that of attracting clients when the overall market is expanding. Figure 2.1 (page 16) compares favourable and unfavourable market conditions for launching a new tourism product or enterprise.

Figure 2.1   Assessing ideas to determine if opportunities may exist

Favourable market conditions	Unfavourable market conditions
Introduction and growth stage of product category life cycle stage	Mature or decline stage of product category life cycle stage
Few barriers to entry	Many barriers to entry
'Immature' businesses	'Mature' businesses
Little customer loyalty among existing businesses	Established customer loyalty among existing businesses
Chaos and confusion in the marketplace	Stability in the marketplace
Favourable externalities	Unfavourable externalities
Inconsistencies or gaps in the current delivery of products	Few or no inconsistencies or gaps in the delivery of products

3 Assumptions

The real research can begin once the idea has been identified. The first step of the vetting process is for the potential operator to list all his or her assumptions about why the idea seems to present a business opportunity. This is a vital preliminary step, for assumptions represent what the potential operator believes to be true about the business. In reality, however, assumptions represent uncertainties and unknowns. They must be resolved before the idea can proceed. The soundness of the idea must first be proven or disproven. Assumptions can be grouped according to the categories identified in Figure 2.2.

Drawing up a list of assumptions makes it easier to organise the research tasks. As the assumptions are written down, it becomes clear that many can be bundled together to form broader, more general research questions. For instance, a series of assumptions about the operations of the travel trade will highlight a need to gain a much better understanding of how this distribution channel operates. In addition, the process of making a list of assumptions helps one identify other unknowns that may not have been considered previously. Finally, a long list of assumptions is a warning signal that the idea needs a lot of work before a definite business opportunity can be confirmed. The more assumptions or unknowns there are at an early stage, the greater is the risk that the idea will prove to be unfeasible.

Figure 2.2   List of assumptions

- The product
- Product category life cycle stage
- The potential market
- Competitors
- Point of differentiation
- Location
- Financial questions
- Operational issues
- Externalities
- Operator's skills

4 The product

Stages four and five of the filtering process are usually conducted concurrently, for the clarification of the product will help define likely markets that may purchase the product and vice versa. Ultimately, these two stages will determine if a suitable product can be developed that will be attractive to enough people at the proposed location at the proposed price to provide the potential operator with the financial goals he or she is seeking. As the research progresses, these four dimensions—product, market, price and location—may be modified. It is important to keep asking: What business am I really in? Di Percy from Dreamtime Outback Safaris warns: 'The business focus will change as you find your market niche and find out what will/will not work. Flexibility of what you do, as well as how you think about what you do is essential.'[11]

What products are actually going to be sold by the business and why would someone want to buy them? These seemingly simple questions are in fact very difficult to answer. Historically, products were developed first and then consumers who might be interested in buying the product were sought. Some of the great product failures can be attributed to the fact that the customers' needs were ignored when the product was being developed.[12] Unfortunately, it still seems that many tour operators develop their products on the naive assumption that if a product exists a natural market must also exist.

Today, the focus of the product–market relationship has changed, and the orientation is now clearly on the provision of products that satisfy existing or latent consumer needs. The change began in the 1970s with the emergence of the societal marketing concept. Four tenets drive societal marketing for tourism: the quality of life of local residents, the well-being of the guest, respect for the natural environment and economic development.[13] In addition, businesses today are striving more and more to form ongoing relationships with their guests and suppliers. Relationship marketing, as it is called, recognises the exchange process between buyers and sellers and the need to develop products that can foster such relationships.[14] The best way to do this is to ensure that the products satisfy the customers' needs, wants or desires. The logic is infallible. The easiest and most profitable products or services to sell are the ones that the customers want to buy.[15]

Other factors have to be kept in mind when deciding on the final product:

- To be successful, products must have a long enough life cycle to recoup the owner's investment and return a suitable profit.
- Tourism products must have the potential for a high value-added component.
- They must also have the potential for a sizeable and durable margin.
- They need to be marketed and delivered in a cost-effective manner.
- They must offer some competitive advantage over existing products.[16]

The steps to define the product are as follows:

1 Isolate the core attributes of the product or the core consumer needs it will satisfy.
2 Assess whether existing products can satisfy similar needs. If they can, how or why is the proposed product unique? If existing products cannot satisfy these needs, is there sufficient consumer demand for the needs that have been identified?
3 Describe in detail the specific component parts of the proposed product. This step will be useful for developing accurate costs, which will help at the financial analysis stage of the proposal.

5 The potential market

Clearly, products cannot be developed in isolation from the wants of the prospective market. Two factors must be considered: the size and habits of the potential market segments to be targeted and the ability of the operator to reach that market.

Segmenting the potential target market

The challenge for small tour operators is to define sufficiently large and profitable market segments that want to purchase the product. It is a fatal mistake to assume that speciality tour operators can adopt an undifferentiated or mass market approach to identifying their potential markets. The market for an ecotourism business that hopes to attract 500 clients a year is not 'Japan', 'Australia', 'Queensland' or even 'Brisbane'. If the business is to succeed, the product must appeal to readily identifiable, easily accessible *segments* of these populations. Segmenting the market permits new and existing businesses to develop products, target promotional activities effectively and allocate resources to maintain important existing markets and to identify and penetrate new markets with high incremental sales potential.[17]

Markets can be segmented in a number of ways: according to the demographic profile of the clients (age, gender, marital status); by their psychographic profile (values, beliefs, attitudes, opinions); on a geographical basis; or by their behavioural characteristics (brand loyalty, use rates, activities, benefits sought, and so on).[18] Increasingly, sectors of the tourism industry that used to be regarded as having mass market appeal, like the skiing sector, are now recognising the need to segment their market and target specific subgroups.[19]

Market segments must satisfy a number of key criteria to be attractive. A profitable segment must:

- be clearly identifiable as a discrete, unified market that shares common values and interests
- be easy to reach through a limited number of promotional media at an affordable cost
- be large enough to provide a sustainable flow of consumers and growth potential over an extended period of time
- be affluent enough to afford the price of the product being offered and to provide the economic returns desired from the business
- have their needs, wants and desires satisfied by the product being offered
- have the potential to become repeat users of the product
- have a strong likelihood of preferring the product over competitor products.

Why is the failure to identify target market segments that satisfy all of the above criteria a major problem for many new tour operators? Without a clear definition and understanding of the needs of the potential market, there is a greater likelihood that the end product will be flawed. A flawed product will then be more difficult to sell to the prospective users. From a pragmatic point of view, the costs of reaching the right audience, when that audience has never been defined, can be high. New operators with limited resources often revert to a random approach to promotion, rather than a targeted approach. This method is both more costly and less effective.

An idea is not a business opportunity until the market is identified. If the presumed target markets do not stand up to a rigorous quantitative and qualitative assessment against these criteria, then a business opportunity does not exist.

Accessing the market: the distribution system

Target markets can be reached by two methods: either directly by the operator or indirectly though the travel trade (travel agents, tour wholesalers or inbound tour operators). Before making a decision, the full costs, benefits and efficacy of each distribution option must be considered. Each has its benefits, but each also has substantial risks. Direct marketing is often easier for new operators, but it is limited in its capacity to reach large numbers of potential clients. Further, if delivered incorrectly, advertising and promotion can be an expensive waste of scarce resources. The media outlets selected, the promotional vehicles used and the distribution channels chosen must produce the desired results. Developing a clear, focused and effective promotional strategy is almost as important as developing the right product to promote.

On the surface, the travel trade is very attractive. The tour wholesaler or travel agent assumes most of the costs of promoting the product in exchange for a fixed commission on each sale. If they do not sell anything, the operator incurs no costs. On top of that, the operator gains access to many markets that could not otherwise be reached. But the costs, conditions, lead times and guarantees involved may make this option less attractive. Moreover, what assurances does the operator have that his or her product will be given priority by the travel trade?

The nexus between the market and the product

Products and markets do not operate in isolation. The key to any successful business is the nexus between the product offered and the satisfaction of the consumers' needs, wants and desires. Operators surveyed for this book commented that this was one of their most challenging tasks. An ecotourism destination stated that it had taken a number of years before it felt that it had got the tours right. The tour had to suit a wide range of skills and levels of fitness but still give a high-quality result every time, while not degrading the environment. Another operator thought that a strategic approach to the product market nexus was needed. He suggested that all operators should ask what sort of product was being aimed at what market, which in turn would lead to a number of product planning issues.

6 Competitors

Competition is inevitable, whether it is from direct sources (similar firms trying to sell their products to the same market) or indirect sources (all other firms that may sell leisure, recreation and holiday products to the identified market). One of the key roles of the vetting process is to determine if the idea has the ability to match or outdo existing competitors' products.[20] Newell, in his excellent little book *Secrets of Small Business Success*, states:

> A new business can only hope to compete effectively . . . if it has something more to offer . . . Yet, many newcomers to the business sector shy off getting into the marketing rat race and prefer, instead, to try to make it on their own in an inappropriate location or with scant hope of attracting a sufficient volume of business to survive.[21]

The product has been defined and target markets have been identified. Now it is necessary to see if any other comparable products targeted at similar markets exist and, if so, how successful they are. The competitor analysis is designed to demonstrate that a sufficiently large gap or opportunity exists for a new product to enter the marketplace. Several aspects must be considered: basic information about competitors' products and competitors' strengths and weaknesses.

Basic information about competitors

First, the number of operators, the product lines offered, the size of the operation (the number of clients each serves and the resources each has) and how long each one has been established must be determined. Sources used to gather this information may include personal knowledge, trade suppliers, competitors' brochures, telephone directories, local and state government tourism organisations and tourist trade associations. If the sector is dominated by a small number of well-established, well-resourced operators, then it is going to be difficult for a new entrant to succeed, unless that entrant can either identify a likely niche or compete directly with the major players. On the other hand, if the sector is diffuse, with no dominant players, it will be easier for a new operator to enter.[22]

A large number of competitors may indicate broad market interest in the product. But this may also be a danger signal: a large number of businesses may also reflect an oversupply of product, rather than high demand. Indeed, the profitability of the operators rather than the absolute number of businesses is a better reflection of the attractiveness of a segment. State tourism commissions and sector-specific tourist trade associations are the best source of meaningful trade information.

Competitors' products

Analysis of the competitors' products will offer insights into the development of the proposed product. Identifying the core need being satisfied, the tangible product and the augmented product and services will indicate the quality of the experience consumers have come to expect. The proposed product must at least match the existing products. By the same token, the prices currently being charged by competitors tell a lot about both the costs of doing business and the market's willingness to pay.

Strengths and weaknesses of competitors

Finally, Reynolds, Savage and Williams suggest that prospective operators should analyse the relative strengths and weaknesses of each of the competitors. They recommend examining competitors' good points and their strengths as an indication of the minimal standards that will have to be met in order to compete successfully. Then their weaknesses should be examined to see what is not being offered and to see how existing businesses are not satisfying customer demands. This analysis will help identify inconsistencies or gaps in the delivery of products, emerging trends where client needs may not be met, or chaos in the marketplace, each of which may provide an opening.[23]

7 The point of differentiation

To succeed, the proposed idea must offer something new or different in the marketplace. In marketing jargon, the proposed product must be differentiated in some meaningful way from all other products. The first thing customers usually do when they hear of a new product or service is compare it to existing alternatives. They will only try the new product if they feel that the perceived value of the new product is greater than the value provided by the existing alternatives.[24]

Differentiation can come from many sources. It can be based on the product itself (wildflower ecology walks), the location of the product (the Victorian Alps or the Daintree forest), the quality of the service provided (personalised small group tours), the expertise of the service provider (tours run by recognised ecologists), the market segments targeted (members of birdwatching clubs), the distribution channels used (the Internet), the price–value relationship (backpackers' tours versus high end tours) or many other factors.

The great benefit of differentiation is that it helps give the product a unique position in the marketplace. In doing so, it effectively brands the product, making it more attractive to consumers.[25] Aaker identifies three key features of differentiation:

- The point of differentiation must be substantial enough to make a real difference in the mind of the consumer. Being marginally superior may not be enough to make a real difference.
- The advantage offered must be real or be seen to be real by the consumer. This point drives home the need to adopt a consumer's

perspective when developing products. The potential operator should always ask: Why would someone buy this product?

- The point of difference must be sustainable in the face of competitor reaction. If existing competitors can match or surpass the point of differentiation, then it never really existed.[26]

8 The location

Next, the potential tour operator should examine where competitors operate in respect to the proposed location. This will determine the effect that market access may have on the competitive attractiveness of the location. Market access relates to the comparative advantage that one destination has over another due to its more favourable position vis à vis its main markets. Market access theory argues that a destination that has easier relative access to a market will enjoy higher use levels than a destination that offers similar products but has more difficult access.[27] This idea is based on the distance decay concept, according to which demand for travel varies inversely with the distance travelled or with an increase in time or money costs.[28] The rate of decay in market demand varies with travel time availability and is most extreme for people with the shortest amount of time.[29]

In practical terms, this means that most people will purchase domestic travel products that are most readily available to them, unless the more distant product offers a number of features that are unique. Thus, if the product being proposed can be consumed at other locations closer to the main market, demand will be low. It is important, therefore, to ensure that the planned location is the best place for the delivery of the product, rather than simply being a location that is convenient to the proposed operator. Because the operator lives in an area does not automatically make it an attractive tourist destination.

9 Capital requirements

No idea, regardless of how brilliant is, can be translated into a sound business without the necessary financial resources. Under-capitalising a business starves it of resources right from the start, significantly reducing the likelihood that it will survive. Without sufficient start-up capital, the product cannot be developed fully, the quality of the service will suffer and, importantly, the promotion of the business will always be constrained. Further, a lack of initial operating capital means that many follow-up marketing and product development ideas will be delayed, as needed capital is spent on such unimportant things as the operator's own existence. Indeed, research has shown that under-capitalised businesses constrain the operators to the extent that most never become fully viable.[30] Unless the right amount of capital exists to develop the idea fully, the project should be abandoned.

It is vital, therefore, to know what the capital investment and initial cash-flow requirements are before any decision can be made to proceed with the business. How much it will cost and how long it will take the business to generate a positive cash flow are just two of the questions to be answered. The next question is, obviously: Do I have that amount of money? If the answer is no, the prospective operator will have to examine where finance can be acquired and at what cost. Given that small nature-based tourism activities are considered high-risk investments, it is likely that the costs of borrowing money will be high.

10 Making the sums work

If the idea does not provide the prospect of achieving a desirable financial outcome within a prescribed period of time, then it is not practicable. Ultimately, the financial feasibility of an idea is the only factor that will determine if the project is to proceed. The purpose of the vetting process to this point has been to ascertain if a commercially successful product can be developed to satisfy the needs of a market. The next stage is to determine if the sums add up. The concept is straightforward, but the proliferation of 'how to' books[31] and the repeated requests for financial planning advice by existing operators suggest that this issue is a vexed one.

At this stage, the vetting process must take into account:

- the profitability of the idea
- the ability of the business to achieve the operator's financial goals in a specified time frame
- whether an acceptable return on the investment can be earned
- whether sufficient cash flow will be generated to cover expenses during the off season and still leave enough money for promotional activities
- the true costs of operating the business (including fixed and variable costs)
- whether the generally accepted market price is high enough for the project being planned
- whether a suitable volume of clients can purchase the product
- whether the logistics of running a certain number of trips with a certain number of clients at a certain price are sound.

If the costs are too high, if the income is too low, if the returns are not satisfactory or if the logistics dictate that it cannot be done, then the idea must be abandoned. Clearly, these questions involve the production of detailed financial plans and the integration of the market research conducted above. Chapters 5 and 6 deal with many financial planning considerations. The following chapter discusses how the myriad issues can be integrated and assessed through the formal business planning process.

11 Externalities

Events that occur beyond the direct influence of individual tour operators may have profound effects on their business environment. Being aware of externalities and able to predict their impact will help proactive operators capitalise on opportunities or defend themselves against threats. Reactive operators, on the other hand, may miss out on new opportunities or may be put out of business by adverse changes to their external operating environment.

The State of Victoria's changing attitude to tourism in national parks is a classic example of how externalities can create significant nature-based tourism opportunities. During much of the 1980s tourism in parks was tolerated but certainly not encouraged.[32] However, changing societal attitudes and the emergence of ecotourism prompted the then Departments of Forest and Lands and Conservation and Environment to begin to encourage greater tourist use of the State's parks.[33] The change of government in the early 1990s accelerated commercial interest in protected areas. The Tourism Victoria Strategic Business Plan identified public lands as being among the State's greatest tourism assets.[34] Since 1993 the department charged with the management of national parks has recognised tourism as a major business for the department and has adopted a stronger business focus.[35]

As a result, the number of tourist businesses licensed to operate in the Alpine National Park has increased fivefold between 1992 and 1996 to more than 150. Now, however, there is growing recognition that some areas are being over-used. Limits have been placed on the size of tourist parties, the areas that may be visited and the number of trips that some operators can take. Further attempts are being made to restrict the granting of new licences. In this instance externalities, in the form of changing public policy, created more than 100 business opportunities in four years. However, a new set of externalities—fear of environmental degradation from too much tourism—has served to reduce the attractiveness and potential viability of some businesses.

12 Personal skills and abilities

Successful tour operators need a wide variety of skills. Being an avid bushwalker does not immediately qualify an individual to become a tour operator.

One adventure tour operator advises:

> Be prepared to be very multi skilled! You and whoever else is in the
> business need to have the abilities, or be prepared to learn, to handle all
> aspects, from interpreting legal or governmental documents to marketing,
> to budgeting and record keeping, to first aid, navigation, customer service,
> etc., etc.[36]

Having a variety of skills in operational, business management, administrative
and customer service areas helps the business operate more efficiently.
Importantly, institutions may specify certain skills before an individual is
allowed to operate. Liability insurers are requiring more and more that all
tour leaders have adequate first aid and crisis management qualifications and,
if the tour leaders are involved in high-risk or specialist activities (such as
canoeing or horse riding) may insist on specialist skill accreditation. Most
states will not allow commercial tour operators to enter national parks unless
they can provide evidence of $5 000 000 liability insurance. Banks and finan-
cial institutions are demanding that prospective operators produce detailed
business plans and submit regular reports thereafter. Industry accreditation
schemes require operators to provide evidence that a variety of systems are in
place.

The owner-operator can either acquire the skills personally, or staff can be
employed who possess them. Either way, a cost is involved. It is preferable to
identify and address skill deficiencies before the business commences than to
have to take time out of the business to acquire skills (a cost in terms of lost
opportunities) or to have to employ staff to cover for the operator's deficiencies (a direct cost).

13 Personal qualities

Finally, the last and arguably most important question must be asked: Does
the operator possess the necessary personal qualities to be in business? Not
everyone is suited to the tourism industry. While owning a business can be
a very gratifying experience, it can also be tremendously stressful and trau-
matic if people discover that they do not have the traits necessary to succeed.

Successful small business operators tend to share certain personality characteristics. English, summarising some of them, maintains that successful
small business operators have drive and energy, are willing to work long hours,
are moderate risk-takers, are tolerant of uncertainty, are competitive, resource-
ful and self-confident, deal with failure well and are assertive, ambitious and
independent.[37] Other researchers highlight the need for a stable personality
and strong family support.[38] The National Executive of Small Business
Agencies has produced a checklist to help prospective new business people

ascertain their suitability for such a life. The questions in the checklist ask if the person is reliable and predictable, has initiative and drive, is a good leader who can influence employees, has analytical and organisational abilities, is sensitive to other people's needs, works well with others and, importantly, is in good health.[39]

To these qualities, a few more can be added. Tour operators must have strong social skills and genuinely like to be around new and different people. They must be able to put people at ease, especially if the activity is new to participants or involves some risk. They must have the capacity to gain the trust and confidence of clients and the ability to mould a group of strangers into a cohesive team. Because most nature-based tours involve using the services of other tourism businesses, prospective operators must also be strong negotiators. They must be good communicators and have well-developed public relations skills.[40] The author would also add high ethical standards to this list.

[1] Pers. comm.

[2] D. Samson (1994) *Preparing a Business Plan*, AusIndustry, Canberra.

[3] G. Meredith (1988) *Small Business Management in Australia*, 3rd edn, McGraw-Hill, Sydney.

[4] M. Newell (1995) *Secrets of Small Business Success*, Stirling Press, Old Noarlunga, SA.

[5] National Executive of Small Business Agencies (1991) *Checklist for Starting a Business*, Managing the Small Business Series no. 1, NESBA, AGPS, Canberra.

[6] Saxon & Allan-Kamil, op. cit.

[7] NESBA (1991) op. cit.

[8] C. Bransgrove (1992) *Tour Operators Business Guidebook*, Small Business Development Corporation, Victorian Tourism Commision, Melbourne.

[9] J. A. Timmons (1989) *New Venture Creation: Entrepreneurship in the 1990s*, 3rd edn, Irwin, Boston.

[10] D. Aaker (1995) *Strategic Marketing Management*, 4th edn, John Wiley & Sons, Brisbane.

[11] Pers. comm.

[12] P. Kotler & R. E. Turner (1989) *Marketing Management*, Prentice Hall, Scarborough.

[13] R. C. Mill (1996) Societal marketing: Implications for tourism destinations, *Journal of Vacation Marketing*, 2(3), pp. 215–21.

[14] A. J. Palmer & R. Mayer (1996) Relationship marketing: A new paradigm for the travel and tourism sector? *Journal of Vacation Marketing*, 2(4), pp. 326–33; D. C. Gilbert (1996) Relationship marketing and airline loyalty schemes, *Tourism Management*, 17(8), pp. 575–82.

[15] English (1995) op. cit.

[16] Timmons, op. cit.

[17] R. R. Perdue (1996) Target market selection and marketing strategy: The Colorado downhill skiing industry, *Journal of Travel Research*, Spring, pp. 39–46.

[18] V. O'Brien (1996) *The Fast Forward MBA in Business*, John Wiley & Sons, NY.

[19] G. Richards & K. Friends (1995) The UK ski market, *Journal of Vacation Marketing*, 1(3), pp. 259–64; Perdue (1996) op. cit.

[20] Reynolds, Savage & Williams, op. cit.

[21] Newell, op. cit., p. 93.

[22] Reynolds, Savage & Williams, op. cit.

[23] ibid.

[24] M. D. Reilly & N. L. Millikin (1995) *Starting a Small Business: The Feasibility Analysis*, Montguide, Montana State University, Bozeman, Montana.

[25] H. Taylor (1996) How to develop a strong hotel brand strategy with a weak branding budget, *Journal of Vacation Marketing*, 2(1), pp. 63–7.

[26] Aaker, op. cit.

[27] D. Pearce (1989) *Tourist Development*, 2nd edn, Longman Scientific, Harlow, UK.

[28] A. Bull (1989) *The Economics of Travel and Tourism*, Pitman, Melbourne.

[29] T. Greer & G. Wall (1979) Recreational hinterlands: A theoretical and empirical analysis, in Wall, G. (ed.), *Recreational Land Use in Southern Ontario*, Dept of Geography Publication Series no. 14, Waterloo University, Waterloo, Canada, pp. 227–46.

[30] NESBA (1995) *Sources of Finance for Small Business*, Managing the Small Business Series no. 2, NESBA, AGPS, Canberra.

[31] J. W. English (1990) *Small Business Financial Management in Australia*, Allen & Unwin, London; L. Hopkins (1993) *Cash Flow and How to Improve It*, Wrightbooks, North Brighton, Vic.; P. Stanley (1994) *Accounting for Non Accountants: The Plain English Guide to Accounting*, Business Library, Melbourne.

[32] National Parks Service (1983a) *National Parks Service Policy on Tourism*, NPS, Melbourne; (1983b) *Bogong National Park: Proposed Interim Management Plan*, NPS, Melbourne.

[33] Victorian Department of Conservation, Forests and Lands (1990) DCE *Presenting Victoria: CFL's Tourism Policy*, CFL, Melbourne; Victorian Department of Conservation and Environment (1992a) *Ecotourism: A Natural Strength for Victoria — Australia*, DCE, Melbourne.

[34] Tourism Victoria (1993) *Tourism Victoria: Strategic Business Plan*, TV, Melbourne.

[35] Victorian Department of Conservation and Natural Resources (1995) Tourism guidelines, internal DCNR document forming part of the *National Parks Service Guidelines and Procedures Manual*.

[36] Pers. comm. The operator wishes to remain anonymous.

[37] English (1995) op. cit.

[38] Saxon & Allan-Kamil, op. cit.
[39] NESBA (1991) op. cit.
[40] Bransgrove (1992).

Chapter 3

Business plans

*r*esearch will have yielded a variety of information about the potential business opportunity. The next step is to integrate this array of material, make some sense of it and put it into a meaningful form. Then it will be possible to make an unbiased decision about whether or not it really does present a business opportunity. The formal business planning process serves this function. A business plan is defined as a document that details the activities of a prospective business and examines how and when various objectives will be achieved.[1] It is a future-oriented document that is focused on specific goals and results and consists of a series of sections, each designed to answer key questions about the nexus between the business opportunity and the market.

Business planning is a process that helps an organisation set its goals across all functional areas and decide how to attain them.[2] It summarises the business opportunity and shows how to pursue it. In essence, it predicts the future of the business, describes where it will go, how fast it will get there and what it has to do along the way to make the path as smooth as possible. A business plan is not the business; it is a *plan* for the business. Business planning is a demanding, difficult, time-consuming task requiring commitment, dedication and practice.[3] It is also one of the most creative endeavours an owner-operator can embark on.

Business planning is essential for established as well as for new businesses. The preparation of a business plan allows existing operations to assess their present position and desired future position in an objective manner. The principals can gain a better understanding of the organisation when they are forced to examine all aspects of the business. They can identify the operation's strengths, weaknesses, relative competitive position and potential competitive advantages. The plan also helps the organisation identify gaps in the delivery of products or services or emerging trends that may affect its future trading position. In short, it is a valuable strategic tool for any business.

The purpose of a business plan

There is much confusion about the role that business plans play. Some see the business plan as a document for raising money. Others see the preparation of the plan as a rite of passage, to separate 'serious' business people from the rest. Others again see it as an interesting intellectual exercise or as an 'I told you so' document to produce if the business fails.[4] A business plan, however, is most useful as an internal management tool or as a map to help guide a venture from a reasonably competitive position to an improved competitive position. Business plans serve seven main functions, as outlined in Figure 3.1. Each will be discussed briefly below.

Figure 3.1   The main purposes of a business plan

- A tool for integrating ideas
- A decision-making tool
- An internal analytical tool to assist in short-, medium- and long-term planning
- A dynamic 'flight plan' for reaching stated objectives
- A tool to measure performance
- A tool for raising finance
- A tool for assessing ideas

A tool for integrating ideas

A business plan provides an opportunity to formalise the filtering process described in the previous chapter. It integrates the disparate information gathered during the research phases—idea generation, product refinement, target market identification, competitive situation analysis, point of differentiation and financial information—into a discrete, coherent document. It provides a structure for distilling and refining the information gathered, clarifying and modifying ideas and identifying where further information is needed. Importantly, it details the operational considerations in delivering the product and, vitally, it describes the advertising and promotional strategies to be used.[5]

A decision-making tool

The business plan enables difficult decisions to be made about the new or existing business by allowing a number of scenarios to be tested in a low-cost, low-risk environment. The planning process provides the information and tools needed to make a number of decisions related to price, capacity, operating season, trip size, service level, types of accommodation required, ancillary services to be offered and the validity of the target market that has been identified. For example, a series of pricing scenarios can be run to determine which ones will achieve the desired financial objectives. Competitors' costs and prices can be analysed to help identify where competitive advantages or disadvantages may exist. It permits the development of accurate cost and value comparisons to determine the price of the product and where to position it in the marketplace.[6]

An analytical tool

A business plan is an analytical tool that can be used to plan how the business should be conducted. It allows the idea or the existing business to be analysed in as unbiased a way as possible. People have a tendency to lose their perspective when they begin to develop a new idea. They can become seduced by the idea and its seemingly unlimited business prospects. In the process, they all too often ignore obvious risk factors or fail to consider latent risks. By stepping back and rationally assessing the opportunity, they can avoid making costly mistakes.[7]

People in existing businesses often feel that they do not have the time to develop a business plan or may feel that their business is running along smoothly enough. But when they are so involved in the day-to-day operations of the business, they are unable assess whether the business is heading in the desired direction. Speaking colloquially, they cannot see the forest for the trees. This is especially true of small tour operators, who may be working seven days a week and spending much of their time in the field. The business planning exercise allows them to stand back and take a holistic view of the entire business. It is a chance to refine strategies and make mistakes on paper, rather than in the real world.

A 'flight plan'

A business plan is a dynamic document that provides a 'flight plan' for guiding the business to an improved position in a specified period of time.[8] It maps out the future and identifies a possible direction to follow. A flight plan describes the desired or intended route, but the pilot can change it if externalities emerge that make the chosen path less desirable. A business plan must likewise be adjustable to changed business conditions.

A tool to measure performance

A business plan furnishes short-, medium- and long-term indicators against which the performance of the organisation can be measured. It provides a mechanism for measuring the growth of a business and for keeping the business on track to reach its targets. It may also serve as a means of keeping growth to sustainable levels. Rapid expansion can threaten a business's viability just as much as low sales.[9] In monitoring growth, the plan is also a powerful management tool, identifying the organisation's goals, objectives and tactics. All people involved in the organisation can become aware of the direction the business wishes to take and the means used to achieve its broader goals.

A tool for raising finance

Business plans can be used to raise money for the venture.[10] They demonstrate to spouses, potential partners, parents and other likely sources of finance that a possible business opportunity exists and that lenders have a strong chance of getting their money back. They also allow potential investors or lenders to examine the proposed business in detail and make constructive comments that may enhance its viability.

A tool for assessing ideas

Finally, and arguably most importantly, a strategic analysis through the business planning process will allow operators to identify potentially fatal flaws before they destroy the business. All it takes is one serious oversight to render a venture non-viable. Michael Porter, one of the gurus of strategic thinking, has identified five fatal flaws or errors that he has seen repeatedly in business. These are:

- Misreading industry attractiveness. Many people think that the most attractive industries are the ones that are growing fastest or are the most glamorous. In fact, Porter says the most attractive industries are those with high barriers to entry and for which few substitute products are available.

- Failing to identify a real competitive advantage. Too many businesses simply imitate their rivals or assume that they have a real point of difference where none really exists. To succeed, businesses must find different ways of competing.

- Identifying unsustainable competitive advantages. A small point of difference, or a point of difference that can be matched easily by competitors, is not a satisfactory point of differentiation.

- Compromising strategy to grow faster. A strategy is a plan to achieve a desired goal. Often some success breeds a feeling of invincibility in operators. They expand their businesses in directions not considered, lose their focus and often lose their core clients, while arousing the competitive instincts of other businesses.

- Failing to make the strategy explicit and to communicate it to all staff. Too often people have ideas, but never formalise them into a specific strategy. Without a specific strategy, it is impossible to set and assess targets or to modify them over time. Furthermore, if the staff do not know what the objectives are, how can they achieve them?[11]

The components of a business plan

Dozens of books have been written on how to draw up business plans. Each one adopts a slightly different format for the plan. (This may be *their* point of differentiation.) However, the basic principles are similar. A business plan usually consists of a description of the idea, sections arguing that a business opportunity exists, a financial analysis demonstrating that financial goals can be met, marketing strategies, operational considerations and evidence of the ability of key people to deliver the stated objectives. The business plan pro forma reproduced in Figure 3.2 is the Tourism Accreditation Program developed by the Australian Tourism Operators Network (ATON).

Figure 3.2   Components of a business plan

1   **Table of contents**
2   **Introduction**
     Business and objectives
3   **Assumptions (internal or draft document only)**
4   **History and background**
     Business structure
     Training and experience
5   **Situation analysis**
     Aims and objectives
     SWOT analysis
6   **Financial analysis**
     Financial considerations
     Budgets—income/costs
     Break-even analysis
     Cash-flow projections
     Financial statements
     Investments

7 **Market analysis**
Market research/trends
Market strategies/competition
Target markets
Consumer characteristics

8 **Marketing strategies**
Products and services
Promotion/advertising
Distribution channels
Projections

9 **Operational strategies**
Resource management
Quality standards
Training
Environmental factors
Maintenance

10 **Conclusions**

11 **Appendices**

Source: ATOA (1995)[12]

Introduction

The plan generally begins with a brief description of the business, the products to be offered and the business objectives. Although it appears simple, this is actually the hardest task for the business planner. It forces the writer to identify clearly the core needs being satisfied by the product and the markets that will be targeted. This brief statement will indicate how the product will be positioned in the marketplace, who the competitors will be and the point of differentiation of the product.

The introductory section also specifies the financial and non-financial objectives, the performance targets and the time frame in which these objectives will be met. The objectives must be SMART: Specific, Measurable, Attainable, Realistic and Timely. An objective of 'earning $50 000 a year by year 3' is a SMART objective. A specific financial target has been set within a specified time frame that can be measured easily. The business plan will demonstrate whether the objective is realistic and attainable. Too often people state meaningless objectives like 'to achieve a desired lifestyle', 'to make enough money to live on' or 'to attain a 10 per cent market share'. What is a desired lifestyle? A rented shack in the bush or a mansion in Vaucluse? What is enough money to live on? Is $10 000 enough or is $100 000 insufficient? How can one gain a share of any market if the size of that market is unknown and its parameters have not been defined?

Assumptions

If the document is intended to be an internal document only, or if it is still a draft document, a section on assumptions or current unknowns is recommended. No plan is written with complete information. The number of assumptions that have to be made with new businesses is higher than for existing businesses. Listing assumptions identifies information gaps that need to be addressed as planning progresses.

History and background

The introduction is followed by a brief description of the business or products offered and a broader background of the industry in which it operates. It is important to clearly identify the type of business and the specific nature of the product and, in doing so, to identify the point of differentiation. It should be very clear what products are being sold and who the primary and secondary users of the products are. For example, an ecotourism operator taking day trips to the Daintree wilderness north of Cairns may indicate that the primary users of the product will be people vacationing in Cairns who are looking for an interesting day trip to see a well-known rainforest. The secondary users may be the true ecotourists, who have come to far north Queensland specifically to learn about rainforest ecology. Implicit in this section is an identification of the products not being sold, the markets not being targeted and the competitors being avoided.

Situation analysis

The next stage is the strategic thinking or situation analysis stage. This section is by far the most important aspect of the plan, for it will define the organisation's sustainable competitive advantages, its point of differentiation in the marketplace and how its products will be positioned. The situation analysis presents a fair, detached and realistic assessment of the business in relation to other businesses offering similar products and services (Strengths and Weaknesses) and in relation to the broad trends in the industry or marketplace (Opportunities and Threats) that may influence the future business environment. Its purpose is to demonstrate a strong understanding of the dynamic business environment that will be entered. Further, it will indicate gaps that the new business can fill. This part of the strategic business planning process is discussed in greater detail in the next section of this chapter.

Financial analysis

The financial analysis section should demonstrate that the business will provide acceptable returns for investors. The financial strategy is the means by which the marketing strategy and the product strategy can be implemented.[13] This section normally considers profit and loss calculations, cash flow projections and a balance sheet for the current year and for three to five years in the future. It also includes a break-even analysis that shows what sales levels must be achieved before any profit occurs.

Market analysis

The size of the market and major trends likely to affect the market are identified in the next section. The market analysis section demonstrates that the proponent has a clear understanding of who the intended clients will be, their motives and their reasons for buying the product, the absolute size of the relevant target markets and an indication of future market trends. Evidence of having conducted suitable research must be presented. The more precise the information presented, the better.

Marketing strategies

The marketing strategies section will describe how the product and the market will be linked. This section will include a discussion of the four Ps of marketing: Product, Price, Promotion and Place (distribution channels). Indeed, it may be beneficial to write a separate, detailed marketing plan and insert it into the business plan.

Operational strategies

Operational strategies are self-explanatory. A range of operational issues must be considered, including the development of systems and the management of on-site operations. It is also in this section that you will address the ethical obligations of a nature-based tour operator.

The business planning process

The business planning process is an iterative process that involves developing ideas, testing scenarios and constantly reviewing all aspects of the proposed or operational business. Meredith suggests that the planning process has three main stages: identification, resolution and revision.[14] All new businesses and most existing businesses operate under a number of unknowns or assumptions. Identifying these at an early stage will provide a clearer idea of the type of information needed before a decision can be made. The substitution of assumptions with knowledge developed through valid, accurate and unbiased research will facilitate progress towards the next stage of the plan. It is likely, though, that most early assumptions will prove incorrect. As such they will need to be rejected, or revised and re-tested, before a business opportunity can be confirmed.

The business planning process involves two main feedback loops, as is shown in Figure 3.3. These enable the individual to eliminate as much of the guesswork, fudged figures and uncertainties of business planning as possible. The inner loop allows a number of possible scenarios to be tested, rejected, revised and tested again before the preferred option is selected. The outer loop represents the formal preparation and testing of the preferred business option.

It is important to treat the entire process as a holistic exercise. A revision of one aspect of the plan may require a revision of the entire plan. Changing the financial goals, for example, may make it necessary to reconsider the market being targeted and the product being offered. A lowering of financial goals may mean lowering the proposed price, possibly creating opportunities to target a larger, but less affluent, audience. Lowering the price will require a review of the costs of the product to ensure that it can still be delivered in a cost-effective manner. Targeting a different market may require a different marketing strategy and the use of different promotional tools and media. All of these factors will require a review of the profit and loss and cash flow projections.

Problems and pitfalls

A business plan cannot guarantee the success of the business. It is designed to identify uncertainties and reduce the risk to acceptable levels. While business plans have proven to raise the odds of operating a successful business,[15] the planning process is not without its problems and pitfalls. Some include:

1 **An obsolete plan.** In a rapidly changing or volatile business environment, a plan may become obsolete before it is introduced. The planning process may take many months to complete, and during that time the business environment will have changed.

2 **Inflexibility.** A business plan predicts the future and identifies a desired path to reach a future direction. To be effective, it must be able to respond to changed conditions on the way to the goal. Some people, though, regard the plan as a forecast of the end result and, once it is written, commit the organisation to the prescribed path come hell or high water. Their inability to be flexible may have planned the business into oblivion.

Figure 3.3   The business planning process

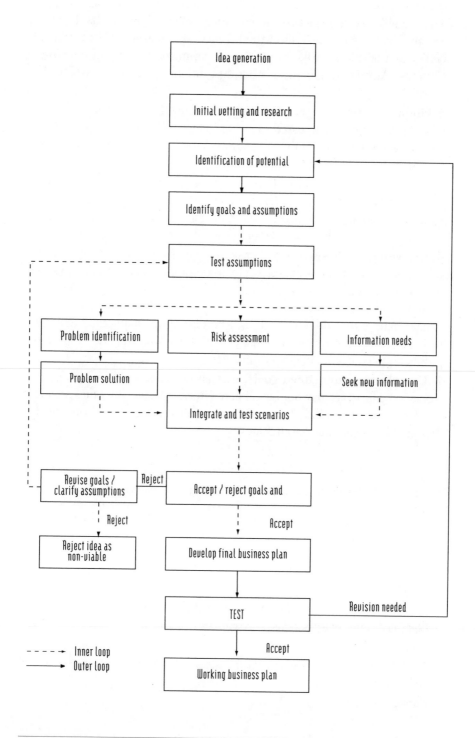

3 Extraordinary events. Business plans are designed to reduce the element of risk and to identify as many risk variables as possible. However, there is always the risk of variable X occurring and nullifying the plan. No one knows what variable X will be or when it will strike. All they know is that it is there and that some time it will affect the business. Extraordinary events like the Gulf War, the pilots' strike of 1989 and the introduction and collapse of Compass Airlines rendered all existing tourism business plans obsolete overnight.

4 Finding the time. To plan effectively takes time. How do small businesses whose principals are engrossed in trying to make a living and may be working 70-hour weeks find the time to plan? Can they afford to take the time away from their business? Can they afford not to?

5 Over-planning. Remember that the planning process is a means to developing a stronger business; it serves no other purpose. Some people are in danger of spending all their time planning and not enough actually running the business. The risk is that planning can be carried to an extreme.

6 The wrong emphasis. There is a risk that the owner-operator will place the wrong emphasis on the plan and will focus on product lines that are no longer relevant or wish lists that are not functioning yet, or else become too focused on one aspect of the plan rather than adopting a holistic view. The greatest danger here is that the emphasis will be placed on 'marketing' activities, which in reality means promotional activities, without fully developing the product, price or other business strategies.

7 Unrealistic or undefined goals. Unrealistic goals may be developed or, worse, specific goals may not be defined. Unless specific outcomes are identified, the plan is invalid. To succeed, the plan must be based on specific, measurable and attainable outcomes.[16]

[1] Maitland (1994) *The Business Planner*, Butterworth Heinemann, Oxford.

[2] Samson, op. cit.

[3] Timmons, op. cit.

[4] Brandt, op. cit.

[5] Saxon & Allan-Kamil, op. cit.

[6] Timmons, op. cit.

[7] E. Siegel, L. Schultz, B. Ford & D. Carney (1987) *The Arthur Young Business Plan Guide*, John Wiley & Sons, Brisbane.

[8] Timmons, op. cit.

[9] D. M. Vogelaar (1994) *How to Write a Business Plan*, Australian Business Library, Melbourne.

[10] Hopkins, op. cit.

[11] M. Porter (1991) Know your place, *Inc*, 13(9), pp. 90–5.

[12] ATOA (1995) *ATOA Accreditation Program*, Melbourne.

[13] Samson, op. cit.

[14] Meredith (1995) op. cit.

[15] Reynolds, Savage & Williams, op. cit.

[16] Timmons, op. cit.

Chapter 4

Legalities, accreditation and other considerations

*t*he organisation and legal operation of nature-based tourism businesses is governed by a variety of Commonwealth, state and local government laws, regulations and conventions. In addition, a number of tourism industry bodies have developed codes of practice and accreditation programs designed to enhance the quality of the tourism experience. Laws exist to protect the public and to provide a fair and orderly environment for the operation of businesses. Operators who run afoul of the law, feel overwhelmed by the intricacies of meeting legal requirements, get frustrated by the complexities of the bureaucratic process, or fail to satisfy industry-driven accreditation standards may feel otherwise.

This chapter reviews some of the considerations affecting the formation, management and operation of nature-based tourism businesses.[1] It provides a lay person's overview of such issues as the legal structure of the organisation, choosing and registering a name, laws affecting the operations of the business, consumer protection laws and some of the unique features of operating on public land. Readers are advised that many of the examples cited in this chapter refer to New South Wales and Victoria. Regulations in other states may vary from these examples. Taking this into account, the reader is advised to seek qualified legal assistance before proceeding with a business.

The legal structure of the business

Businesses in Australia can be structured in one of almost a dozen formats, or variations on existing formats. The most common for tour operators are sole traderships, partnerships or proprietary limited companies. Less common forms include trusts, public companies, companies limited by guarantee, co-operatives, closed corporations and limited partnerships. The merits and deficiencies of the three most common types of business structures are summarised in Figure 4.1.

Figure 4.1 Comparison of different business structures

SOLE TRADERSHIP

Strengths	Weaknesses
Ease of establishment	Maximum personal liability
Maximum personal control	Fewest tax advantages
Ability to write off business losses against other income	Least likelihood of sourcing external capital
Least capital required	Narrow management base
All profits to owner	Difficulty in attracting capital
Least start-up paperwork	

PARTNERSHIP

Strengths	Weaknesses
Similar to strengths of sole proprietorships	Inability to add or remove partners
Skills of potential partners	Potential for problems with partners
Opportunity to reduce taxes and split income	Unlimited liability of all partners for the acts of one partner
	Less flexibility in transferring ownership

CORPORATION OR COMPANY

Strengths	Weaknesses
Existence of the business as a separate entity	High set-up costs
Limited liability of shareholders	Operation highly regulated
Ease in transferring shares	Constraints on management
Control of directors' actions	Arm's-length relationship demanded
Greater ease in attracting capital	Expensive to organise and manage

Sources: Bransgrove; English; Meredith; Reynolds, Savage & Williams[2]

Sole tradership

A sole proprietorship or sole tradership is the easiest and simplest form of business to establish. A single proprietor becomes the sole owner of the business and carries on the business in his or her own right, either under a personal name (Jane Smith) or under a business name (Jane's Wilderness Tours). If the person chooses to trade under a business name, the name must be registered with the appropriate state authority. The person owns the entire business, receives all the profits and assumes all the risks. This format does not preclude the proprietor from hiring staff or entering into most types of contracts.

Simplicity and ease of establishment are the greatest advantages of this form of business structure. In addition, the operator exerts maximum control over the enterprise and enjoys all the profits. The administrative and regulatory requirements of a sole tradership are also minimal. Shut-down of the business is simple if the operator decides to stop trading.

Being a sole trader has a number of tax implications. Because the business and the individual are not seen as separate entities, one tax return is filed for the total income of the proprietor. Taxable income is taxed at personal rates. If the business registers a loss during its first few years, this loss can be written off against other income the proprietor may earn from a full- or part-time job. If the business is profitable, the proprietor may have to pay tax at the highest marginal rate. There is less opportunity for tax avoidance, as profits cannot be spread to other principals or shareholders who may have lower marginal tax rates.

However, a number of significant risks and disadvantages must be recognised. As stated above, in law the business and the individual are not seen as separate entities, as the law does not distinguish between the sole trader as a business and the sole trader as a person. A sole trader therefore assumes unlimited personal liability for all debts incurred by the business or for negligent acts and any other wrongs committed by the business or its employees. Thus, a sole trader risks the assets of the business plus all personal assets, including house, car, furniture, private superannuation plan and savings if things go wrong. For example, if the business defaults on a business loan, the trader may lose his or her house. Similarly, if a catastrophic accident occurs and the insurance pay-out exceeds the amount of liability insurance the operator has, or (more commonly) the claim is declined by the insurer, the sole trader may be personally liable for the full payment of the settlement. If the potential sole trader has a substantial personal asset base or if the venture has a high element of risk, an alternative business structure is recommended.

In addition, sole traders generally find it more difficult to access finance or raise capital, especially if the proprietor has few personal assets. The business cannot be continued if the owner dies or is incapacitated, as the sole proprietorship is then deemed to be automatically terminated. Finally, sole traders, who may be fiercely independent and unwilling to hire staff, may not have the management skills to make their business perform.

Partnership

A partnership is defined as a relationship between owners or potential owners who are carrying on a business in common with the view of making a profit.[3] Partnerships are regulated under various state Partnership Acts which allow two to twenty people to come together to operate a business that is expected to last at least a year. States generally require that some evidence of the partnership be presented, usually in the form of a written partnership agreement.

Generally, three conditions must be satisfied before a partnership is deemed to exist:

- The partners must be carrying on a business.
- They must be working in common.
- The business must be profit oriented.

The first condition implies that the business must be an ongoing entity. A one-off venture, such as a church fete, may not be considered in law as satisfying the criterion of carrying on a business. The 'in common' criterion requires that there be proof that the business is being carried on, by, or on behalf of the partners. While the partners do not have to take an active role in the day-to-day operations of the business (in which case they are silent partners), they are still responsible for its actions. The third condition confirms that the partnership is carrying on a business.

A partnership operates in law in essentially the same manner as a sole tradership, except that there are two or more people involved in the venture. Like sole traders, partners have no existence in law as separate entities; the individuals who form the partnership *are* the partnership. As such, each partner has the same legal obligations to the organisation that a sole trader would have to her or his business. The assets of the business are viewed as belonging to the partners and the partners assume unlimited liability for all debts incurred by the partnership. Further, each partner is an agent of the firm and of the other partners. Thus, a partner who is not particularly experienced or skilled in business has the power to enter into contracts or other transactions that will be binding on all co-partners.[4]

Partnerships can be structured in any number of ways, with the terms and conditions spelt out in the formal partnership agreement. The major investor may become a majority partner, owning a larger percentage of the business than minority partners. Some partners may be actively involved in the day-to-day operations of the business; others may not. Some partners may have their personal liability limited to the amount of their investment (although the courts may choose to disagree).

In the author's opinion, the risks of entering into a partnership far outweigh the limited benefits for all but a few prospective tour operators. Like sole traderships, they are simple and inexpensive to form. Their main benefit is that they can bring together the complementary skills and talents of more than one stakeholder. Partnership agreements can be structured to describe each partner's duties and functions in such a way that the partners can develop their own skill bases. Because more people are involved, it is often easier to acquire the necessary capital for the venture, either through the partners' own assets or by using them as collateral for loans. Finally, the structure of the partnership may provide tax benefits to partners, especially if the partnership is formed between family members.

However, partnerships can also be extremely dangerous and, in the author's opinion, should be avoided under most circumstances. First, because each partner has the right to make contracts and commitments on behalf of all other partners, the business may lack clear focus. Secondly, and most alarmingly, all partners legally assume unlimited liability for the actions of any other partner. Thus the actions of one partner legally bind all other partners to his or her debts. If one partner, without the approval of the other partners, embarks on a risky venture that fails, all other partners are liable to cover the debts created by the actions of that individual.

Further, in practice, the operation of partnerships may not work as smoothly as first envisioned. Partners may enter the partnership in good faith and with a clear idea of how the functions performed in the business will be delineated. However, as the business evolves, the roles are likely to evolve too, with one partner possibly assuming a greater share of the workload but not of the fruits of the business. Newell states that the problems with partnerships, like marriages, is that they often come under stress and the parties concerned may disagree to the point of splitting up. It is difficult to divide an ongoing business two or more ways and still retain its viability.[5]

Importantly, the partnership arrangement cannot be altered unless all existing partners agree to the move. No new partners can be admitted and, by the same token, non-performing existing partners cannot be removed, nor can they leave the business if they wish to. A number of very close friendships have been destroyed by partnerships gone wrong.

In some cases, partnerships work extremely effectively; however, the general advice is to avoid entering into partnerships unless they are with family members with whom a strong, stable relationship exists. The risks associated with partnerships are otherwise too great. It is recommended that anyone considering a partnership investigate the options of entering into a sole tradership and then employing prospective 'partners' as salaried or commissioned staff or, if a partnership is desired, form a limited company.

If a partnership format is chosen, a clear, unambiguous, legally binding partnership agreement should be written and this should be signed by all partners. The agreement must outline the expected duties and functions of each partner, profit and loss sharing, drawings and banking procedures, voting rights, parameters by which the partnership may be dissolved and, if more than two people are involved, a structure that allows the business to function in the case of a disagreement with one or more partners. This document should be written by a lawyer experienced in business law.

Proprietary limited company

The third form of business structure is the proprietary limited company, which exists as a legal entity in its own right, separate and apart from the shareholders who own it. A company is formed when a group of people or firms combine as shareholders and incorporate under the provisions of the Companies Act.[6] The structure of the business is stated in its Memorandum and Articles of Association, which states what types of activities the business can engage in. While the shareholders own the company, subject to any personal or directors' guarantees given, liability is limited to the assets of the company. Thus, the risk assumed for most shareholders is limited to their contribution of capital to the business and does not involve their personal assets.

There are a number of advantages in structuring a business as a corporation, apart from limiting personal liability.[7] The management of the enterprise can be centralised in a board of directors, thus permitting the selection of experts as managers. The enterprise has continuous existence, which means it is not dissolved by the death, insanity or withdrawal of an owner. An interest in the business can be bought and sold, allowing the owner to withdraw from the company without jeopardising its continuity. Capital is usually easier to attract, as the business itself has assets. The owners can become employees of the company, which provides a number of tax and superannuation benefits.

As with all business structures, though, there are some disadvantages. The greatest relate to cost, complexity and the regulatory and reporting requirements of operating a limited company. It is expensive to start and operate a corporation, costing $1000 or more to establish a business and another $1000 a year in fees.[8] The real costs are likely to be much higher. Moreover, the process is time-consuming and bureaucratic; starting a business from scratch involves working with the Australian Securities Commission. The alternative is to buy a shelf company—an existing structure waiting for someone to buy it. But again, the time and costs of changing the company name and amendments to the Memorandum and Articles of Association may be prohibitive.[9] With this in mind, many new small nature-based tour operators with limited capital may opt to start their business under a different structure, only incorporating when the complexity of the business and the increased risk involved demand it and the financial resources permit it.

Selecting a suitable structure

Figure 4.2 summarises the key factors that must be considered when selecting the business structure. Most new nature-based tourism businesses begin life as partnerships or sole proprietorships, primarily because of the ease of establishment and the low costs involved. However, these may not be sufficiently compelling reasons, given the medium-to-long-term implications of the decision. A range of other factors must be considered to determine if the structure selected best fits the type of business, or if it really is the cheapest and easiest option.

Figure 4.2   Factors affecting choice of business structure

- The nature of the business operation
- The degree and complexity of the venture sought
- The risk involved
- The number of people involved in the venture
- Taxation considerations
- The need to acquire capital for establishment or expansion
- The desire to admit new partners into the venture
- The potential liability exposure of the principals
- Available finances and the cost of establishing and continuing the structure
- Continuity of the business entity
- Transferability of interest
- A range of personal factors
- Reliability of the partners

Sources: Bransgrove; English; Meredith; Reynolds, Savage & Williams[10]

Choosing and registering a name

The business name will have to be registered unless the business is trading under the name of the proprietor. Thus 'Peter Jones' does not have to be registered, but 'Peter Jones's Adventures' does, as would a name like 'Alpine Cycling Tours'. Business names for sole traderships and partnerships must be registered with the appropriate state's Corporate Affairs Office, Registrar of Business Names division or equivalent, while companies must resister their names with the Australian Securities Commission. Names are registered for a number of reasons, some for the benefit of the consumer, others for the benefit of the operator. The certificate of registration must thereafter be displayed in a prominent position in the place of business.

Selecting an appropriate name is one of the bigger challenges facing new tour operators, for the name will convey much to the travelling public. English explains that a business name creates an image of the new business, aids in customer recall and tells potential customers much of what the business is about.[11] It also helps give the business respectability and differentiates it from the myriad other businesses that may be offering similar products. A good business name, therefore, should be short, convey the main theme of the business, be easy to say and spell, be amenable to various forms of publicity and constitute a symbol of quality, service and reliability.[12]

Names like 'Gary's Ecotours', 'Jill's Nature Rambles', 'Champagne Sunset Tours' and 'Bogong Jack Adventures' convey a clear message to potential travellers. On the other hand, some names should be avoided. Humorous names like 'Crash Airlines' may be offensive, while others may be too obscure for the public to understand. Names that are difficult to pronounce or have unusual spellings, such as 'Ptarmigan Arctic Expeditions' (where the 'p' is silent) may confuse people and be hard for telephone operators to find. The name must convey an idea of what is being offered without constraining the business. 'Fred's Guided Bushwalks' may be suitable if Fred only plans to offer bushwalks. But if he expands his product range to offer bicycle tours, ski tours and hang-gliding adventures, then the name is inappropriate. In this instance a more generic name, such as 'Fred's Adventure Unlimited', may be more appropriate.

Licences and other legal considerations

Selecting the appropriate business structure and registering the name of the business represent only the start of the bureaucratic process for most tour operators. Throughout the life of the business, operators will be required to comply with a variety of regulations, laws and government policies. In addition, the industry, through various accreditation programs, is striving to improve the quality of the tourism product available in Australia. Accreditation incorporates the legal requirements for a business and also includes business planning, crisis management and ethical operational components.

Licences and statutory requirements

A variety of licences, permits and registrations may be required for tour operators. Tour operators must comply with the same types of statutory legal requirements as all other businesses pertaining to business name registration, fire, health and safety, signage and regulations surrounding dangerous goods and consumer and trade practices. The ATON accreditation document also sets out that tour operators may require specialist commercial passenger vehicle drivers' licences, food premises or restaurant licences, liquor licences, marine board licences, high frequency radio licences and Civil Aviation Authority licences for pilots and aircraft.[13]

In addition, insurers may insist that all staff present evidence of skill qualifications for the type of work they do. As a minimum, all staff involved in leading trips will require first aid training certificates. Guides may also have to provide evidence of certification in their speciality areas through accredited bodies such as the Outdoor Recreational Council of Australia (ORCA) or the National Outdoor Recreation Leadership Division (NORLD); they may need nationally recognised scuba diving, surf lifesaving or appropriate horseriding qualifications.

Finally, depending on the type of business and the state in which the business operates, prospective nature-based tour operators may be required to register themselves as licensed travel agents. The majority of retail travel agents and tour wholesalers must be licensed, but state licensing laws may also require other types of tour operators to be licensed. If, for example, the business plans to on-sell others' products, it may need to be registered as a travel agency. Without a licence, the business cannot operate legally. It is advisable to check with the relevant state travel agent licensing authority.

Tax

There is no escaping the reality that small business must pay taxes if it shows a trading profit. Failure to so may result in the proprietor's enjoying an extended stay at the Crown's leisure in one of its many resorts. The views are lousy, the food is worse, the company is poor and the staff are not trained in customer service. Overall, it is an experience that is not recommended. Commentators generally have little positive to say about the tax situation for small businesses. English, for example, states:

> If ever there was a disincentive to organising and operating a small business it is taxes. The problem is not just the cost, but the mountain of paperwork that is required. Taxation is complicated and it is not an area in which do-it-yourself experts find much success.[14]

Reynolds, Savage and Williams add:

> No topic arouses more interest and is more confusing for people in small business than that of taxation. New laws and regulations and an endless stream of court judgements combine to create a climate of continual change.[15]

The concept of provisional tax is the one that seems to cause the most confusion for new operators. Provisional tax is the counterpart to the PAYE (Pay As You Earn) system for individuals who have income other than salaries and wages. It is called provisional tax because the Australian Taxation Office asks business operators to pay their tax provisionally for the current year before they know what the income for that year will be. Businesses are asked to pay this year's taxes in advance based on the previous year's taxable income. Taxes may be paid in a lump sum or quarterly, depending on the size of the business and arrangements made with the Taxation Office. The first time provisional tax is paid, though, can come as a shock to operators, for businesses effectively pay up to two years of tax: tax for the previous year plus provisional tax for the current year.[16] Operators who fail to plan for this event may find themselves in a difficult cash-flow situation.

Worker's compensation and staffing

Most businesses require the assistance of paid staff, be they permanent full-time workers, permanent part-time staff or casual staff who may operate as guides, trip leaders and helpers. The employer has certain duties and responsibilities to all staff, regardless of their employment status. Australian employers are held responsible for any work-related sickness, injury or death of their employees and therefore all employees, regardless of their status, must be covered by worker's compensation insurance. The cost of this insurance can be high, but as with all forms of insurance, the cost of not being covered can be higher still.

It is common for many small tourist businesses to pay staff with cash in hand or by offering in-kind payment (discounted equipment, free trips and the like), rather than go through the hassle, cost and excessive paperwork of placing them on the formal payroll. People get away with this practice (although it is illegal and, therefore, *not recommended*) as long as the staff member does not suffer a serious injury or illness at the place of work or as long as no client suffers any mishap. Bear in mind that the risk of injury is enhanced for tour operators, since the place of work may be found hanging off the side of a mountain, walking though a blizzard, swimming in shark-infested waters or wandering though the desert in 40° Celsius heat. If the person is injured, he or she may have a right to sue for compensation or indemnity. If the injury is serious, the settlement may result in the closure of the business. In the long run, it is easier to put up with some paperwork and do the right thing rather than try to cut corners.

Operators also have other financial obligations to staff. Within guidelines that seem to change with every change of government, employers are compelled to provide a minimum level of superannuation cover and to deduct tax instalments from an employee's wages. Annual leave and long service leave entitlements of staff must also be budgeted for. Depending on the nature of the work and the hours of operation, employers may be required to pay penalty rates. Further, to be competitive in the marketplace and to retain staff, employers are offering a variety of other benefits, ranging from personal disability insurance to subsidised accommodation. As a minimum, the on-costs of employing staff add about 20 per cent to the total wage cost.

Licences to operate on public land

Virtually all states require tour operators who wish to operate on public land to be licensed. The licence protects both the operation and the environment in which it operates by limiting both the number of businesses and the number of clients in a given area. Although targeting common goals, licensing requirements vary from state to state. The information below gives a general picture of the situation across Australia. Readers wishing for more specific details are advised to contact the appropriate state department.

Today, state natural resources departments recognise the contribution of commercial tourism to government policies on public land access.[17] National park management plans now include sections that deal specifically with commercial tourism use issues.[18] Tourism is being credited with having a significant role to play in the enjoyment of protected areas. However, it is also recognised that tourism can have a deleterious impact on fragile environments. By licensing and controlling the number of tour operators, the number of clients they can carry and where they can go, states can optimise the benefits of tourism while minimising its adverse effects.

Permits are generally required for a variety of tourist activities on public land, including water-based recreation, horse and camel riding, rock-climbing, hunting, hang-gliding, sightseeing bus tours, four wheel drive tours, bushwalking, cross-country skiing, photography and nature observation.[19] Licences identify which activities are acceptable, specify where the businesses can operate and set limits on party sizes. In addition, certain conditions may be set for specified activities. For example, four wheel drive operators may have to provide a detailed itinerary of the roads and tracks they plan to use, provide the registration number and type of each vehicle and adhere to set maximum tour sizes.

Other requirements normally include:

- a minimum of $5 000 000 in public liability insurance
- specifications as to where tour operators can and cannot go
- controls on the lighting of fires
- site maintenance, including the removal of garbage
- limits on the use of huts
- current licences and other permits
- a current paramedic qualification for guides.

Operators who contravene the terms of their licences may be penalised or excluded from operating. Penalties are usually exacted on a sliding demerit points scale. For instance, one demerit point may be given for minor infringements. Two points may be incurred for exceeding party size limits, running tours outside permitted areas or exceeding the maximum number of permitted tours. Infringements of the Wildlife of National Parks Act or failure to hold public liability insurance may earn, say, three points. An operator who gets the maximum number of points may lose his or her permit.

Consumer protection and the Trade Practices Act

Ethical businesses adopt a policy of treating their clients and their competitors in a fair and equitable manner. Unfortunately, not all business operators are ethical. Over the years, there have been a number of cases where business owners have colluded to reduce competition or exclude competitors, displayed unfair or misleading advertising, taken advantage of consumers, abused credit practices and produced poor-quality products. In response, the Commonwealth Government passed the Trade Practices Act in 1974 to protect consumers from unethical, misleading or unfair business practices. This Act and the various state Fair Trading Acts form the cornerstone of consumer protection legislation in Australia.

Section 52 captures the essence of the Act. It stipulates that:

> A corporation shall not, in trade or commerce, engage in conduct that is misleading or deceptive or is likely to mislead or deceive. Conduct that is deemed to be misleading or deceiving consists of some form of misrepresentation, which may be conveyed by an express statement or by silence.[20]

Restrictive business practices

The Act regulates certain restrictive trade practices to protect the interests of the consumer, to foster real competition between businesses and, importantly from a small business perspective, to protect the interests of small business operators. Over the years, the Act has been amended to match the changes in Australian consumer attitudes. Recently, new sections have been added to the Act to prohibit unconscionable conduct in consumer or commercial transactions.[21] The Trade Practices Act addresses, among other business practice issues:

- agreements that affect competition
- exclusionary provisions
- price fixing
- market power abuse
- exclusive dealing
- resale price maintenance
- price discrimination
- mergers.

One of its main roles is to ensure that a fair competitive business environment exists in Australia. It is, therefore, illegal for businesses to enter into an agreement (formal or informal) with their competitors that will lessen competition. This stipulation does not preclude businesses working together to enhance their competitive position, nor does it preclude the normal functions of market forces.

Price fixing is the most common method by which competitors can collude to control a market. The Trade Practices Act stipulates that any form of agreement between competitors that is likely to fix, control or maintain prices is prohibited. The Act recognises that businesses offering similar products in a competitive marketplace will likely have to charge similar prices to remain both competitive and viable. Price fixing does not apply if organisations recommend retail prices, even if they recommend them strongly. As long as businesses are free to set the retail price they choose, then price fixing has not occurred. However, when competing businesses collude to influence the market, and in doing so reduce real competition, then they have violated the law. It would not be illegal for all nature-based tour operators in one community to charge a similar price. In fact, market forces dictate that most do. It would be illegal, though, if they agreed to fix prices at an artificially high level and to prevent other operators from charging a different price in order to enhance their own trading position. Recent court cases have upheld these principles.

Protecting the consumer

Sections 53 to 60 of the Act seek to protect consumers from false or misleading representations. The Act stipulates that the consumer must be able to do business with an organisation without being defrauded, that he or she must be able to make an informed choice, that there must be equality in dealing with the trader (that the relationship must be equally powerful) and that the product being sold must be safe.[22]

It is illegal to make false representations about the quality, style and rating of goods sold. A tourism lodge cannot claim to have a four-star NRMA rating if, in fact, it has never been inspected by the organisation or if it was rated at two stars. Similarly, clients cannot be told in advertisements that they will travel in the newest, safest four wheel drive vehicles and then be presented with a rusty 1963 mini bus.

Businesses cannot claim sponsorships, approval or performance characteristics that do not exist. It is generally regarded that industry-based accreditation programs, like the ones offered by the Australian Tourism Operators Network or the Ecotourism Association of Australia, will provide accredited businesses with a marketing advantage. It is illegal to claim that the business is accredited, if no such accreditation has been granted.

Operators cannot make false or misleading statements about the prices charged, nor can they engage in bait-and-switch tactics. Sale prices must reflect genuine sales based on real savings in established retail processes or recommended retail prices. It is illegal to offer products for a 'sale' price of $50, if the regular retail price has not been established legitimately beforehand. In a similar manner, it is illegal to promote a 'sale' price of $199 when the regular retail price for the trip is $200. Consumers cannot be attracted by offers of low-priced products when no such products exist, and then be offered a more expensive product to close the sale.

Conditions must be displayed clearly, so that the consumer knows if there are conditions that apply to the purchase of a product at a certain price or if other charges are likely to be levied. Nash and Zullo report on a hotel in Denver, Colorado, that promised a 'Free Hotel Room' but then added in fine print '*Parking $55/night (Parking is Mandatory)'.[23] This type of practice is frowned upon.

Advertising

Many businesses get into trouble by conducting false or misleading promotional campaigns. Sometimes this happens by mistake; at other times it is deliberate. Whichever is the case, it may be illegal. Smith stresses that operators must be very careful about how the business, product or service is represented in their advertising or promotions.[24] It is not what is said that counts but what is believed by the consumer. Similarly, it is not what is meant by the promotion, but what the consumer understands that will dictate whether the ad is misleading. The protection afforded under the Act applies to all forms of advertising, including press, television, radio and magazine ads, catalogues, brochures, pamphlets and other promotional literature, point-of-sale material and signage.[25]

Activities that are illegal include:

- misleading claims or survey results ('100 per cent of our clients are satisfied' when clients have not been surveyed)
- misleading or false savings ('Book now and save $200' when in fact, if you booked three hours before the trip, you could save the same amount of money)
- undisclosed credit terms
- undisclosed payment schedule
- undisclosed reasonable or likely extra prices (such as the cost of mandatory safety equipment)
- misleading symbols
- 'exclusive' mail advertising when in fact every house in the neighbourhood got a letter
- unlimited or limited time offers when in fact that is not what is delivered
- classified ads that appear to be private sales
- 'like for like comparisons' when the items being compared are not similar (for instance, ads that say 'Why pay $600 for a wildflower tour when you can do ours for $6?' when the $600 tour is a fully escorted, luxury four wheel drive with a world-renowned guide and the $6 product is a photocopied road map)
- use of similar brand names and logos
- false statements about the product or services to be delivered
- suggestions that goods are made in Australia when they are not.

Accreditation

Increasingly, the tourism industry is playing a proactive role in enhancing the standards of the sector through the development of industry-based accreditation programs. Two in particular are relevant to the nature-based tour operator. The Australian Tourism Operators Network program has been designed to establish minimum performance criteria for the industry.[26] In doing so, it sets quality parameters that the tourism industry can strive to meet. The ATON program focuses primarily on the business aspects of tourism, addressing such issues as business planning, compliance with legal requirements, the establishment of operations procedures, the development of risk management plans, the preparation of marketing plans and quality assurance programs.

The Ecotourism Association of Australia launched its accreditation program in late 1996.[27] Designed to dovetail into the ATON program, this program accredits products rather than businesses and ensures that ecotourism businesses operate in a socially and ecologically sustainable manner.

Accreditation programs serve a number of useful purposes. They:

- help businesses focus their product offerings and develop formal business plans
- provide marketing benefits, especially to the travel trade
- ensure that systems are formalised, making businesses operate more efficiently
- provide a means to assess and alter business practices
- provide real cost savings, especially for insurance premiums
- help operators differentiate the business from non-accredited businesses
- give businesses greater credibility.

Anyone wishing for further information should contact their appropiate state tourism body or relevant industry organisations.

---

[1] The material presented in this chapter is summarised from a number of sources, including ATOA (1995); Bransgrove; English (1995); A. Hiam (1990) *The Vest Pocket CEO: Decision Making Tools for Executives*, Prentice Hall, Englewood Cliffs, NJ; Hopkins; Meredith (1988; 1995); NESBA (1993) *Costing and Pricing*, Managing the Small Business Series no. 42, AGPS, Canberra; Newell; R. W. Peacock (1993) *Small Business Success: Your Home Based Business*, McGraw-Hill, Roseville; J. Ratnatunga & J. Dixon (1993) *Australian Small Business Manual*, 3rd edn, CCH Publishing, Sydney; Reynolds, Savage & Williams; Saxon & Allan-Kamil; G. Smith (1996) *Do-It-Yourself Marketing: Practical Hints and Tips for Marketing in Australia*, Prentice Hall, Sydney; Trade Practices Commission (1993a) *Unconscionable Conduct in Consumer Transactions*, AGPS, Canberra; (1993b) *Unconscionable Conduct in Commercial Dealings*, AGPS, Canberra; and VTOA (1995c) *Tourism Accreditation Program: Tour Operators and Attractions*, VTOA, Melbourne. As much of the information presented in these sources is similar, specific references to individual authors will be omitted unless they are quoted or paraphrased directly.

[2] Bransgrove, op. cit.; English (1995) op. cit.; Meredith (1988) op. cit.; (1995) op. cit.; Reynolds, Savage & Williams, op. cit.

[3] Meredith (1995) op. cit.

[4] English (1995) op. cit.

[5] Newell, op. cit.

[6] Reynolds, Savage & Williams, op. cit.

[7] English (1995) op. cit.

[8] Saxon & Allan-Kamil, op. cit.

[9] Reynolds, Savage & Williams, op. cit.

[10] English (1995) op. cit.; Meredith (1995) op. cit.; Peacock (1993) op. cit.; Reynolds, Savage & Williams, op. cit.

[11] English (1995) op. cit.

[12] Newell, op. cit.

[13] ATOA (1995) op. cit.

[14] English (1995) op. cit.

[15] Reynolds, Savage & Williams, op. cit.

[16] English (1995) op. cit.

[17] DCNR (Vic.) op. cit.

[18] DCE (Vic.) (1992b); Victorian Department of Conservation, Forests and Lands (1989) *Alpine Area Bogong Planning Unit Proposed Management Plan February 1989*, CFL, Melbourne.

[19] DCNR (Vic.) op. cit.

[20] In Smith, op. cit.

[21] TPA (1993a; 1993b) op. cit.

[22] ibid.

[23] B. Nash & A. Zullo (1988) *The Misfortune 500*, Pocket Books, Sydney.

[24] Smith, op. cit.

[25] English (1995) op. cit.

[26] ATOA (1995) op. cit.

[27] Ecotourism Association of Australia (1996a) *Ecotourism Accreditation Program*, EAA, Brisbane.

Chapter 5

Planning, budgets and cash flow

*m*any new tour operators have little or no knowledge of the financial realities of running a business. Many lack even the most rudimentary concepts of budgets and have never been confronted with cash flow considerations. Some believe that if money is left in the bank at the end of the operating season, they have had a profitable year. The path of failed tourism enterprises is littered with people who entered the sector for lifestyle reasons and then discovered to their chagrin that the lifestyle they envisioned could not be achieved with the revenue generated by the business. Therefore, it is not surprising that gaining further knowledge about accounting, budgeting, finance, cash flow management and pricing consistently ranks highest among the needs of new tour operators.

The next two chapters will introduce the reader to some of the financial considerations important to the successful operation of a tourism venture. This chapter examines such issues as the financial planning process, the preparation of operational and cash flow budgets and the need to establish control measures. It also makes suggestions for improving the cash position of a business. It concludes by discussing some crisis control measures. The chapter that follows examines a number of matters pertaining to costing and pricing from a financial perspective.

The financial planning process

Developing financial objectives and preparing workable financial plans is a process that is intrinsically linked to the business and strategic planning processes. While the business plan outlines the goals of the organisation and the desired path for achieving them, the financial plans indicate how they will be achieved. An enterprise requires positive cash flow to enable it to keep functioning and a profit to enable it to grow.[1] Without either, the best laid business plans are meaningless. Further, businesses require a series of clearly defined benchmarks against which progress towards their goals can be measured. Monitoring profit and loss and cash flow budgets is the easiest way to ensure that targets are being achieved. The financial planning process thus forms a link between the organisation's goals and its day-to-day operations. Figure 5.1 outlines an eight-step process to develop appropriate financial plans.

Figure 5.1   Steps in the financial planning process

1   Linking the owner's goals with the enterprise's goals

2   Analysing past performance and setting efficiency goals

3   Establishing an overall plan and long-term strategy

4   Completing financial plans and verifying key factors

5   Analysing the performance plan

6   Projecting the financial position

7   Preparing weekly cash plans

8   Preparing control reports

Source: Meredith (1993)[2]

1 Linking the owner's goals with the enterprise's goals

In a very real sense, small tourism businesses are a reflection of their owners. For this reason, a business's financial goals must be compatible with the objectives of the owners, the objectives of family members associated with the owners, and the objectives of the enterprise as a business entity.[3] Too often people get involved in the tourism industry because they enjoy the lifestyle of being tourists themselves. They tend to look at the business from the perspective of the tourist and feel that tourism offers a low-stress lifestyle in a healthy environment and permits the operator to set his or her own hours. Because most people visit during the high season, they think that tourism is easy money.

Oh, how wrong they are! What they do not appreciate is that, while the guests are relaxing, the operator is working. Spending an hour having a drink with a guest means that another hour must be spent somewhere else to catch up on the workload. While guests can sleep in if they have had a busy night, the operator must get up at 6 a.m. to cook breakfast. Furthermore, while the guest may spend a lot of money on the vacation, most of that will flow through the operator's hands into the pockets of suppliers. Finally, as visitors they do not see tourism operators in the off season, when no revenue is generated.

2 Analysing past performance and setting efficiency goals

As with any form of planning, the next year's plans must be based on the organisation's past performance. The best indicator of how the business is performing and where it is likely to go comes from the history of the organisation. Analysing past performance enables the operator to make a comparison with sector norms, identify realistic future targets, and develop SMART (Specific, Measurable, Attainable, Realistic and Timely) goals for the venture.

Importantly, it also allows the operator to analyse the performance of specific aspects of the business. If actual costs vary significantly from budgeted costs, a review is necessary. It may be that the estimate of costs was simply inaccurate, in which case corrections can be made in the next year's budget to reflect reality. It may also be that cost overruns reflect a deeper problem: a business that is out of control.

Clearly, new businesses cannot set financial targets based on their past performance. However, they can set targets based on the past performance of other businesses. Analysing the competitive situation is a key role of the filtering process discussed in Chapter 2. Such an analysis will establish a rough idea of the gross and net revenues generated by established businesses offering similar products. These figures can be used as a guide for new ventures.

3 Establishing an overall plan and long-term strategy

After analysing past performances, the next step is to identify short- and long-term profit objectives. At this point, the details of expense items are unimportant; the key is to identify clearly what the operator wishes to get out of the business. Objectives may include target profits, net profit as a percentage of sales, and desirable sales figures to reach target profits. They should be developed for the current year and for three to five years in the future. These targets identify the parameters for the development of the profit and loss and cash flow budgets.

4 Completing financial plans and verifying key factors

Once SMART goals have been set, the rest of the financial plan can be developed, vetted and verified. The volume of product needed to be sold, the price to be charged and all the expense items can now be calculated to see if the targets are realistic. If the business offers multiple products (or trips), separate gross profits, sales, price structures and costs for each product can be developed. Different products have different market appeal, different cost structures and different prospects for generating profits. A product-by-product analysis will allow the operator to identify profit centres and products that may need some support. This analysis will also help the operator identify the product mix being offered, ensuring that enough volume of high-profit products is offered to carry less profitable lines.

5 Analysing the performance plan

The plan must then be analysed to ensure that it is both feasible and realistic. It is easy to add another trip here, expect a few more customers there and assume that just a little bit more can be squeezed out of the business somewhere else. In the end, the financial plan may be unworkable through the tyranny of small decisions.

6 Projecting the financial position

This next stage relates to projecting the financial position of the organisation for the end of each year. In essence, the operator will develop a draft balance sheet for each year, identifying fixed assets, working capital, long-term and short-term commitments, equity and reserves. The great challenge for many tour operators is to ensure that they have sufficient reserves to carry the business through low or no-cash periods and still have enough revenue to conduct promotional campaigns leading into their next season.

7 Preparing weekly cash plans

Cash flow plans are the penultimate, but arguably most important, step in developing appropriate financial plans for the business. Some people suggest that weekly cash flow plans be developed, but for most tour operators monthly cash flow projections are suitable. Cash flow budgets represent the actual amount of money that flows into and out of the business. Cash has been likened to petrol. Just as a car cannot operate without petrol, a business cannot operate without cash.

Most people who have never operated their own business before feel that developing a yearly operating budget is enough to meet their needs. However, there are significant differences between a profit and loss statement and a cash flow budget. A business may be showing a strong paper profit but be forced to close because it has run out of cash.

8 Preparing control reports

Finally, operators must develop effective control mechanisms to enable them to monitor what actually happens during the period. Control reports include regular cash flow reports, monthly profit and loss statements, bank reconciliation statements, regular assessment of accounts receivable and accounts payable, and various expense forms.

The nature of the small tourism sector makes it essential that workable financial control systems be implemented. It is easy to let a tourism business slip out of control, for the operators often spend long periods of time away from the office running trips. The last thing people want to do after an exhausting seventeen-day trip is spend a number of mind-numbing hours doing accounting. That is not why they went into business. But unless they do this, it will be the reason why they are no longer in business.

The process

The process of financial planning for a small business is shown in Figure 5.2. The vertical arrows reflect the ideal flow of the process linking the enterprise's goals and assumptions with capital needs, budgets, cash flow and control measures. In reality, the process is iterative, requiring minor and possibly major modifications as progress is made through each of the stages. The dotted lines indicate where minor revisions may be needed, while the solid curved lines indicate where major modifications may be required to develop a workable financial plan for the business. Minor modifications can come in many forms. Goals may change as assumptions are confirmed or rejected. Similarly, revisions to the operating budgets may necessitate minor changes to the cash flow budgets and vice versa.

Figure 5.2   The financial planning process

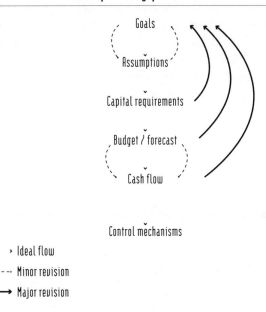

Goals

Assumptions

Capital requirements

Budget / forecast

Cash flow

Control mechanisms

› Ideal flow

---→ Minor revision

⟶ Major revision

Major changes, however, will mean a complete review of the entire financial plan. If any facet of the plan proves to be impracticable, the operator will have to return to the start and revise the overall goals and objectives. There may be important revisions if the operator realises that high capital expenditures will be required that have an adverse effect on the cash flow of the organisation. Similarly, overestimating the volume of clients, assuming a higher use or occupancy rate than is realistic or supposing that an unrealistic number of tours can be run will necessitate a fundamental review of the entire financial plan.

Budgeting

An operating budgeting process is a document projecting the estimated sales, costs and profit or loss for the upcoming year. It is not to be confused with a cash flow budget, which is a separate document outlining the cash in and cash out for the business over the same period. A budget is a planning document, a co-ordinating document, a motivator for the organisation and a control document all in one.[4] Moreover, it will form the basis for the profit and loss statement prepared at the end of the year for taxation purposes.

A budget contains a number of sections as outlined in the pro forma developed by the Department of Tourism and reproduced in Figure 5.3. Budgets specify all sources of income for a business, including sales income from tours, rebates received from suppliers or agents and all income from other sources, such as interest earned, souvenir sales and the like. The next section generally outlines the direct cost of goods sold (COGS) involved in generating the income flow. The COGS represents the costs incurred in providing the components of the product. For example, the gross profit for a wildflower tour in the Kimberleys involving the use of commercial lodging and transport would be calculated by deducting the costs of accommodation, food and transport from the price.

A $600 tour that incurs direct costs of $400 for the above items will produce a gross profit of $200. The gross profit must be sufficient to cover all other expenses incurred by the business and to produce a satisfactory profit. Such expenses can include administrative costs, insurance, rent, phones, mortgage and other loan repayments, wages and salaries, rates, rents and interest expenses. In addition, depreciation expenses for equipment are included, even if the business will not incur any cash outlay for articles being depreciated during the financial period.

Figure 5.3   Components of a profit and loss statement

INCOME

    Sales
    Rebates, discount, commission received
    All other trading income

      Total trading income

EXPENSES

    Cost of goods sold
    Opening stock
    Plus purchases
    Less closing stock

      Cost of goods sold

Gross profit

      = Income less cost of goods sold

Overheads/operating expenses

    Advertising and promotion
    Bad debts
    Bank and credit charges
    Depreciation—equipment and vehicles
    Electricity and gas
    Insurances
    Interest
    Lease payments
    Motor vehicle operating costs
    Personal salary/drawings (if incorporated)
    Postage
    Rent on premises
    Rates and taxes
    Repairs and maintenance
    Salaries, wages and taxes on same
    Superannuation, long service leave
    Telephone and fax
    Travel and entertainment
    Other expenses

      Total overheads/operating expenses

TRADING PROFIT

      = Gross profit less overheads/operating expenses

NET PROFIT

      = Remainder after tax considerations

Source: DOT (1993)

Just a brief note on depreciation. Property, plant and equipment eventually wear out over time. The Australian Taxation Office recognises that the use of these assets to generate income consumes their economic potential. At some point of reduced potential, these assets will need to be disposed of and usually replaced.[5] As a consequence, the ATO permits businesses to charge a paper expense equivalent to the amount by which the asset depreciates over the budget period. In this manner, businesses can develop a theoretical cash reserve that will allow them to replace the items when their useful life ends.

An example will clarify the concept of depreciation. A business may have bought 30 sets of cross-country skis in 1995 for a cash outlay of $15 000. Under normal working conditions, the skis should have a useful life as rental skis of five years. Thus, the operator can depreciate this asset at a rate of 20 per cent per annum. The 1995 cash flow budget would record the $15 000 actual expense that has been incurred. However, the income or operating budget would show a depreciation value of $3000 (20 per cent loss of the asset value). In a similar manner, the 1996, 1997, 1998 and 1999 budgets would include depreciation expense for the equipment, even though no cash outlays were made. After five years, the depreciation expense item has allowed the operator to 'save' $15 000, which can then be used to replace the equipment.

Monthly or quarterly operating budgets need to be prepared to reflect the variability in demand over the year caused by seasonal fluctuations or different product offerings. These can then be agglomerated into an annual operating budget. The great benefit of spending a little extra time drafting monthly budgets is that it establishes a series of regular benchmarks against which the performance of the business can be measured. If the actual income and expenses vary significantly from projected figures, the operator can adjust the business.

The budgeting process

There is no magic formula for developing a budget. Some businesses do not prepare a budget at all. Many others simply take last year's budget and adjust all income and expenses by a fixed percentage. Others begin by calculating their expected expenses and then force the income to fit in order to provide a suitable profit. Still others begin by estimating revenue and then look for ways to make the costs fit. All of these approaches work to a certain degree, but all have their limitations. Lack of a budget means that the business cannot have any goals. Adjusting last year's budget may not be appropriate for changed business conditions this year. Beginning with either revenue or expenses forces the business to adopt a product-oriented approach, which is out of line with current consumer demands. None of these methods is recommended.

1 Establish the goal: the bottom line

It is advisable to begin with the bottom line—the desired profit for the venture—especially if the business is to operate as a sole tradership and the profit represents the owner's income. Unless the financial goals are specified, the operator is at great risk of sacrificing profit to make the rest of the numbers fit. Goals must specify the desired financial return ($60 000) and can also relate to the volume of product to be sold (say, 15 extended tours and 37 day trips), bed-nights or customer nights (say, 3000 client nights). Setting goals lays the foundation for the rest of the budget planning process and, once the goals are determined to be feasible, establishes targets against which the performance of the business can be measured.

2 Identify fixed costs

Once financial objectives are established, it is a matter of working up through the budget from knowns to unknowns. The next step is to identify the fixed costs, or costs that the business will incur regardless of whether it sells one trip or 1000 trips. Fixed costs are generally easy to estimate accurately, for they represent predictable and necessary expenses. They include such items as rent, mortgage or loan repayments, insurance costs, electricity and telephone bills, marketing expenses, salaries and wages, including the owner's drawings, legal and audit fees, depreciation and the like. The operator's desired income from the business should also be included as a fixed cost for the budget planning exercise. Many neophyte tour operators do not budget for their own living expenses, assuming naively that they can live off the profits. If the numbers do not work, they make them work by reducing the profit figure, not appreciating that they are also reducing their own wages.

3 Estimate variable costs

The next step is to estimate the variable costs on a per client or per client-day basis for the products being offered. Variable costs are expenses that are incurred only when a product is purchased. In the nature-based tourism sector, these may include commissions paid to the travel trade and the costs of components of the tour, such as lodging, meals, vehicle costs or the costs of additional staff and the like. The product development, market research and distribution phases of the vetting process will help identify the types, quality and quantity of variable costs incurred in delivering an appropriate product to the target markets.

Different products will incur different variable costs depending on the length of the trip, the use of external goods and services, the amount and quality of ancillary services used and the involvement of the travel trade. A three-hour driving tour sold directly by the operator may incur virtually no variable costs, except for vehicle operating expenses. The variable costs for a two-night wilderness educational tour will be higher, involving transport, two nights' accommodation, meals and additional staff. On the other hand, a five-night Red Centre tour targeted at the overseas market may incur substantial variable costs in the form of a 25 to 30 per cent commission to the travel trade, five nights of accommodation, all meals, special equipment, entry passes to Aboriginal sites, hire of local guides and hire of transport.

Cash flow

A cash flow budget differs from an operating budget in that it shows the actual amount of cash inflow and outgoings of the budget. Efficient cash management assures the business of sufficient liquidity to keep it running. Cash is necessary to cover monthly expenses and to fund future growth. As well, for many seasonal tourism operators, cash is needed to cover off-season expenses and to provide an adequate cash reserve to do the marketing required in the lead-up to the next season.[6] The objective of a cash flow budget, then, is to project the expected cash receipts and cash payments. This will indicate a monthly surplus or deficit of cash for the period. If a deficit appears likely, the operator will have to ensure that alternative sources of finance are available so that the business continues to operate smoothly.[7]

Cash flow budgets are often not prepared, under the mistaken impression that an operating budget showing a profit will ensure that sufficient cash is available. However, profits are not cash. Profits are calculated in accordance with accounting principles, by matching revenues and expenses. Cash flow, on the other hand, represents the movement of cash through the business.[8] The financial accounting process does not distinguish between financial transactions and cash transactions, nor does it consider the substantial delays that may occur before cash is received.[9]

The following simplified example will highlight the differences between an operating budget and a cash flow budget. In this case, the operator runs a seasonal business over a four-month period with initial sales of $10 000 in Month B, which grow by $10 000 per month until they peak at $40 000 in Month E. The operator sells the product through the travel trade and has agreed to receive payment 30 days after the trip has taken place. The operator's suppliers, accommodation houses and vehicle rental firms have been burned by the tourism industry before and insist on payment in full 30 days prior to the trip. The fixed costs for the business are $3000 a month and the variable costs (or supplier costs) are 60 per cent of the total revenue the operator received ($6000 for every $10 000 in sales).

Abridged operating and cash flow budgets are shown in Table 5.1. On the basis of the operating budget, the operator appears to be trading well, generating a pre-tax profit of $22 000. While the operator expects to run at a loss for the first two months, by Month C the business will be trading in a surplus position.

Table 5.1   Abridged operating and cash flow budgets

ABRIDGED OPERATING BUDGET

	Mth A	Mth B	Mth C	Mth D	Mth E	Mth F	Total
Sales revenue ($)	0	10 000	20 000	30 000	40 000	0	100 000
Expenses							
COGS	0	6 000	12 000	18 000	24 000	0	60 000
Operating expenses	3 000	3 000	3 000	3 000	3 000	3 000	18 000
Profit (loss)	(3 000)	1 000	5 000	9 000	13 000	(3 000)	
Cumulative profit (loss)	(3 000)	(2 000)	3 000	12 000	25 000	22 000	22 000

ABRIDGED CASH FLOW BUDGET

	Mth A	Mth B	Mth C	Mth D	Mth E	Mth F	Total
Cash receipts ($)	0	0	10 000	20 000	30 000	40 000	100 000
Cash disbursements							
COGS	6 000	12 000	18 000	24 000	0	0	60 000
Operating expenses	3 000	3 000	3 000	3 000	3 000	3 000	18 000
Cash surplus (deficit)	(9 000)	(15 000)	(11 000)	(7 000)	27 000	37 000	
Net cash surplus (deficit)	(9 000)	(24 000)	(35 000)	(42 000)	(15 000)	22 000	22 000

An examination of the business's cash position for the same period, though, reveals an entirely different situation. Remember that the operator must pay the suppliers 30 days before the trip occurs, but does not receive any revenue until 30 days after the trip has taken place. By the end of Month A, the operator has a cash deficit of $9000. This cash deficit grows steadily until Month D, when it peaks at $42 000.

The operator has a major problem—he cannot pay his bills when they come due, even though he is owed a great deal of money. To stay in business in Month D, the operator must begin the year with at least $42 000 of surplus cash in the bank—an unlikely event for a business that generates a pre-tax profit of $22 000. Alternatively, the operator must have a friendly bank manager who is prepared to give the business an overdraft of more than

$40 000 (at full commercial rates). Again, this is unlikely, given that the business will only gross $100 000. Without either, though, the operator will be forced to cease trading. Suppliers, leery of being burnt again, will cancel bookings 30 days before they are to be used. Being ethical in his dealings, the operator will have to advise the travel trade of his inability to accommodate the clients that have booked, and will thus lose revenue.

How can a business showing a trading surplus of $12 000 in Month D have a concurrent cash flow deficit of $42 000? The answer is simple. The operator has an effective two-month lag between the time that cash disbursements must be made and when revenue is received for delivering the trip. Month B's expenses must be paid in Month A, while revenue is not received until Month C. In short, the operator has negotiated a payment scheme that is detrimental to his interests.

This simple scenario happens all too frequently in the tourism industry. For this reason, cash flow budgets assume a greater operational importance than the annual profit and loss budgeting process. Cash flow problems are probably the greatest challenge facing small tourism businesses. Most small tour operators do not have the buying volume or collective sector history of success to be able to negotiate favourable terms with suppliers of component parts of the trip. Many accommodation houses, for example, require non-refundable deposits up to 60 days prior to the trip's departure and full payment 30 days before. Others demand cash on arrival. By the same token, significant delays in receiving revenue are common, especially if the operator uses the overseas travel trade. It is not uncommon for overseas tour wholesalers to pay up to six months after the trip has finished. In the meantime, the operator must carry the accumulated debt until he or she receives payment. Without cash, the business cannot function, even if it is showing a strong paper profit.

Cash flow budgeting

It is recommended that monthly cash flow budgets be prepared and then combined to give an idea of the annual cash flow for the business. The procedure for developing cash flow budgets involves six stages:

1 estimating cash receipts for the budget period
2 estimating cash payments for the budget period
3 calculating net cash gain (or loss): (1) − (2) = (3)
4 adding the surplus (or overdraft) from the previous period
5 computing cash surpluses (or shortages): (3) + (4) = (5)
6 projecting extra cash needed in the future.

There are a few issues that must be remembered when developing a cash flow budget. The cash flow budget represents actual revenue received during the period and actual cash expenses incurred. As such, the revenue and disbursement columns must reflect this reality. Revenue from one month's trips may arrive at different times throughout the year. Some people may book directly and the revenue will come in at the time of the trip. Credit card payments may result in revenue being received in the following month, while arrangements with the travel trade may result in revenue coming some months later. The revenue section of the budget must reflect this variability, as is shown in the cash flow budget sample.

In a similar manner, expenses will occur at various times during the year. One-off expenses, such as insurance, licence fees and association membership fees, must be recorded in the month when they were actually paid. Likewise periodic expenses, such as phone, electricity and fuel, will also be recorded only in the months paid.

Controlling cash flow

There are some tools available to businesses to control their cash flow situation. Essentially, they fall into one of three categories: methods to accelerate the receipt of revenue, methods to delay payments and methods to eliminate peaks and troughs in cash flow.[10]

Accelerating payments

It is essential to negotiate a collection period that is beneficial to the operator, especially if the business is seasonal or if it is reliant on the inbound travel trade. Small operators often are unaware of how the travel trade system works and acquiesce to unreasonable demands made by their suppliers. However, like all business dealings, there is room for negotiation. In some cases, inducements can be offered to encourage prompt payment. It is common in some sectors to offer a 2 per cent discount if payment is received in less than 30 days. By the same token, some businesses have successfully negotiated surcharge penalties for late payments. Ultimately, if the operator is faced with unfavourable conditions, he or she can take the business somewhere else.

It may be beneficial to work with an Australian-based inbound operator as an alternative to dealing directly with an overseas-based wholesaler. In this situation, the Australian inbound tour operator is responsible for paying promptly and then collecting from the overseas-based business. The cash flow problem becomes theirs, not the small operator's.

One of the best tools available to control cash incomings is to develop a clear, unambiguous cancellation policy. An examination of the cancellation policies of the major players provides many lessons for smaller tour operators. Qantas Vacations had the following policy in 1996:

- deposit of $100 on confirmation of booking
- final payment 45 days prior to departure
- bookings made within 45 days of departure to be accompanied by full payment
- no refund after commencement of the tour
- a $100 administration charge for cancellation prior to 45 days
- a $100 fee plus the risk of having to pay any non-refundable costs incurred by Qantas for cancellation within 45 days.[11]

Goway Travel is even more succinct in its cancellation policy. Its 1995–1996 Canadian brochure included the following warning:

> Cancellations received more than 6 weeks prior to departure will incur loss of non-refundable deposit . . . Cancellations received less than 6 weeks and more than 3 weeks prior to departure will be levied a fee of 25%. Cancellations received less than 3 weeks prior to departure will be levied a fee of 75% of the tour cost unless the booked seat is resold. There will be no refund for unused land arrangements after departure from North America.[12]

Adjusting outgoings

Adjusting cash outgoings can have a dramatic effect on the cash situation of many businesses. Proper cash management is a tool that operators can use to enhance their cash position. It is wise business practice to make excess cash work for the operator. Instead of leaving a large sum of money in a non-interest-bearing cheque account, it may be beneficial to invest it in term deposits, cash management accounts or, if the money will be needed in the near future, simply placing it in an interest-bearing savings account. Reasonable cash reserves should always be set aside for unforeseen emergencies before investing large sums of money.

Eliminating peaks and troughs

Operators may adjust their business to eliminate peaks and troughs in cash flow. One such method is to lease equipment. Leasing is an attractive option for many businesses, for it removes the need to incur major cash expenses by purchasing items. Instead, the business pays a monthly or quarterly lease fee.

If a business knows it is going use a certain number of rooms at an accommodation property, it may be able to negotiate a block booking and then pay for the rooms on a flat rate basis over the course of the year. For example, a business wanting 1200 room nights during the summer may be able to negotiate a payment schedule whereby the operator pays for 100 room nights a month over the entire year. This has obvious cash flow advantages for the tour operator, but may also provide a needed source of cash for the accommodation property during its off season.

In some cases, reducing sales volume serves to lessen cash flow needs. In the example cited earlier in this chapter, cash flow problems were caused by the rapid seasonal growth in the business. Capping the volume of business would have diminished the problems.

Finally, seasonal tour operators may wish to develop cash cow programs —high-volume, high-profit programs that will provide a sizeable cash reserve heading into a low season. One tour operator that the author is aware of runs a long weekend bicycle tour, bushwalk and interpretative tour on the last long weekend before the winter. The operator normally attracts 10 to 15 people on each trip, but will attract up to 100 clients on this trip. The massive influx of cash provides the operator with sufficient revenue to survive the off season and to fund the spring marketing campaign.

Some seasonal tour operators have striven to shorten their operating cycle by developing programs in the off season. In doing so, they generate some cash during periods that would otherwise produce no revenue. Alternatively, operators can increase their net profit margins either by raising prices or by reducing costs. The higher profit provides a greater cash buffer.

Records

Anyone entering business must make sure that accurate and reliable records are kept of all financial activities of the business. As Hopkins states: 'Unless you know what is owing you, you have no hope of collecting it.'[13] The corollary is that, unless you know what you owe, you have no way of knowing how the business is performing. Accounting systems must be accurate enough to allow the operator to chase payments and detailed enough to reveal the origins of debts. Further, in the event of disputes, the operator must be able to trace and retrieve documentation.[14]

Appropriate recording systems should be able to serve at least three other vital purposes for the business:

- They must be accurate and current enough to allow the operator to make valid assessments of the state of the business and then make appropriate adjustments.
- They must have built-in warning systems to alert the operator to emerging problems. If the sales or cost figures diverge unacceptably from the budget, the operator should be able to establish the reason for the divergence.

- Finally, they must be able to address any potential problems with the liquidity of the business. Liquidity problems can snowball quickly, as is shown in the cash flow example used in this text. Recognising a problem only when a crisis emerges is a sure way of risking loss of the business.[15]

In addition, having accurate records will lead to operational efficiencies and will reduce auditing costs. The operating budget establishes the framework for the profit and loss statement. Having to prepare monthly profit and loss and cash flow statements forces the operator to process the paperwork that flows through the office. If this is done, the likelihood is that the operator will also be able to store it in an ordered manner. Accountants prefer to work through an organised set of records rather than be presented with shoe boxes full of receipts. The less work they have to do, the less it costs the operator. Many excellent and simple-to-use computerised accounting spreadsheet packages are on the market that will make this task less onerous.

Stanley suggests that there is a need to record all cash received and paid out; what has been purchased, at what price, quantity and amount; the names of all suppliers who purchased goods or whom the business purchased goods from; what was sold, at what price, quantity and amount; and to whom goods and services were sold. As a minimum, he suggests that every business should have:

- a cash receipts journal and a cash payment journal to record receipts and payments of cash and the balance at any time
- a bank deposit book
- reconciliations of bank accounts
- a journal to record transactions not involving cash payments, such as credit purchases
- a ledger that integrates cash and non-cash transactions
- a record of accounts receivable and their age
- a record of accounts payable and their age.[16]

It is highly recommended that monthly reports be prepared for the business outlining the trading and cash situation, accounts payable, accounts receivable and bank reconciliations. These reports should then be compared to monthly projects made during the budgeting process to track the progress of the business towards its goals. If significant positive or negative variations occur, their cause must be established and the impact they will have on the business must be considered. At this point, adjustments to the operating or cash flow budgets may be required.

Crisis management

Even the best laid plans sometimes do not work as hoped. From time to time, internal or external factors may cause a crisis. Perhaps the distribution network did not perform as well as expected. Perhaps adverse weather conditions have slowed trading. Perhaps suppliers increased their prices without giving any advance warning. Perhaps the pilots went on strike. Perhaps the Gulf War happened. Perhaps the operator's assumptions proved to be invalid. Perhaps the dreaded 'X' factor has reared its head. Perhaps any of a thousand things that could happen to the business have happened. What can be done? A number of sources offer sound advice on managing a financial crisis. Their findings are briefly summarised below.[17]

The first piece of advice is to act quickly to identify potential problems before they snowball into business-threatening emergencies. Hopefully the records that the business keeps are accurate, appropriate and up to date, allowing the operator to react promptly to any emerging crisis. The next step is to accept that the business has a problem. Too often businesses choose to figuratively hide their heads in the sand when potential crises arise, explaining them away as anomalies or seasonal fluctuations. Astute operators, though, know when a change in the business environment transcends normal business cycles. Besides, there is usually some forewarning of change. Observing trends, having discussions with other operators, reading the newspaper and talking to trade associations or government agencies will indicate whether the crisis is general to the tourism sector or specific to the business in question.

A number of options may be available, but one that must always be considered is the closure of the business. It may hurt in the short term to close it, but it is a lot less painful than bleeding a dying business dry while trying to resurrect it. However, if it is felt that the business can survive the current crisis, a number of actions are suggested.

1 **Assessing the business's strengths and weaknesses** to learn or find the skills to trade out of the problem. Among these desirable skills are the abilities to lead, to think clearly and to develop a strategic focus to the business or problem.

2 **Implementing strict financial controls** to stop or slow the cash flow crisis. In some cases, it may be worthwhile moving from a monthly reporting system to a weekly system. Personal and business expenditures need to be reviewed to find ways of reducing costs or initiating efficiencies. No expenditure should be incurred unless it is necessary. Staff levels can be reduced.

3 **Concentrating activities on the most profitable areas.** Efforts should be focused on those activities that the business does best, that are the most

profitable, or that can generate the quickest cash flow. The number and range of products may be reduced. Further, a policy of minimal trip sizes or purchase-by dates may be introduced to stop the organisation from operating unprofitable trips.

4 Reviewing pricing. The problem may be caused by a pricing regime that is not reflective of either the costs or the industry norm. In many instances, prices can and should be increased. In some instances, discounts may be required. But this should only be a short-term measure: discounting is not a recommended long-term solution.

5 Tightening credit lines and extending payment time frames. Cash crises often occur, even though the business is ostensibly trading profitably, because clients have not paid their debts. There is nothing wrong with spending a few weeks on the phone calling debtors and reminding them to pay their bills. By the same token, if an operator has an established relationship with a creditor, there is nothing wrong with asking for an extension.

6 Finding new sources of finance. Loans may be renegotiated. Short-term financing may be provided by the bank. Partners or family members may be able to inject capital into the business. Further, if large amounts are owing from clients who will eventually pay, it may be possible to borrow money against these debts.

7 Not becoming involved in illegal or unethical activities to save money. Any form of illegal or unethical trading or illegal business practice should be strictly avoided. The spate of accidents involving small, non-viable airlines that have cut corners illegally to keep flying should be a lesson to all in the tourism industry. If the business is insolvent and has no realistic chance of paying its debts, it is illegal for it to keep trading.

[1] D. Hey-Cunningham (1993) *Financial Statements Demystified*, Allen & Unwin, St Leonards.

[2] Meredith (1993) *Small Business Management in Australia*, 4th edn, McGraw-Hill, Sydney.

[3] ibid.

[4] Stanley, op. cit.

[5] M. Gaffikin (1993) *Principles of Accounting*, 3rd edn, Harcourt Brace, Sydney.

[6] J. A. Tracy (1994) *How to Read a Financial Report*, 4th edn, John Wiley & Sons, Brisbane.

[7] Stanley, op. cit.

[8] Hey-Cunningham, op. cit.

[9] English (1995) op. cit.

[10] ibid.

[11] Qantas (1996) *Qantas Vacations Brochure*, Sydney.

[12] Goway Travel (1995) *Goway Canadian Vacations*, Melbourne, p. 47.

[13] Hopkins, op. cit, p. 57.

[14] ibid.

[15] Newell, op. cit.

[16] Stanley, op. cit.

[17] Australian Bankers' Association & Commonwealth Department of Tourism (1993) *The Business of Tourism: A Financial Management Guide for Tourism Related Businesses*, ABA & DOT, Canberra, pp.127–34; J. E. Boritz (1990) *Approaches to Dealing with Risk and Uncertainty*, Canadian Institute of Chartered Accountants, Toronto; English (1995) op. cit.; Hopkins, op. cit.; K. Keasey & R. Watson (1993) *Small Firm Management, Ownership, Finance and Performance*, Blackwell, Oxford; Newell, op. cit.

Chapter 6

Costing and pricing

*t*he price charged for nature-based tourism products is set according to financial and strategic considerations. Most new tour operators, however, do not have a clear idea of either. This chapter will discuss the financial considerations involved in determining a profitable price for nature-based tourism products. The reasons why nature-based tourism products are more expensive than mass tourism products will be examined. In addition, the chapter will deal with break-even analysis, yield management and a method of developing the optimal price mix for the products on offer.

As a minimum, the price charged for nature-based tourism products must generate sufficient revenue to cover the costs of providing the product and yield a suitable profit for the operator. Prices of tourism products, in general, are affected by:

- the costs of delivering the product
- the impact of state or local legislation
- the level of competition and competitors' pricing strategies
- the marketing strategy of the business at that time
- types and uniqueness of products and services offered to clients
- demand factors affecting products and services
- the life cycle stage of the product
- the extent to which customers can be influenced by advertising and promotion, rather than price
- the perceived value of the product in the consumer's mind
- the desired image of the business or product
- the elasticity of demand for travel and tourism products.[1]

In addition, nature-based tourism operators must also consider these factors:

- the primary market (domestic and/or international)
- the location of the enterprise
- seasonality factors and the volume of visitors
- the price mix
- the level at which the travel trade is used
- the primary goal of the enterprise (profitability, provision of services, lifestyle).

The challenge is to determine what volume of product has to be sold at what price to break even. The competitor analysis will offer insights into the price range that can be charged for similar products, provided that a number of cautions are considered. The costs incurred by other operators may differ significantly, especially if they are well established, take many clients or use the travel trade. Further, the product being considered may be different in some significant way from existing products, which means that the costs may also differ.

The break-even analysis

In an open market, the operator has no real limits on the amount of product that can be sold. In these instances, the key factor in determining how much the operator will need to sell to break even will be influenced by the price charged for the product. The operator can consider scenarios to determine how much product must be sold to achieve the desired goals by adjusting the proposed price.

The easiest way to determine the volume of product that needs to be sold to break even involves two steps.

1 Determine the gross profit for each unit sold as follows:

Gross profit = proposed price – variable costs per unit sold

2 Then divide the fixed costs by the gross profit, as follows:

Volume of units to be sold = fixed costs ÷ gross profit

A simple example illustrates how these two equations should be used. In the following example, an operator has estimated her fixed costs to be $20 000, while the variable costs are $200 per unit sold. The operator wishes to know how many units of the product must be sold at what price to break even. At an estimated price of $2200 per trip, only 10 units would need to be sold to break even, as is shown below.

Gross profit = \$2000 = \$2200 (price) – \$200 (variable costs)
Volume   = 10 units = \$20 000 (fixed costs) ÷ \$2000 (gross profit)

Repeating these calculations at the proposed prices of \$600 and \$400 per unit reveals that the operator must sell 50 packages and 100 packages respectively to break even.

In certain instances, though, the absolute volume of product that an operator can sell may be fixed. This situation often occurs with operators who are licensed to conduct their business in national parks. The terms of the licence may stipulate that an operator can only bring a certain number of people into the park. To be viable, then, the operator must charge a high enough price to cover all expenses. When the absolute volume of product is predetermined, the operator can determine the minimum price to break even as follows:

Break-even price = (fixed costs ÷ volume) + variable costs

In the above scenario, let us say that the operator is limited to 50 clients a year. What price must she charge to break even?

Price = \$20 000 (fixed costs) ÷ 50 (volume of trips) + \$200 (variable
        costs)
      = \$400 + \$200
      = \$600

Thus, if the absolute number of trips the operator can offer is limited to 50, and demand indicates that all 50 can be sold, the operator must charge \$600 per trip to break even. If the operator's licence stipulates that the operator may take 200 clients a year into the park, the minimum price that must be charged is \$300 (\$20 000 ÷ 200 + \$200).

The break-even analysis establishes the minimum price that must be charged and the minimum volume of goods that must be sold to achieve the business's goals. The break-even analysis also enables the operator to assess the validity of the assumptions made about the size and the willingness of the market to pay the price required for the product, as well as the operator's ability to deliver the product.

Coping with multiple product offerings and adjusting to seasonality effects

Of course, few tour operators offer only one product line. It is likely that the product mix for the business will vary significantly throughout the year. The number and types of trips offered will reflect seasonal demand, climatic conditions, the operator's own need for a holiday and a range of other factors. The variation can be as basic as offering five-day and two-day trips or as complex as offering weekend camping trips to a local park and four-week overseas tours to Africa.

While the overall fixed costs for the business may not change, each of the activities offered incurs different variable costs and each may appeal to different market segments with differing price sensitivities. To achieve the desired financial goals, the right mix of products must be developed at the right prices. Essentially, businesses with multiple product lines or those faced with seasonal fluctuations in demand must develop some sort of yield management program. Yield management is a revenue-maximising technique that aims to increase net profit through the predicted allocation of the firm's capacity to predetermined market segments at an optimal price.[2] Businesses can afford to offer an array of prices because they know the average yield they need to get from the entire product range, the composition of their client mix, and typical use levels. The various prices charged are calculated carefully to ensure the profitability of the business. Excess capacity is often sold at highly discounted rates on the assumption that users paying a higher rate will cover most of the costs of the trip.

Most tour operators embark on some type of informal yield management program by varying rates in low seasons or scheduling different types of tours over the course of the operating year. The challenge is getting the right mix of tours at the right price. Each of these tours incurs different variable costs, each has different resource implications for the business, each has different demand levels and each has different price sensitivities.

Figure 6.1   Break-even costing for multiple product lines

Product A	Product B	Product C	Product D
Price A	Price B	Price C	Price D
Variable cost Product A	Variable cost Product B	Variable cost Product C	Variable cost Product D
Gross profit Product A	Gross profit Product B	Gross profit Product C	Gross profit Product D
% of fixed costs allocated to Product A based on relative volume of total user days	% of fixed costs allocated to Product B based on relative volume of total user days	% of fixed costs allocated to Product C based on relative volume of total user days	% of fixed costs allocated to Product D based on relative volume of total user days
Number of units of Product A to be sold to break even (fixed costs A ÷ gross profit A)	Number of units of Product B to be sold to break even (fixed costs B ÷ gross profit B)	Number of units of Product C to be sold to break even (fixed costs C ÷ gross profit C)	Number of units of Product D to be sold to break even (fixed costs D ÷ gross profit D)

Given the variety of product lines that may be offered by a business, it is recommended that each product be costed separately, taking into account the desired volume of visitors per product, the desired product mix and the desired price to be charged per product (Figure 6.1). Once a desirable and potentially profitable product mix has been determined, the separate work sheets can be combined to form the business's budget. The process is basically the same as for single-product businesses, except that a separate break-even analysis must be completed for each product.

Fixed costs are allocated across product lines on a pro rata basis according to the expected share of total user-days for each product. This figure can be calculated by estimating the total number of user-days per product multiplied by the duration of each trip. Thus, an operator who expected to sell an equal volume of seven-day tours, two-day trips and day trips would allocate 70 per cent of the fixed costs to the extended tours, 20 per cent to the shorter tours and 10 per cent to the day tours. If, on the other hand, the operator expected that 80 per cent of the total user-days would come from day trips, the allocation of fixed costs would be adjusted accordingly.

In the examples shown in Table 6.1, an operator offers a seven-night extended tour, a two-night weekend escape and day tours. The total fixed costs for the business of $100 000 have been allocated across the three product lines according to the desired volume of business. Using the formulae discussed above, the operator must sell 200 extended trips at $700 each, $300 weekend trips at $250 and 167 day trips at $110 to break even.

Table 6.1   An example of break-even costing for multiple product lines

	Tour A 7-night tour	Tour B 2-night tour	Tour C 1-day tour	Totals
Proposed price	$700	$250	$110	
Variable costs	$400	$150	$50	
Gross profit	$300	$100	$60	
% of fixed costs allocated to product type	60%	30%	10%	100%
Fixed costs	$60 000	$30 000	$10 000	$100 000
Number of units to be sold (fixed costs ÷ gross profit)	200	300	167	667

Different pricing and product mix scenarios can be tested using this model. The impact of altering the prices charged can be seen in Table 6.2. A $100 reduction in the price of the extended tours means that the operator must sell 50 per cent more tours to break even. Similarly, a $30 reduction in the cost of day tours means that twice as many tours must be sold to achieve desired targets.

Table 6.2   Varying the price

	Tour A 7-night tour	Tour B 2-night tour	Tour C 1-day tour	Totals
Proposed price	$600	$350	$80	
Variable costs	$400	$150	$50	
Gross profit	$200	$200	$30	
% of fixed costs allocated to product type	60%	30%	10%	100%
Fixed costs	$60 000	$30 000	$10 000	$100 000
Number of units to be sold (fixed costs ÷ gross profit)	300	150	334	784

The operator may wish to test different scenarios by altering the product mix as reflected in the share of fixed costs attributed to each product (Table 6.3). In this instance, the operator hopes that 30 per cent of the client-days will be day trippers, with 40 per cent of client-days coming from two-night tours. Five hundred day trips and 400 short break holidays will need to be sold to break even, while the operator will only have to sell 100 extended tours.

Table 6.3   Varying the product mix

	Tour A 7-night tour	Tour B 2-night tour	Tour C 1-day tour	Totals
Proposed price	$700	$250	$110	
Variable costs	$400	$150	$50	
Gross profit	$300	$100	$60	
% of fixed costs allocated to product type	30%	40%	30%	100%
Fixed costs	$30 000	$40 000	$30 000	$100 000
Number of units to be sold (fixed costs ÷ gross profit)	100	400	500	1000

Running different break-even scenarios by adjusting the price of each product, the relative volume of each product sold or both the price and volume allows the operator to select the mix of products at a price that best suits his or her needs and resources as well as consumer demand. The key is to develop a program that is both feasible and practical. On paper, it is easy to add more trips, take more clients per trip or adjust the prices that are charged. In practice, it may be much more difficult. Unless the figures are vetted thoroughly, the operator may be making unrealistic assumptions about the operations of the business and the consumers' willingness to buy the products.

One of the risks is that the operator may 'need' to run 60 weekend trips to achieve the target, forgetting that there are only 52 weeks in a year. Similarly, the author has seen people develop budgets on the false assumption that every trip will sell out. To be viable these operators need a 100 per cent occupancy rate, leaving no room for any error. Alternatively, the prices may have to be adjusted upward two or three times by 'a little bit' each time. The final price may bear no resemblance to the price the market will accept.

It must be remembered that different products have different profit potential. The product mix must allow for the potential profitability of each product as well as its ability to generate revenue. English recommends that businesses analyse the contribution margin (the gross profit per product divided by the sales of that product, presented as a percentage) as well as the actual dollar amount of profit.[3] This analysis will tell operators which products generate the greatest *rate* of profit and which provide the greatest *amount* of profit. It will also tell operators which products are not performing. Further, it will offer insights into which products could be encouraged. Again, the risk may be that an operator may 'need' to sell a large number of high-profit products when consumer demand may be higher for lower-profit products.

Why are nature-based tourism products so expensive?

The reason why most nature-based tourism products are priced well above the standard price of mass tourism products is a function of the realities of running a small business. For a start, most nature-based tourism businesses cannot achieve the economies of scale that larger tourism enterprises can. As a result, fixed costs represent a higher proportion of the cost of a trip than they would for businesses taking a larger volume of clients.

The effect of seasonality is the second factor. Most full-time nature-based tourism operators have a less than six-month effective operating season during which they must make an annual income and ensure that they have sufficient cash reserves to deliver their marketing programs for the following season.

The third reason is that they often face higher variable costs for the purchase of component parts of their trips, like accommodation and food. Suppliers are typically less willing to offer nature-based tour operators the standard trade discounts they would offer larger players, simply because they cannot guarantee the volume of traffic to make discounts worthwhile for the supplier. An inbound tour operator preparing to guarantee 20 000 room nights at a major hotel will probably be able to negotiate a price that is 40 to

50 per cent lower than the published price. A small nature-based tourism operator who might bring 50 room nights to a similar property may not be able to negotiate any discount. As a result, the nature-based operator may be forced to include the full retail price of the accommodation and food in the cost of the product.

Finally, if the operator chooses to use the travel trade to distribute the product, the 10 to 30 per cent commission must be taken into consideration.

Pricing: a case study

A pricing case study will explain why nature-based tourism prices are so high. In this case, a couple want to offer one product to the marketplace: a six-day, five-night alpine eco-adventure. The trips involve four wheel drive interpretative tours of the Bogong High Plains in north-eastern Victoria. Each night the guests will come off the mountains and stay in commercial accommodation in surrounding towns. All meals are included in the trip. Assume also, for simplicity, that the client group will consist entirely of inbound visitors who buy the product through the travel trade.

Some basic issues need to be resolved in order to calculate the lowest price that can be charged to break even.

1 Volume of business

- **Number of trips taken.** The effective operating season for this business is deemed to be 32 weeks, for the operators cannot drive through the Alps in winter. However, the operators realise that not all trips will run and are, therefore, budgeting on running 25 trips for the season. More will be a bonus; fewer will lead to financial problems.
- **Number of clients.** The maximum capacity of the vehicle is 8 clients per trip. The total annual capacity, if all 32 trips are filled completely, is 256 passengers. Again, though, the operators realise this is unlikely and have decided to budget on an annual use level of 60 per cent of the business's capacity. As such, the break-even point will be calculated on the basis of 150 clients per annum (6 per trip × 25 trips).

2 Fixed costs

The following is a partial list of fixed costs that the operators will incur over the year. The income they want to earn from the business has been included as a fixed cost.

Cost of vehicle lease payments	$7 000
Office rent @ $250 per month	$3 000
Brochure production and advertising	$5 000
Insurances, liability, auto, etc.	$3 000

Phone/fax/computer @ $500 per month	$6 000
Depreciation	$3 000
Legal and accounting	$1 000
Desired salary	$35 000
Licence costs	$500
Total fixed costs	$63 500

3 Variable costs

- **Per client.** The variable costs incurred for every client who buys the trip are summarised below. Included in the summary of variable costs is a 25 per cent commission to be paid to the travel trade. Variable costs equated on a per person basis include:

Accommodation (5 nights @ $40)	$200
Food costs ($20/day × 5 days)	$100
Travel agency commissions (10% travel agent, 10% wholesaler, 5% inbound operator)	25% of the retail price
Total variable costs per client	$300 per trip, plus 25% of the retail price

- **Vehicle.** The operators will also incur variable costs for the use of the vehicle while on tour. These costs include vehicle operating costs, staff salaries for interpretative guides and so on, and are summarised below.

Vehicle operating costs @ 60c per km, 500 km trip	$300
Guide @ $90 per day (salary and expenses)	$450
Total vehicle costs per trip	$750

The total expenses for the business for the year are $127 250, as summarised below, based on the amount of fixed costs plus the variable costs of 150 clients per annum and 25 trips per annum.

Fixed costs	$63 500
Variable costs per client (300 × 150)	$45 000
Variable costs per trip (750 × 25)	$18 750
Total expenses	$127 250

The price the operators must charge to break even is determined by calculating the break-even cost per client and then factoring in travel industry commissions. Remember that the travel trade takes its commission from the retail price, not from the cost. To account for a 25 per cent commission, the retail price is determined by multiplying cost price by 4/3 to get a retail price. In a similar manner, to determine the retail price when the operators are paying a 10 or 20 per cent commission will require multiplying the cost by 10/9 and 4/3 respectively.

Break-even cost per client = total expenses as above ÷ volume
= $127 250 ÷ 150
= $848

Retail price = break-even price per client x 33% mark-up
for travel trade commissions
= $848 x 133%
= $1128

Thus, just to break even, which includes an annual wage for the couple of $35 000, the business must charge $1128 per person for its trips. This figure seems high when it is remembered that the component parts of accommodation, food and vehicle use cost the operators less than $450. They also seem high when one remembers that visitors from overseas will incur airfare expenses and almost certainly other travel expenses while in Australia. If the business's target market was Germany, the total cost to the customer of this five-day ecotour adventure for them would be more than $5000.

The high price that must be charged for nature-based tourism products highlights the need to offer high-quality products, services and interpretation. In this instance, choosing backpacker-style accommodation that costs $20 per person per night would reduce the total cost of the trip by only $133. Would prospective clients who are still paying close to $1000 for this trip feel that backpackers' accommodation represented value for money? On the other hand, better-quality accommodation at $60 ($120 for a room for two) would result in a price increase of only $130 to $1250. Better accommodation may enhance the perception of value for money.

[1] Sources: Meredith (1995) op. cit.; NESBA (1990) *Cash Flow: Cash Management, Managing the Small Business Series* no. 23, AGPS, Canberra; J. C. Holloway & C. Robinson (1995) *Marketing for Tourism*, 3rd edn, Longman, Harlow; A. Morrison (1996) *Hospitality and Travel Marketing*, 2nd end, Delmar Publishers, Albany, NY.

[2] Donaghy & McMahon, op. cit.

[3] English (1990) op. cit.

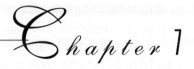

Chapter 1

Strategic marketing

*t*ourism marketing is a management process that is used by organisations to develop destinations, facilities and services as tourism products, identify potential travellers and their needs and wants, price their products, communicate their appeals to target markets and deliver them to their customers' satisfaction, in compliance with organisational goals.[1] Clearly, marketing involves far more than selling products; it is an overriding management philosophy that tries to link consumer desires with appropriate goods and services.[2] Yet few tourism businesses appear to have developed a marketing orientation and even fewer prepare any kind of formalised marketing plan.[3]

The process of marketing tourism products is driven by the marketing mix, which is 'the mixture of controllable marketing variables that the firm uses to pursue the sought level of sales in the target market'.[4] The marketing mix is generally regarded as having four elements: price, product, promotion and place (that is, the distribution system used). They reflect the practical decisions that marketers must make when matching consumer needs and wants with the goods and services provided. Each of these elements must be consistent with the organisation's broader aims and objectives and must be directed clearly at defined markets and goals. How to use the elements of the marketing mix to market nature-based tourism products will be discussed in subsequent chapters.

Successful tourism businesses recognise that they cannot be everything to everyone. Instead of trying to reach an undifferentiated market with undifferentiated products, businesses are adopting a more tactical or strategic approach by identifying and capitalising on their sustainable competitive advantages in the marketplace. This way, they can more effectively target specific market segments and position their products to appeal to these segments. The various elements of the marketing mix can then be applied in a concerted manner to reach the desired market in the most appropriate way, thus enhancing the comparative competitive position of the product.[5]

This chapter examines the concept of strategic marketing. The principles of strategic marketing management and the concept of identifying and capitalising on sustainable competitive advantages are discussed. The chapter concludes by investigating the role that a situation analysis can play in helping organisations develop and apply strategic marketing principles.

The need to think strategically

Competition in the tourism industry is intense. The latest estimate is that there are over 45 000 businesses in Australia, all vying for a share of the tourist dollar. In fact, there are literally millions of other tourism enterprises throughout the world that people can choose from. What is worse is that many of these businesses offer largely comparable products, ostensibly targeted at similar markets. Moreover, many competitors are well established in the marketplace, have a high level of awareness and are well resourced.

How can a new nature-based tourism business hope to compete against all other tourism ventures in the global marketplace? The answer is that it cannot. To survive, it must make some strategic decisions about which markets it wants to target and which businesses it wants to compete against. It must further differentiate itself from its competitors by promoting a real and consistent difference between its attributes and those of its competitors. In doing so, it must highlight its own strengths or the weaknesses of its competitors, target a slightly different market, or target the same market in a different way, and modify the product to satisfy the needs of the market.

The *New Webster's Dictionary* defines a strategy as 'the science and art of conducting a military campaign in its large-scale and long-term aspects'. The *Australian Oxford Dictionary* defines a plan as 'a method or way of proceeding thought out in advance'. A strategic plan for marketing, therefore, is a method of conducting a campaign in its large-scale and long-term aspects that is well thought out in advance. But here is the key: it involves both science and art. Not only must an organisation decide upon a method, but it must also have the finesse to apply that method. Put another way:

> [Strategic marketing] is the process of formulating long-term objectives and strategies for the entire business or business unit, by matching its resources with its opportunities. Its purpose is to help a business set and reach realistic objectives and achieve a desired competitive position within a defined time. It aims to reduce the risk of error and place the business in a situation in which it can anticipate, respond to and even create change to its advantage.[6]

Strategic thinking involves understanding the structure of the industry and how it is likely to evolve, as well as understanding fully the company's relative position in that industry.[7]

Key elements of strategic marketing

The key elements of strategic marketing management, as identified by Aaker, are discussed below.[8]

1 Defining product markets

The first element of strategic tourism marketing is to determine the product markets the business will compete in and, by extension, determine those it will not compete in. In essence, any tourism operation wishing to adopt a strategic marketing approach must first define:

- the products it chooses to offer
- the products it chooses not to offer
- the markets it chooses to target
- the markets it chooses not to target
- the competitors it chooses to compete with
- the competitors it chooses to avoid.

The act of defining the products offered and the markets targeted dictates the types of businesses the operator will be in direct competition with. Defining the geographic area of operation will determine who the indirect competitors are. However, by the same token, defining these aspects explicitly also defines implicitly what the business does not do, who it does not target and who it will not compete against in the marketplace. Too many tourism businesses try to do too many things. As a result, they lose their focus, and in doing so forget what their core product is and who their core markets are. Moreover, the features of the product usually have to be compromised in order to broaden the appeal of the product to as wide a market as possible. As a result, the quality and uniqueness of the product is diminished.

It is erroneous to think that any business or destination is in competition with all other tourism businesses or destinations. Thinking like that essentially provides a handy excuse to explain failure. The adoption of a 'shotgun' marketing approach is a sure way to waste scarce marketing resources while gaining limited benefits. The Australian Tourist Commission, with its $80-million-plus international marketing budget, carefully chooses which markets to serve and which ones not to. Should not a smaller venture do the same?

Al Ries and Jack Trout, two US marketing gurus, have identified 22 immutable laws of marketing that apply to all businesses.[9] Two of them, the

Law of Sacrifice and the *Law of Focus*, are especially relevant to nature-based tourism.

The *Law of Sacrifice* says that a business has to give something up in order to get something. It is argued that the more narrow the focus of the business or product, the easier it is to create a positive image in the client's mind.

Sacrifices can be made in two ways. The first is to sacrifice product lines. By focusing on a few clearly-defined products, a business can create a unique position in the marketplace. This is especially true in destination marketing. Not every destination can be everything to everyone. Just because a country town has an 18-hole golf course, a regional museum, an art gallery and restaurants does not mean that it is a golfing, heritage and cultural destination. Other destinations that may offer more, or better, services will be able to outcompete it. By the same token, no nature-based tourism product can satisfy all the needs of all clients.

The second sacrifice to be made is in the target market. A business may have broad market appeal, but it will go broke targeting all the potential markets that may buy its products. Rather, it is suggested that marketing campaigns target a limited number of high-value markets. This strategy acknowledges that the market being targeted does not necessarily represent the entire user base. Indeed, quite the opposite is true. If the marketing campaign is directed at the values of the target markets, members of other market segments may buy the product to receive similar personal benefits. For years, Queensland has been focusing its ads on the 18-to-25 sea, sun and sand market, knowing full well that a large share of its winter market comprises seniors. It does this because it realises that the 70-year-old who wants to feel 30 again will respond positively to a campaign promoting a young, active lifestyle. The same happens with nature-based tourism products. Values-based marketing, directed at segments that want a nature-based holiday, will spill over into other market segments.

The *Law of Focus* states that the most powerful concept in marketing is owning a piece of the prospect's mind. A company can become successful if it can find a way to own a word or a concept in the mind of the prospect. The best way to burn an image into the mind of a prospective client is to narrow the focus to a single word or concept. The benefit of a clearly-defined focus is that, if one benefit is established strongly, it is likely that the consumer will find other benefits. Three varieties of focusing tactics can be used: benefit-related (McLean's toothpaste: whiter teeth), service-related (home delivery) or sales-related (Kleenex the preferred brand).

Most tourism activities use words to relate benefits to the consumer. Think of a few popular destinations or eco-businesses. The Queensland motto, 'Beautiful One Day—Perfect the Next', implies perfect weather, which also suggests a relaxed, sexy, exotic, tropical paradise. 'The Red Centre' implies finding the heart of Australia and, in so doing, finding the core value of being Australian. 'Ecosummer Expeditions' creates a clear image of exploration, summer relaxation and environmental consideration. 'Quest Nature Tours' brings a clear image to the consumer's mind of nature, a meaningful search and a holiday at the same time.

2 How much to invest?

The costs of different marketing strategies will vary depending on the goals desired for that strategy. Investment decisions will be driven by the age of the business, its competitive position *vis-à-vis* other businesses and the plans the operator has for the business. A strategy to foster growth, for instance, will require an increased investment of resources, while a milking or divesting strategy may involve a reduction of resources. Depending on the state of the competition, a maintenance strategy will involve less, the same or more money. Launching a new product, a new service or an entire new business will entail higher costs than supporting an existing product, service or business.

The rule of thumb is that an established tourism enterprise will spend 5 to 7 per cent of its gross on marketing activities. A study of new tourism ventures in Victoria revealed that most spent 10 per cent or more of their gross on marketing. The reasons for this are self-evident. On the one hand, the costs of attracting new clients are substantially higher than those of retaining existing users. As new businesses have no existing clientele, the costs will be high. Further, as new businesses generate less revenue than established businesses, the relative costs of marketing as a proportion of total revenues will be higher. A new business that spends $20 000 on marketing and grosses $100 000 spends 20 per cent of its revenue on marketing. An established business spending the same amount on marketing but grossing $400 000 will only spend 5 per cent of its gross on marketing.

Sufficient resources must be provided for the enterprise to achieve its goals if the business is new, if it is planning to launch new products, or if it wishes to expand into new markets. The failure to see that such resources are available is a sure way of choking a business. If the tourism venture is going through a period of resource constraint, it must delay implementing strategies that require a large amount of resources, or it must reallocate existing resources away from some areas to the area requiring additional resources. Insights into how this can be achieved can be gained by conducting a thorough situation analysis.

3 Functional area strategies

The specific way a nature-based tourism venture competes will be characterised by one or more functional area strategies. These include:

- product line strategies
- pricing strategies
- distribution strategies
- logistical strategies
- positioning strategies.

Positioning is a marketing strategy that is designed to create a unique perception of a product or service in the marketplace by describing the product in terms of the attributes and values that are important to particular consumer groups.[10] The desired position of the product is reinforced by the elements of the marketing mix used to promote that product. Marketing has been wrongly described as a battle of products. In fact it is a battle of perceptions. Owning a position in someone's mind is better than owning a better product. As Ries and Trout illustrate, there is no objective reality.[11] There are no facts; there are no best products. All that exists in the world of marketing are perceptions in the mind of the customer or prospect.

Most marketing mistakes stem from the assumption that businesses are fighting a battle rooted in reality. Too many people base their entire marketing strategies on the premise that the merits of the product will determine the success or failure of the product. In fact, marketing is about getting a better position, or a perception of superiority in the consumer's mind. If merit were absolute instead of relative, global companies would have the same market position in each country. Yet this is patently not true. What is the better hot beverage, coffee or tea? In the UK tea is preferred; in the US it is coffee. What is the better code of football? In New South Wales it is Rugby. In Victoria it is Australian Rules. Surely both cannot be better. Who is right and who is wrong? The same thing happens in tourism. Australia has a strongly favourable image in the Japanese market, but is not a highly sought after destination in Brazil. Yet if the tourism product were absolute, one would expect that Australia would enjoy equal levels of popularity in both countries.

The beauty of positioning is that, because there are no absolutes, the marketplace is open to create new positions to suit the needs of different products. One rule of positioning is that if a business or product is not first in the prospect's mind, then it is in trouble. The second rule is that if it is not first in one category, then why not create a second category and be first in that category? Consider popular music. There must be at least a dozen top 10s in country, easy listening, jazz, blues, pop, alternative, techno, dance and other forms. Each number one song has a legitimate right to claim that it is number one, even though the absolute sales may vary significantly between lists. It is more important for a country singer to have a number one song on the country hit parade than to peak at 57 on the mainstream charts.

The same type of positioning strategy can be used for nature-based tourism products or destinations. Especially with domestic travellers, Australia is not seen as one single destination. The public perception is of a diverse destination with many products. Alice Springs has successfully positioned itself as Australia's premier desert destination. In New South Wales it is Broken Hill. Byron Bay is the premier alternative destination. The Sapphire Coast is the premier family destination on the south coast. Tamworth is the home of country music. Coffs Harbour has the subtropical Big Banana. Each of these destinations has created a new category and has gained pre-eminence in that category.

Ecotourism, nature-based tourism, alternative tourism, adventure tourism and sustainable tourism are all different categories in which an operator can successfully position his or her product. In fact, the Tourism Council Australia, through its annual awards for excellence, encourages the industry to position its product in at least 30 different categories, including special events and festivals, environmental tourism, heritage and cultural tourism, Aboriginal and Torres Strait Islander tourism, unique accommodation and regional tourism. Identifying a business's sustainable competitive advantages plays a key role in determining which position it could occupy.

4 The organisation's strategic assets or skills

A strategic skill is something an organisation does exceptionally well. Within a tourism organisation, strategic skills may include staff or directors with strong contacts in the travel trade, expertise in international marketing or a flair for promotion. A strategic asset is a resource, such as a brand name or an existing customer base that is strong in comparison to those of its competitors. From a tourist perspective, strategic assets are easier to identify and usually more permanent than strategic skills. Strategic assets can include proximity to water, beaches or mountains, the history or culture of an area, proximity to population bases, transport links and the like.

Strategic assets and skills are the backbone of any tourism organisation. The key to identifying strategic skills or assets is in their relative superiority compared to those of competitors. Exploiting them will help the operator adopt a more strategic approach to positioning the business in the marketplace. In turn, this will influence the range of products offered and not offered, the markets targeted or avoided and the competitors the business will fight against or avoid.

Sustainable competitive advantages

The goal of strategic marketing is to identify and exploit those attributes of the business that give it a sustainable competitive advantage (SCA) in the marketplace. An SCA is defined as a real competitive advantage that is sustainable over time in the face of competitor reaction.[12] Indeed, the process of strategic marketing is becoming focused increasingly on managing competitive advantages. It is a strategy that involves an organisation-wide plan to excel in its strengths or to reduce or hide its weaknesses. Why is it so important to be able to identify SCAs? Regardless of the sector, some businesses always seem to perform better than others. Superior performers always possess something special that is hard for others to imitate and gives them a competitive advantage in the marketplace.[13]

SCAs have a number of attributes:

- They must be substantial enough to make a difference; a marginal superiority may not be enough to make a real difference in the consumer marketplace.

- They must be sustainable in the face of competitor reaction. The advantage that is identified must be as immune as possible to competitor reaction.

- They should be linked with the positioning of the product. As a central theme of the entire strategy, they will influence how the product is positioned in the marketplace. Remember Queensland's SCA of beautiful subtropical weather and its positioning statement 'Beautiful one day— perfect the next'.

- They must be real, or perceived to be real by the consumer, and must be valuable to the consumer. An insignificant advantage or one that the consumer does not value is no advantage.

- They must be rare among the firm's current and potential competitors, with no strategically equivalent substitutes.[14]

What the consumer believes to be true about a product is the truth, regardless of the facts. Further, differences must be substantial enough or perceived to be substantial enough to position the product uniquely in the consumer's mind. Work done by the author comparing operators' perceptions of why clients bought their products and the reasons stated by the clients for buying them revealed a substantial gap, which suggests that the operators did not have a clear understanding of their potential competitive advantages in the market.

There are no hard and fast rules for developing SCAs, although they are generally regarded as being the core competencies of the organisation. SCAs can be things that a business does extremely well, or things that competitors do poorly. Sources of competitive advantage for businesses in general have been identified as a reputation for quality or excellence, cost advantage, technological superiority, product design, superior customer service and product support, name recognition (for larger players), systems, geographic locations and superior resources.[15]

In addition, competitive advantages in the tourism industry can come from a number of other areas. Companies that adopt a packaging strategy, focusing on either providing superior packages or by bundling components from a variety of suppliers into a comprehensive package, tend to have more competitive advantages and higher performance that companies that do not package well.[16] By the same token, the ability to develop co-operative marketing programs, create strategic alliances with fellow businesses and capitalise on the natural synergies that exist among businesses with complementary products can provide co-operating businesses with a strong competitive advantage, especially if the businesses are targeting inbound markets.[17] A commitment to quality and to continuous service improvement is seen as an asset for businesses that have a high proportion of repeat clients,[18] as is a commitment to develop new products to serve these clients. Many nature-based tour operators have developed strong competitive positions by promoting environmental preservation as a key feature of their tours.[19]

Identifying SCAs is not an end in itself; it is a tool that helps a business develop a strategic approach to marketing its products. Ultimately, the greatest benefits of SCAs lie in their ability to help a firm develop a differentiation strategy that will position it uniquely in the marketplace and, in doing so, to market its products most effectively. The strongest points of differentiation— those features of the business or product that are truly unique in relation to other products or services in the industry[20]—will form the basis of successful marketing strategies. The application of elements of the marketing mix will reflect and support the SCAs that have been identified.

The situation analysis

How does one identify SCAs and apply them to strategic marketing? How does an operator decide which functional area strategies to highlight? Moreover, how is this done when it is recognised that the tourism business environment is always changing and that, to remain competitive, operators must be able to adjust to these changes?[21]

The answer is: by conducting regular and rigorous situation analyses. A situation analysis uses systematic methods to analyse the external and internal factors affecting the business.[22] Its usefulness lies in its ability to enable strategic actions that will exploit the business's own strengths, neutralise its weaknesses, capitalise on the weaknesses of other businesses or offset the strengths of competitors. It is also used to identify gaps in the delivery of products, or to identify imminent changes in the business environment that will affect the business's trading position. Conducting a situation analysis is, therefore, vital for both new and existing operations.

To a large extent, the success of any situation analysis depends on three factors: the quality of the information to be assessed; the ability of the assessors to examine information in an unbiased manner; and their ability to think laterally and conceptually when analysing the material. If there is not enough information the analysis will be incomplete, making it more likely that the actions identified will be inappropriate. Similarly, if someone is too close to the organisation, he or she may lack the necessary perspective to gain fresh insights from the material presented. The effectiveness of a situation analysis thus depends on the ability of the person or people doing the analysis to think conceptually about the story gained from the information. Not everyone has this skill, so care should be taken in selecting the analysis team.

External analysis

A situation analysis is carried out on both the external and internal factors that affect the business. The external analysis usually consists of four general dimensions: competitor analysis, market analysis, customer analysis and environmental analysis. The purposes of an external analysis are to examine the likely impact that factors lying outside the direct control of the business will have on it and to gain insights about how to plan for and adjust to them.

Competitor analysis

The competitor analysis involves an assessment of both direct and indirect competitors. Direct competitors are those organisations offering similar products. Indirect competitors are those organisations offering products than can be substituted for the ones offered by the business. Nature-based tour operators are in the unique position of competing directly with both commercial and non-commercial enterprises such as clubs, outdoor recreation groups and environmental organisations.

Competitors will react in different ways depending on their market position, their own strategic strengths and weaknesses, their perception of how much competition the proposed venture will give them, the similarities and differences in their product offerings, their market share and the resources available to them. A great deal can be learned by understanding what products they offer, the markets they target and why they do what they do. In a similar manner, operators can gain insights into differentiating their products by comparing a competitor's relative strengths and weaknesses business with those of their own business.

Market analysis

A market analysis examines the entire market of consumers who use products similar to those offered by the operator. The goals of the market analysis are to determine the attraction of the market or submarket to the products offered by the operator and to understand the dynamics of the market in order to anticipate, react to and plan for change.

Market analysis usually involves consideration of the following points:

- the size and life cycle stage of each market
- the potential for new markets, or growth prospects for existing markets
- the market profitability, which can be assessed on the basis of the number and intensity of competitors, the impact of powerful players on profits, the threat posed by new competitors, the threat posed by new or substitute destinations, and the power of consumers to affect price
- the cost structure of the market
- distribution channels, especially if the destination is highly dependent on one or two dominant players
- market trends: are current fads going to have legs or will they have a short life cycle?

The key success factor in any market analysis is to look for things that the competition does well which give them an advantage over the operator's business, or for things that the operator does extremely well which give them an advantage over the competition.

Customer analysis

The customer analysis examines who uses the product, why they use it and what trends are emerging among clients. One of the objectives of a customer analysis is to identify alternative markets for existing products or alternative products for existing markets. A second objective is to identify unmet needs in the marketplace. Gaps in the delivery of products, areas where other operations are not satisfying customer demands or consumers who have previously been overlooked can offer ideas about new and emerging markets or business opportunities.

Environmental analysis

The goal of any environmental analysis is to look at those forces that will affect the organisation, its markets or its competitors. Essentially, this step tries to identify macro trends that will affect all businesses in the future. The first organisation to successfully identify and capitalise on emerging trends can often gain a sustainable advantage over its competitors.

Environmental analysis usually has six major components. These components are:

- technological
- governmental/political
- economic
- cultural
- ecological
- demographic.

The aging of the Australian population, improved health care and the higher take-up rate of self-funded superannuation plans, for example, have created an affluent seniors market that is interested in a variety of travel experiences. This market will continue to grow for the foreseeable future, creating a variety of tourism opportunities that did not exist ten years ago.

Internal analysis

The internal, or self, analysis examines those features of the tourism organisation over which the operator has direct control. It usually involves three components: an analysis of the performance of the organisation, an assessment of the product portfolio and an analysis of the resources available to the organisation.

Performance analysis

The performance of the business over the recent past will indicate what the business is doing right or wrong. Also, longer-term trend lines can be identified which can point to issues that will need to be addressed in the future. Performance analysis looks at both the financial and non-financial performance of the organisation. Financial indicators include the trend in profitability, market share, gross revenues, the achievement of goals against targets, and the like. Important non-financial considerations include customer satisfaction, customers' desire to return and loyalty to the tourism product and the types of associations they make with the tourism product. In many instances, non-financial performance indicators can point to emerging financial issues. If the satisfaction level of guests declines, repeat business will suffer, which will result in a loss of revenue or the need for higher marketing costs to attract new clients.

Product portfolio assessment

The goal of a portfolio analysis is to examine how effectively the product mix is achieving the organisation's goals. Each of the individual products a business offers will evolve through its own life cycle. Some will have enduring qualities and enjoy a long period of popularity. Some will be faddish and progress through their life cycle quickly. Others will simply not work. An operator must be conscious of the life cycle stage of the products on offer. Successful businesses have a variety of products in different life cycle stages. Thus, as the popularity of one product wanes, new products can be introduced to retain existing clients or attract new ones. Further, the profits from popular, mature products can be invested in the development of new products. Unsuccessful businesses, on the other hand, rely on the same few tired products. As the product progresses into the decline stage of its life cycle, consumer interest will wane and revenues will dwindle.

A number of product portfolio models have been developed to assess the performance and strategic mix of an organisation's products *vis-à-vis* life cycle stages, growth prospects, financial objectives, non-financial objectives, competitors and goals. Any introductory marketing text provides a number of models.

Resource analysis

Finally, it is always worthwhile to assess the resources available to the business. The resource analysis examines issues relating to staffing and financial support for the organisation. The business evolves through a life cycle just as surely as its products. Over time, the resource needs of a business will change. Unless they are reviewed at regular intervals, organisations can become unbalanced. Resource analysis assesses, for example, whether the right numbers of staff are employed in the right jobs and whether staff have the ability to perform the jobs required. It also looks at the level of financial and non-financial support for the organisation and assesses whether or not the goals that have been identified can be accomplished with the current resources.

The SWOT analysis

The summary of the data collected from the internal and external analysis phases is often best presented conceptually in the form of a SWOT analysis. 'SWOT' is an acronym for Strengths, Weaknesses, Opportunities and Threats. A SWOT analysis is usually presented as a one-page summary, with the page divided into four. The top quadrants of the page list the Strengths and Opportunities, while the bottom quadrants show the Weaknesses and Threats.

- **Strengths** are features of the business, product or internal assets that are unique, strong or done very well by that business. They may also be features of the business or product that the operator does reasonably well, but that the competition does poorly. Strengths provide clear insights into the development of and capitalisation on SCAs, which will enable the business to be positioned effectively against competitors.

- **Weaknesses**, on the other hand, are those features of the product, market or internal organisation that are deficient or weak in comparison with the competition. Weaknesses provide insights into what features of the business or product must be improved to enhance its competitiveness. In addition, they provide valuable information on how not to position one product against another. However, weaknesses may also be unrealised strengths. The nature-based tourism industry cannot compete against mass tourism on the basis of price. This is clearly a weakness. However, it can compete easily by using that weakness—high prices—to its advantage by promoting the reasons why prices are higher: smaller group sizes, more personalised experiences and better value for money.

- **Opportunities** are those external factors that provide favourable circumstances for future business development. Remember that opportunities are factors, not options that can be developed. The option development phase occurs after the SWOT analysis. The example of the aging of the Australian population discussed above is an opportunity, as it means there will be more people entering this demographic group. Providing new tourism products for this group is an action that evolves from the opportunity; it is not an opportunity itself.

- **Threats** are those external features that may threaten the present position of a tour operator. Examples of threats include new competitors entering the marketplace, changing government policy on tourism, climate change, or changing government policy on the use of public land. The advent of each or any of these may have an adverse effect on the future viability of the business.

SWOT analyses work only when the business is compared rigorously to other businesses or to industry norms with a specific goal in mind. The goal may be to see how effectively it competes, to compare products, to see if it markets its products as well and the like. Indeed, the value of the SWOT exercise comes from the outcomes it produces, not the exercise itself. A SWOT is successful if it provides insights into solving specific problems. Too often, though, people do not appreciate the tactical role of a SWOT analysis. Instead, they use it in an unfocused manner to prepare a rambling list of items that will solve no problems. Like any tactical marketing analysis tool, SWOTs must be goal oriented.

Analysis provides the framework for the identification of the key strategic issues that will affect the business in the short, medium and long term. It provides insights into strategic thinking, analyses and decisions that will ultimately be made. The strategic thinking phase involves the identification of key issues to be considered and the development of a number of strategic options to address these key issues. The options can then be assessed to determine which ones provide the best benefits for the business. At this stage, it is possible to begin to identify goals and strategies to achieve those goals. Finally, the decision-making stage identifies which options have been selected, formalises the strategy to achieve the goals and objectives identified and sets performance criteria by which these goals can be measured.

[1] J. I. Richardson (1996) *Marketing for Australian Travel and Tourism: Principles and Practice*, Hospitality Press, Melbourne, p. 6.

[2] Kotler & Turner, op. cit., p. 4.

[3] G. E. Greenley & A. S. Matcham (1990) Marketing orientation in the service of incoming tourism, *Marketing Intelligence and Planning*, 8(2), pp. 35–9.

[4] P. Kotler (1984) quoted in Middleton, V. T. C. (1994) *Marketing in Travel and Tourism*, 2nd edn, Butterworth Heinemann, Sydney.

[5] G. Eccles (1995) Marketing, sustainable development and international tourism, *International Journal of Contemporary Hospitality Management*, 7(7), pp. 20–6.

[6] L. Brown (1995) *Competitive Marketing Strategy*, 2nd edn, Thomas Nelson, South Melbourne, p. 1.

[7] Porter, op. cit.

[8] Aaker, op. cit.

[9] A. Ries & J. Trout (1993) *The 22 Immutable Laws of Marketing*, Harper Collins, London.

[10] S. Dibb & L. Simkin (1993) The strength of branding and positioning in services, *International Journal of Services Industry Management*, 4(1), pp. 25–35.

[11] Ries & Trout (1986) *Positioning: The Battle for Your Mind*, Warner Books, NY.

[12] Aaker, op. cit.

[13] S. G. Bharadwaj, P. R. Varadarajan & J. Fahy (1993) Sustainable competitive advantage in service industries: A conceptual model and research propositions, *Journal of Marketing*, 57(4), pp. 83–99.

[14] Aaker, op. cit.; Bharadwaj, Varadarajan & Fahy, op. cit.

[15] Aaker, op. cit.

[16] D. A. Edgar, D. L. Littlejohn & M. L. Allardyce (1994) Strategic clusters and strategic space: The case of the short break market, *International Journal of Contemporary Hospitality Management*, 6(5), pp. 20–6.

[17] T. Hill & R. Shaw (1995) Co-marketing tourism internationally: Bases for strategic alliances, *Journal of Travel Research*, 34(1), pp. 25–32.

[18] S. M. Cherasky (1992) Total quality for sustainable competitive advantage, *Quality*, 31(8), Q4, Q6–7.

[19] R. Weiland (1995) Market trends, *Successful Meetings*, 44(5), p. 54.

[20] M. R. Evans, J. B. Fox & R. B. Johnson (1995) Identifying competitive strategies for successful tourism destination development, *Journal of Hospitality and Leisure Marketing*, 3(1), pp. 37–45.

[21] Edgar, Littlejohn & Allardyce, op. cit.

[22] Aaker, op. cit.; Brown, op. cit.

Defining products and markets

*t*he key to any successful business is to develop products that effectively match the consumer's desires. On the surface, such a match seems easy; many successful businesses appear to do it effortlessly. In reality, though, the product–market match is far more difficult than first imagined. It is driven strategically by an intrinsic understanding of the core needs and wants of the market being targeted and of the ability of the core attributes of the product being offered to satisfy these needs. This chapter examines the nexus between tourism products and the nature-based tourism market. It begins with a discussion of what a 'product' is and what purpose it serves for the travelling public. The nature-based tourism market is then profiled and the key motivations of nature-based tourists are discussed.

Products

Products have been defined as 'anything that can be offered to a market for attention, acquisition, use or consumption that might satisfy a need or a want'.[1] The key words are *satisfying the consumers' needs and wants*. From the tour operator's perspective, the product is often seen as the set of tangible and intangible components that are packaged together and sold to the consumer. An operator selling a seven-day ski trip, for example, may feel that the product includes transport, trail notes, camping gear, the services of a qualified guide, instruction, food and accommodation at the beginning and end of the trip. From the consumer's perspective, however, the product being purchased may be perceived in an entirely different manner. Consumers may regard the same ski tour as a chance to challenge themselves, be with like-minded people, see the Australian Alps in winter and travel in safety with a qualified guide.

So who is right? The consumer, of course. As with everything else in tourism, operators must always think of their product from the perspective of the person who is buying the good or service. Major casino and resort chains realise that when they sell a package to their property, they are really selling hospitality and entertainment, not a room and food.[2] Likewise, when consumers buy nature-based tourism products, they are buying a range of personal benefits.[3] Increasingly, tourists are buying products that satisfy their lifestyle preferences, and the quest for adventure or the desire to see nature is becoming an increasingly important part of that lifestyle.[4] The component parts of the trip facilitate this need satisfaction, but in and of themselves do not provide it. A hotel room facilitates the satisfaction of the need for sleep; it does not provide sleep. Applying a consumer perspective to product development forces the operator to answer the questions 'Why is someone buying this product?' and 'What needs are being satisfied by purchasing it?' Applying the operator's perspective only answers the question 'What component parts am I selling?'

The Australian Tourist Commission explains this concept more fully:

> It is important to remember that the data shown [in the ATC's market segmentation research] is from the potential traveller's point of view. To look for groups of travellers that may represent potential customers for a particular product, look at the product from the potential traveller's viewpoint: To you it may be a 4WD Tour. To the traveller it is an 'Adventure', a possible way to 'See Australia', experience 'The Outback', or see 'Big Nature'. Depending on the way your product is perceived it can also be seen in a number of ways: 'Active', and 'Adventurous', or 'Safe', and 'Comfortable' and these aspects can be desirable to some groups of travellers and totally undesirable to other travellers.[5]

Components of a product

All products exist at three levels: core product, tangible product and augmented product, as shown in Figure 8.1 (page 107). The *core product* represents the heart of any product and answers the question: What is the consumer really buying? To be successful, then, at its heart, any product must provide a range of personal benefits that satisfies the individual's needs, wants or desires. In the ski touring example used at the start of this chapter, the underlying benefits sought by clients were safety, an adventure, the opportunity to experience the Alps in winter and the social pleasure of travelling with others who wanted to share similar experiences. That is why they bought the trip. They did not buy it because the operator labelled it 'Tour XYZ'.

The core product can vary among similar product categories just as it can across different market segments using the same product. For example, a person buying a used car may be satisfying the core need for transportation. Someone buying a Volvo may want to buy safety, while someone purchasing a Rolls-Royce may want to buy prestige. Great Barrier Reef tour operators provide a product that satisfies the needs of people who seek to develop a greater understanding of reef ecosystems, people looking for the excitement and adventure of snorkelling on a reef, and people who want to 'do' the reef for the prestige such a trip offers.

Once the operator has defined which core personal benefits the product will provide, the next challenge is to transform them into something tangible that the consumer can purchase. Hence, the second level of a product is defined as the *tangible product*. In the tourism industry, this task is accomplished by assembling a number of component parts into a single entity. In many ways the tour operator is like a small manufacturer assembling the component parts of transport, accommodation, guides, food, experiences, transfers, admissions to attractions, extensive research and the operator's own personality into a tangible product for sale.

The appeal of purchasing a commercial package is that the consumer is offered a one-stop shopping option. The type of person who buys an extended commercial nature tourism holiday is usually an extremely busy professional who does not have the time to negotiate departure dates, research the trip route, book all accommodation, food and services, obtain the equipment that may be needed and, in many cases, develop the skills required to make an independent trip. Further, because their interests or their holiday availabilities may differ from those of their friends, they may have problems finding suitable travelling partners. All these concerns can be alleviated with one phone call to a tour operator.

Research on the packaged adventure tourism sector in Victoria showed that the ease and convenience of participation provided by the commercial sector was the attribute mentioned most frequently by clients. The opportunity–cost savings provided by a relatively low-involvement purchasing decision enabled clients to overcome real or perceived time constraints that could otherwise have blocked their participation. Similarly, the safety and security provided by an organised trip led by a professional guide helped many clients overcome potential fear or anxiety barriers concerning the activity itself. Of special interest to women travelling without a partner, the commercial option provided a socially enjoyable and acceptable opportunity to partake in outdoor recreation.

There is a challenge in developing the tangible component of the product when the good being sold is experiential or non-material in nature, for the consumer cannot inspect the product and assess its value.[6] New entrants into

Figure 8.1   Components of a product

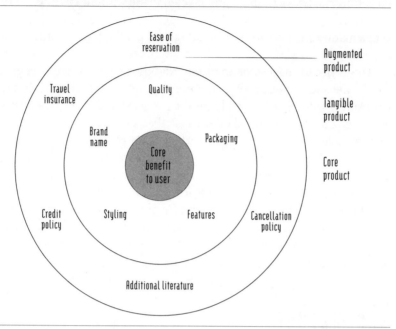

Source: adapted from Kotler & Turner (1989)

a marketplace face an additional challenge in that they must persuade clients to switch from another product to their own; yet they cannot conduct a direct comparison of the relative quality of each product. Making the tangible component of the product attractive will help allay concerns about the quality of the product.

Tangible products have five main characteristics that distinguish them from core products:

- They have a quality or value-adding level that makes the product as a whole more valuable than the sum of the individual component parts.
- They have distinctive features that distinguish them from other similar products.
- They have some styling that usually reflects the operator's personality.
- As a separate entity, they can be branded.
- They have some level of packaging (such as a brochure) that can be used to make the product attractive.

It is common for tour operators to become too focused on the tangible product while ignoring considerations of the core needs the product will satisfy. This focus is understandable, for operators agonise for many hours about the best itineraries, selecting the right type of accommodation, providing those special extras that make a trip memorable and trying to create a range of tours that will be very attractive to clients. Unfortunately, this product-driven focus on getting the package 'just right' is often made without considering the real reason why people may buy the package: the core need being satisfied. As such, many tour operators develop 'great' products with little consumer appeal.

This is not to suggest for an instant that the tangible product is unimportant in the successful delivery of tourism products. Far from it. In fact, the opposite is true. If the tangible product is substandard or deficient in any way, clients will not be satisfied because their core needs are not being met. The tangible product is, therefore, a reflection of the core product and, as such, should be developed to fully satisfy core needs.

Finally, additional features and services may be provided to make the product complete. These *augmented products* provide extras above and beyond the tangible product being sold as the trip. Augmented products for the tourism industry may include easy reservation services, credit or cancellation policies, the provision of travel insurance, the inclusion of wildlife manuals on the tour, or the sale of film.

The market

The nature-based tourism market is a very attractive one for, as marketers say, it has the right demographics. Nature-based tourists are generally affluent, independent travellers with high disposable incomes, who eschew normal packaged tours aimed at the mass market.[7] Many are women and many travel on their own. Moreover, they are experienced travellers who seek new adventures and are keen to try things at least once. Most importantly, this market is felt to be growing by 10 to 30 per cent per annum.

However, the market also has three features that sound a note of caution to people planning to enter the nature-based tourism industry. First, no one knows how big the nature-based tourism market is. What is certain is that the absolute number of purely nature-based tourists is quite small. Many existing nature-based tour operators contacted during the research phase of this text commented that they wished they had known how minuscule the market was for their product before they entered business. Some 'lifestyle' operators commented that, even after seven years, the market had not grown to the point where they were making a reasonable living. At the same time, the operators commented that competition for a share of this modest market was intense. To survive, they had to broaden their market base by tailoring their products to more 'mainstream' tourists.

Second, the nature-based tourism market is not a single unified market. Numerous studies have shown that different market segments are attracted to different activities.[8] Thus, the market for one operator providing a similar service to that of another may be quite different.

The third feature is that this market is evolving rapidly. Six or seven years ago, ecotourism was a niche product that appealed to an elite, allocentric type of traveller. Today, it is much more of a mainstream activity[9] and, as such, appeals to a near-allocentric or midcentric audience. This expansion of the market has resulted in the emergence of a large group of new nature-based tourists who are seeking more mainstream, recreational experiences rather than purely educational or adventure holidays. This new market is also more interested in shorter, high-intensity trips than in extended tours.

Australian and New Zealand research has demonstrated that the profile of the domestic nature-based tourist is atypical of the travelling population as a whole.[10] As a rule, this cohort of travellers are more likely to be university educated (often holding postgraduate qualifications), to work as professionals and to include women than are mainstream travellers. The age range varies significantly, depending on the activities undertaken. Experiences requiring greater physical activity tend to attract a younger market, while more sedate activities appeal to older travellers. Ecotourists fall into two distinct income categories. On the one hand, the main market represents high income earners, with family incomes of over $A40 000 or $NZ60 000 being common. These people are generally older travellers in their mid-30s to mid-50s. On the other hand, a second significant market consists of young travellers earning lower incomes. These people often see nature-based tourism as just one of many activities they can participate in while on holiday.

Nature-based tourists are very active. They belong to bushwalking clubs and birdwatching clubs and are more likely to be members of environmental organisations than the Australian population as a whole. Their involvement in environmental and public interest organisations means that they not only have a keen interest in environmental issues, but they also tend to have a greater knowledge of these issues than most Australians.

Overseas research has identified the emergence of two distinct nature-based tourism markets: specialists and generalists.[11] Specialists are the more committed group, seeking the experience because it provides them with an intense nature-based tourism activity. They are likely to take longer trips, be knowledgeable about the experience offered and be seasoned travellers. The nature-based experience is the main purpose of the trip for these people. They do not mind making sacrifices to have this experience. They are prepared to travel long distances to participate in the activity and neither want nor expect luxurious accommodation, food or night life.[12]

Generalists, on the other hand, are those people who participate in nature-based tourism as just one of many things they will do while on holiday. They are likely to take short-duration trips, have limited knowledge about the area they are visiting, book at the last minute and, in the case of wildlife viewing, may only have a casual interest in the activity. These people are less likely to travel long distances explicitly for the nature-based tourism experience, but may be prodigious consumers if an experience is easy and close to their current destination. This category of nature-based tourists is the primary market for the over-abundance of ecotourism operators in Cairns who specialise in day trips to the Reef and the Daintree forest.

A word about the inbound market

Demand for nature-based tourism from overseas markets is highly variable, being influenced by the level of industrialisation of the society and the length of time it has been industrialised. Demand is highest among post-industrialised Western societies, where an awareness of the fragility of the environment has changed societal attitudes to nature from one of use to one of preservation. The result is that many tourists are now motivated to see and help preserve environmentally sensitive areas. Residents of recently industrialised or currently industrialising countries, on the other hand, do not seem to have the same environmental ethos. The natural environment is still regarded as a non-performing economic resource. In these countries, there is little interest in visiting such areas. While many people from these nations may call themselves environmentalists, few will choose green tourism products if offered a mainstream alternative.[13]

New Zealanders, Swiss, Germans, Scandinavians, Britons, Canadians and Americans represent a disproportionate number of inbound nature-based tourists. Market research by the Australian Tourist Commission and Tourism Victoria suggests that these types of travellers are motivated to come to Australia for the adventure opportunities.[14] By contrast, relatively few Japanese, Korean and South-East Asian travellers purchase nature-based tourism products. They are more interested in Australia for its wholesome, safe, sun-sea-and-beach vacation experiences. A study of visitors to New Zealand back country areas found that people from different countries have different perceptions of what constitutes a wilderness or natural experience.[15] Visitors to New Zealand from Japan and Hong Kong, for example, are far more tolerant of a non-purist wilderness experience than visitors from North America, Australia or the UK.

The potential size of the market is reflected by the activities reported by inbound tourists while in Australia. The International Visitor Survey reveals, for example, that:

- 13 per cent of inbound tourists over the age of 15 go bushwalking
- 12 per cent go on rainforest walks
- 2 per cent go on outback safaris
- 3 per cent go wildflower viewing

- 12 per cent go coral viewing
- 8 per cent visit Aboriginal sites
- 50 per cent visit national parks, state parks, reserves or caves during their visit to Australia.[16]

However, these figures must be treated with caution, for only a relatively small 5 per cent of all inbound visitors indicated that experiencing outdoor or nature-based activities particularly influenced their decision to travel to Australia. Further, while the participation rates in many activities seem high, the potential for commercial involvement in the delivery of services may be low. There is no way of knowing if the 13 per cent of inbound visitors who went bushwalking went on five-day wilderness treks or walked along a two-kilometre scenic trail near their destination. The likelihood is that far more did the latter than the former.

This research also illustrated that the mean expenditure for nature-based tourists was significantly higher than for other types of travellers. People who visited national parks some time during their trip, for example, spent an average of $2132, which is about 19 per cent higher than the background expenditure rate. Bushwalkers spent $2842, or 58 per cent more than the average visitor, scuba divers 42 per cent more and people who identified viewing wildflowers 49 per cent more.

It is adventure tourists, though, who are the biggest spenders. Horse riders and outback safari tourers had average expenditures of more than twice the national norm, while rock climbers spent about 75 per cent more than the typical visitor. It must be recognised that the line between adventure tourism and nature-based tourism blurs in many cases. Horse riding trips and outback safaris involve a substantial adventure and eco-experience.

Motivations of nature-based tourists

Nature-based tourists have different travel motivations from mainstream tourists. To a large extent, this can be explained by the fact that they are seeking to have different needs satisfied. Stanley Plog's psychographic profile of tourists, made in 1974, is still relevant to understanding the motivations for participation in nature-based tourism today. Plog's research identified tourists along a bell curve continuum (Figure 8.2, page 112).[17] At one end are psychocentric travellers, who seek safety and security when travelling. In the middle are the midcentrics, who represent the bulk of travellers and are typified by the conventional mass tourist. At the other end is the allocentric traveller. Allocentrics are adventurous travellers who seek change and want an authentic tourism experience.

Figure 8.2   Psychographic profile of tourists

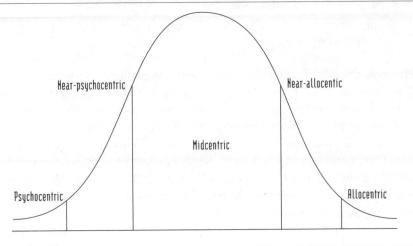

Source: Plog (1974)

Some of the motives for travel among allocentric and near-allocentric travellers include:

- educational and cultural objectives, the chance for learning and increased appreciation, scientific or purposeful trips, trips with expert lecturers or leaders
- a search for the exotic
- opportunities to develop new friendships in foreign places
- religious pilgrimages and inspiration
- travelling as a challenge, a personal test
- exploring, mountain climbing, hiking
- a chance to try a new lifestyle.[18]

To a great extent, these are the same motives identified by various studies examining adventure, eco- and nature-based tourism. An early study of Canadian nature-based tourists identified a variety of environmental, cultural and social objectives.[19] Environmental motives included wilderness, lakes and streams, mountains, national or provincial parks, rural areas and oceanside. Cultural features such as local crafts and historic sites were also important. Social motivations that ranked highly were being physically active, experiencing a new and simpler lifestyle, meeting people with like interests, having a change from a busy job, seeing cultural activities, buying local crafts, and having fun.

More recent research has recognised that some differences exist in the motivations of specialist nature-based tourists and generalist nature tourists who may participate in an activity as just one of the many facets of their trip.

The specialist traveller is motivated to seek scenery and nature, have new experiences or visit new places, view wildlife, visit wilderness areas and have an uncrowded tourist experience. Generalists, on the other hand, are less concerned with crowding and wildlife viewing, but are more interested in revisiting familiar places and in learning about nature or culture.[20] Further, ecotourists will often base their nature-based tourism purchase decisions on their perception of how 'sustainable' the product is, how ethical the activity is and what effect their presence may have on local communities.

Finally, it should be remembered that, above all else, these people are on holiday. As Emanuel de Kadt said in the 1970s: 'The normal tourist is not to be confused with an anthropologist or other researcher. Tourists are pleasure seekers, temporarily unemployed and above all, consumers; they are taking their trip to get away from everyday cares.' This maxim still holds true for today's nature-based tourist.

Segmenting the market

Segmenting the market, or identifying those sectors of the overall market that are most likely to purchase a product, is vital to the success of nature-based tourism businesses. Middleton defines segmentation as:

> . . . a process of dividing a total market such as all visitors, or a market sector such as holiday travel, into sub-groups or segments of the total for marketing management purposes. Its purpose is to facilitate more cost-effective marketing, through the design, promotion and delivery of purpose-designed products, aimed at satisfying the needs of target groups.[21]

Markets can be segmented in many ways. They can be segmented geographically, by identifying the specific region (Australia, Western Australia) or subregion (Perth, Nedlands) from which the largest number of clients are likely to come. Segments can be defined by the demographic profile of key user groups, using such elements as age (seniors, under 18s), gender, ethnicity (Japanese, Australian-born Chinese), marital status, family status (couples with no children, young families), life stage (single young, seniors), education, sexual orientation, occupation or income. Many nature-based tour operators define their key markets by the psychographic profile of the consumer, segmenting the market according to its values (environmentalist), beliefs (pro-conservation), attitudes (healthy, fit), opinions, religion, interests and hobbies (birdwatchers, rock hounds), or other affiliations. Others still define the market by its behaviour, in terms of usage rates (repeat as opposed to one-off visitors), perceived benefits (education, fun, excitement), or buyer readiness.[22]

Segmenting provides a means for the small to medium-sized tour operator to cater for specific groups of consumers and, in doing so, to offer products that will satisfy their needs and wants. Many tour operators make two fundamental mistakes when identifying their product–market match. The first is to think they are catering for an undifferentiated market and that their specialist product will have wide consumer appeal. As a result, they adopt a 'shotgun' approach to advertising and promotion. The consequence is that they attract clients almost by happenstance, wasting scarce resources chasing markets that are not interested in their product. The second mistake they make is to identify several market segments but then try to sell the same undifferentiated product to each segment. The risk is that, by trying to provide one product to satisfy many segments that may have different needs and wants, the operator will end up satisfying none. A sure way to business failure is to develop an undifferentiated product and target it at an undifferentiated market.

The task of effectively segmenting markets is difficult because there are literally millions of ways that any market can be divided.[23] It is advisable to adopt the approach of using fewer, rather than more, variables to segment a market. Regardless of how markets are segmented, each segment has to be:

- discrete; each group must be sufficiently separated by such criteria as purpose of visit, income, location, motivation or some other meaningful factor
- measurable; the size of each group must be able to be measured using available market research data. Segments that cannot be measured cannot be effectively targeted
- viable; the segment must be sufficiently large and must have enough potential to generate a sustained flow of customers (and therefore revenue) to the organisation
- appropriate; the segment must be relevant to the organisation.[24]

Matching products with the market's needs and wants

The process of effective product development begins with an understanding of the personal benefits the client will gain from purchasing the product. It appears, though, that most tour operators really do not have a strong understanding of the core product they offer, instead focusing on the tangible products they develop. This may help explain why many tour operators are struggling to attract a large enough clientele to keep their business viable.

The challenge, then, for nature-based tour operators is to move away from the traditional method of providing products operators want, to developing products that meet the needs of their clients. This task can only be achieved through a thorough understanding of the underlying motives of the consumers, and this knowledge can only be obtained by conducting detailed market research. The Australian Tourist Commission and most state tourism bodies are good places to start, for they have commissioned many attitudinal surveys of inbound markets.

Many tour operators appreciate that women are the dominant consumers and, even when travelling with partners, are the main decision-makers. Yet, to date, most tourism products have been targeted at men, or have been non-gender-specific (which is a euphemism for 'aimed at men'). Research examining gender differences in tourism has found that men and women have substantially different needs. Women are very interested in the social aspects of the trips, seek the security of a guide, do not feel they have enough confidence to do the trip independently, are keenly interested in the trip as an adventure and, if they do not have travelling partners, see packaged tours as a socially attractive means of taking part in an activity. These are all requirements that are especially suited to packaged commercial tourism activities, yet few operators capitalise on satisfying core needs with their marketing.

Furthermore, astute operators appreciate that the same product, if properly designed, can satisfy the core needs of different types of travellers. In doing so, the business can broaden its market base and enhance its viability. However, it is vital that the different market segments that are identified are compatible. High adrenalin junkies may not want to participate in the same trip as people expecting a low-key, relaxed outing. This synchronicity can only happen if the core needs of each potential market can be identified and if the benefits of the product can be successfully transmitted to the market segment. Businesses may need to develop different marketing tactics and promotional tools to target the segments effectively. A high-adrenalin advertisement in a magazine like *Wild* will not be likely to work in *Seniors Today*.

The maturation of the nature-based tourism market has led to the emergence of two distinct market segments, each with substantially different core needs. Specialist or hard nature-based tourists are committed consumers who purchase the products for the intense experiences offered. These people want longer excursions, are willing to make a greater personal and financial commitment to participate and expect a high-quality experience. Soft or generalist nature-based tourists, on the other hand, may purchase their tourism experience as something to 'do' while on holiday because it is fun. They want shorter-duration experiences that are easy to consume, require little effort to participate in, are not too taxing emotionally or intellectually, yet may be fun, exciting, adventurous and educational.

Tailoring products exclusively for the specialist market will, by necessity, limit the market appeal of the business. If this path is chosen, a greater onus is placed on the operator to differentiate the product to ensure that the core product is correct at the same time as being able to compete effectively against other businesses targeting the same market. If the generalist market is targeted, by definition the market should be larger. However, direct and indirect competition will be greater. Moreover, the integrity of the product may have to be altered to cater to the needs of this less committed market. These tours will have to involve shorter trips, more superficial interpretation, an emphasis on thrill over skill and a focus on entertainment instead of education. Clearly, it may be impossible to cater to both markets effectively, since the needs of one may be incompatible with the desires of another.

Ultimately, the product development process involves a consumer-oriented approach of identifying and satisfying the needs of specific target market segments. It entails determining which markets will be served, which ones will be disregarded, which businesses the operator will compete against and which competitors will be avoided, as well as taking into account the business's own abilities. In short, it will require a strategic marketing approach to the business.

[1] Kotler & Turner, op. cit., p. 435.

[2] M. Rowe (1996) Beyond heads in beds, *Lodging Hospitality*, 52(1), pp. 42–4.

[3] D. E. Hawkins (1994) Ecotourism: Opportunities for developing countries, in Theobald, W. (ed.), *Global Tourism: The Next Decade*, Butterworth Heinemann, Melbourne, pp. 261–73.

[4] R. Donoho (1996) Broadening their horizons, *Sales and Marketing Management*, 148(3), pp. 126–8.

[5] Australian Tourist Commission (n.d.) *Asia, Europe, Japan, Market Segmentation Studies: Executive Summary*, ATC, Sydney, p. 5.

[6] Bharadwaj, Varadarajan & Fahy, op. cit.

[7] Sorensen, op. cit.

[8] D. Pearce & P. M. Wilson (1995) Wildlife viewing tourists in New Zealand, *Journal of Travel Research*, Fall, pp. 19–26; Weaver, Glenn & Rounds, op. cit.; Wight (1996a) North American ecotourists: Market profile and trip characteristics, *Journal of Travel Research*, Spring, pp. 2–10; (1996b) op. cit.; ATC, op. cit.

[9] Litvin, op. cit.

[10] B. Weiler, H. Richins & K. Markwell (1993) Barriers to travel: A study of participants and non-participants in Earthwatch Australia programs, in Hooper, P. (ed.), *Building a Research Base in Tourism: Proceedings of the National Conference on Tourism Research*, Bureau of Tourism Research, pp. 151–61.

[11] Wight (1996a) op. cit.; Pearce & Wilson, op. cit.

[12] C. T. Lang, J. T. O'Leary & A. M. Morrison (1996) Trip driven attributes of Australian outbound nature travellers, in Prosser, G. (ed.), *Tourism and Hospitality Research: Australian and International Perspectives*, Bureau of Tourism Research, pp. 361–77.

[13] Litvin, op. cit.; S. Cha, K. W. McCleary & M. Uysal (1995) Travel motivations of Japanese overseas visitors: A factor-cluster segmentation approach, *Journal of Travel Research*, Summer, 34(1), pp. 33–9.

[14] ATC, op. cit.; Tourism Victoria (1995) *Tourism Victoria: International Markets Update*, TV, Melbourne.

[15] J. Higham (1997) Sustainable wilderness tourism: Motivations and wilderness perceptions held by international visitors to New Zealand's Backcountry Conservation Estate, in Hall, C. M., Jenkins, J. & Kearsley, G. (eds), *Tourism Planning and Policy in Australia and New Zealand: Cases, Issues and Practice*, Irwin, Sydney, pp. 75–86.

[16] International Visitor Survey, quoted in Blamey (1996a) op. cit.

[17] S. Plog (1974) Why tourist destination areas rise and fall in popularity, *Cornell Hotel and Restaurant Administration Quarterly*, 1(4), pp. 55–8.

[18] R. W. McIntosh & C. Goeldner (1990) *Tourism: Principles, Practices, Philosophies*, John Wiley & Sons, Brisbane, p. 146.

[19] P. Eagles (1992) The motivations of Canadian ecotourists, in Harper, G. & Weiler, B. (eds), *Ecotourism*, Bureau of Tourism Research, pp. 12–20.

[20] Wight (1996b) op. cit.

[21] Middleton (1994) op. cit.

[22] O'Brien, op. cit.

[23] Aaker, op. cit.

[24] Middleton (1994) op. cit., citing Chisnall.

C hapter 9

Pricing nature-based tourism products

*t*here is much more involved in pricing nature-based tourism products than simply setting a tariff that reflects the accumulated costs of the product and an acceptable profit margin. Price is the only element of the marketing mix that produces revenue; the other elements—place, product and promotion —produce costs.[1] Therefore, selecting the 'right' price must be made for tactical as well as economic reasons.[2] Bearing in mind the need to ensure that the business remains economically viable, pricing is or should be a central theme in the overall marketing and positioning strategy. The price charged for nature-based tourism products is a reflection of the quality of the product being offered, its position in the marketplace and, importantly, its position relative to competing products. Moreover, different pricing strategies can be implemented in different situations that will influence demand, either by encouraging or discouraging use.[3]

This chapter examines a number of strategic points about pricing nature-based tourism products. It begins by discussing why it is important to charge the right price. This is followed by a review of pricing strategies that reflect the price–value relationship the operator is striving to achieve. The chapter then deals with pricing strategies that organisations with multiple products can use to achieve business-wide objectives. It concludes by reviewing some of the methods that can be used to influence demand for nature-based tourism products.

The role of 'value' in selecting the 'right' price

Virtually every 'how to' business planning manual will stress that pricing is not an exact science and that there are no simple ways of establishing the right price for a product. At the same time, they all point out that if the right price is not charged, the business will not perform as well as it could. At its most basic level, the prices that nature-based tourism businesses charge must be high enough to cover all the expenses involved in running the organisation, produce an acceptable income for the principals and their staff, generate enough cash flow to keep the business liquid and provide enough cash reserves for the off season. Taking this into account, the operator enjoys great freedom in setting different prices for the products offered and in varying the price of any product to reflect altered market conditions.

The price that is selected sends many signals about the perceived type and quality of the product being sold and also, importantly, about the type and quality of the person who may buy the product. As such, price is an important strategic tool which acts as a filter to achieve the desired product–market mix of the business.[4] Charging $15 a night for backpackers' accommodation, for example, suggests to the consumer that a basic product with few facilities and little privacy is being offered, which in turn appeals to the price-conscious consumer for whom lodging represents a social experience and a place to sleep. On the other hand, an international-calibre hotel charging a tariff of $500 a night is sending a completely different signal to the marketplace and, rightfully, expects a completely different type of clientele.

Pricing strategies fall within three broad concept bands:

- Premium pricing—setting prices well above the market price—is used to position the product as either unique or of exceptional quality.
- Value-for-money pricing, as the name implies, strives to ensure that the quality of the experience is a reflection of the price charged. Most operators will use this mid-range pricing strategy.
- Cheap-value pricing uses low prices without any pretence of quality to attract clients.[5]

Each of these broad pricing strategies may reflect a fair price for the product being sold and each may be attractive to different market segments. Each also has its weaknesses. A premium pricing strategy that does not offer a premium-quality experience will be seen as exploitative. The main risk of a cheap pricing strategy is that some competitors will always be able to undercut the price charged. The greatest risk in the value-for-money pricing strategy is that the operator is in danger of undercharging for the product. The client may receive very high value, while the operator may not receive much money at all.

Most businesses do not handle pricing well. In general, they tend to base their prices either on competitors' prices or on costs alone; they fail to revise prices often enough to capitalise on market changes, set prices independently of the other factors of the marketing mix, and do not vary prices to satisfy the diverse needs of different market segments or different business conditions.[6] The author's own experience and research into the nature-based tourism industry suggests that the most common pricing mistakes made by tour operators include:

- failing to appreciate cash-flow needs
- undervaluing the experience through an unwillingness to charge a price that reflects the true quality of the experience being offered
- charging low prices for fear that people will baulk at the price that reflects the true worth of the product
- failing to recognise resource scarcity as an asset for which a higher price can be charged
- failing to recognise that some SCAs are unique and that clients are prepared to pay a price premium for them
- being afraid to charge prices that the operator would personally be unwilling to pay, without appreciating that clients are likely to be very different from the operator
- clearly overcharging for the quality of experience received.

In short, too many operators fail to look at the price being charged from the perspective of the client who is buying the product, and in doing so fail to consider the value they are offering the client. If the area being visited is special, if the product being offered is unique, if the value-adding is of high quality and, importantly, if the tour operator can facilitate easy access to the experience being offered, then the clients will perceive that they are getting a premium product, for which they are prepared to pay a premium price. By the same token, if the product is substandard, if the service is poor and if the activity offered is a common one, guests may feel they get little value for money.

This may come as a surprise to many people, but tourists often have little awareness of the prices they actually pay for the products they purchase. In fact, recent research on price awareness has concluded that the prices of tourism activities at destinations are generally unimportant to tourists and that, for all but the most expensive items, price is rarely a reason cited for non-participation.[7] The research also revealed that visitors relate prices to their own frame of reference. If they enjoy an affluent lifestyle, they are less resistant to paying higher prices for products, so long as they feel confident that the value for money is there.

The key feature in any pricing strategy, therefore, is not the price charged, but the value provided for that price. For most tour operators, the true worth of the product comes from the value the operator adds to the total product rather than from the ingredient costs of the trip. People are willing to pay $120 for a day trip to the Daintree rainforest, but not because the operator includes a meal, morning tea, a ferry ride across the Daintree River and return transport in a four wheel drive vehicle. They could see the same sights for $30 per person if four of them hired a car, brought a packed lunch and paid for the ferry themselves. What makes this trip strong value at $120 is the knowledge of the guide, the quality of the interpretation of a World Heritage rainforest, the ease with which the trip can be purchased and the fact that someone else will do the driving.

Adopting a 'costs-plus' pricing method fails to consider the value-adding, the benefits it will provide the consumer or the operator's desired position in the marketplace. Moreover, it fails to consider the psychological buying process involved in targeting an up-market product at attitudinally affluent consumers who understand quality and are willing to pay a premium price for it, even if their incomes are modest.[8] Thus, underpricing a product will undersell it. A lower price implies lower value, which may serve to actually drive clients away from the business rather than attract them. If the going rate for the above Daintree rainforest tour is $120, what will the reaction be to an operator who offers exactly the same product for $80? Some people may feel this is a good deal, but many others will wonder what has been removed from the product to enable such a low price to be charged. After all, a $15 000 car is not perceived as having the same quality as a $35 000 car.

Moreover, lower prices may actually result in lower satisfaction levels among attitudinally affluent clients who are conscious that paying a lower price usually means lower value. Research the author conducted on the accommodation sector showed that people buying three-star accommodation were much more demanding than those who bought four- and five-star accommodation.[9] The reason was that people purchasing the highest standard of accommodation expected to receive a high-value experience for the amount of money they paid, and generally felt they did. Those people who bought three-star accommodation, on the other hand, wanted service that approached the five-star level, but at a discounted price. Because their main reason for buying the product was price-driven, they were acutely conscious of the value they thought they were or were not getting. When the quality of the experience inevitably failed to live up to their five-star expectations, they became dissatisfied, believing that for a few dollars more they could have purchased a superior product. Thus, while high prices suggest a quality product, the premium components that warrant the high price are what deliver the quality expected by clients.[10] If these components are not evident, clients will be dissatisfied.

It is better to seek ways to add value to a product than to look for ways to discount prices.[11] Value-adding can include such simple things as meals, using name-brand soft drinks at lunch instead of cordials, or including home-cooked biscuits and cakes at morning tea. It can also include such features as complimentary pick-ups and drop-offs at convenient locations. It can include a higher guide-to-client ratio, the employment of local experts, and the use of interpreters or multilingual staff. From an operational perspective, value-adding may include the use of newer or better-quality equipment than competitors. Importantly, though, value-adding need not cost anything. Clean, well-groomed, courteous guides who enjoy being with people can add tremendously to the quality of the experience. Similarly, hiring guides with cooking qualifications as well as other areas of expertise can make a trip more enjoyable.

Pricing strategies

At least six different pricing strategies can be used to achieve an organisation's goals. The selection of the final strategy will be influenced by the organisation's objectives, the characteristics of the customers, the demand levels of customers, costs, the number and relative strength of competitors, the distribution channels selected, the complementarity of the services and facilities used with the pricing objectives, and the sophistication of the operator.[12] In addition, the life cycle stage of the product should be considered when setting pricing strategies.[13] Each pricing strategy is discussed briefly below.

Maximising sales growth

A *penetration pricing strategy* is used to achieve maximum sales. This technique adopts a strategy of setting as low a price as possible to reach the mass market and in doing so to win market share. The belief is that increasing sales volume will ultimately lead to low unit costs, greater efficiencies in operations and high profitability. The end result will be a sustainable competitive advantage based on price, because other competitors will not have either the high volume of users or the economies of scale. The market conditions favouring a market penetration pricing policy are high price sensitivity among consumers, unit costs that can be reduced significantly by economies of scale and deterrence of new entrants into the market due to low prices. This strategy is used most often during the introductory and growth stages of a product's life cycle and is most appropriate for those products that will have mass consumer appeal.

It is difficult for all but the largest nature-based tourism operators to adopt a penetration pricing strategy, for few have the potential size and scale of operation to become market leaders. Such a strategy is essentially useless for smaller players, for they simply will not achieve cost advantages. Small four wheel drive ecotour operators, for example, who can accommodate six people per vehicle will not achieve significant profit growth by slashing their prices to try to get ten people per trip. To do this would require the additional capital costs of another vehicle, extra equipment and the added variable costs of staff and food.

Market skimming

Most small operators striving to position themselves as niche tour operators will want to consider a market skimming pricing strategy. This technique sets high prices to try to skim the 'cream' off the market. By setting a high price and delivering a high-quality product, the operator positions the product for only some segments of the market. Market skimming works best when there are a sufficiently large number of buyers willing to pay a higher price for the product. The high price supports the image of the product and acts as a disincentive for other competitors, who may feel that they cannot compete at the same quality level.

Product-quality leadership

An alternative to market skimming is to adopt a high price strategy supported by an intention to be recognised as the product quality leader. This technique is reserved for only a small number of companies that offer a truly exceptional product. The price charged reflects the superb quality of the experience offered. Such a strategy is used by Rolls-Royce and Ferrari.

If nature-based tour operators wish to adopt this pricing strategy, they must ensure that the quality of the product reflects the high prices being charged. A guide-to-client ratio as low as one-to-one, silver service dining at the campsite, the best equipment, the newest vehicles and the use of world-renowned experts will all be needed to deliver the experience.

Maximising current profit

A profit-taking pricing strategy is designed to provide a short-term surge in profit for the organisation. This technique is often used by nature-based tourism businesses at the end of their operating season, when their primary business need is to ensure they have sufficient revenue for the off season. Businesses may run either high-profit trips or trips that can accommodate a large volume of clients. The risk of a profit-taking exercise is that the operator will reduce the quality of the service to such an extent that the clients will be dissatisfied. The longer-term consequences of such an action may be more damaging than the short-term profit benefits. Therefore, if a profit-taking strategy is adopted, the operator must ensure that the overall quality of the product does not diminish to the point where it damages the image of the business.

Maximising current revenue

This strategy is designed to maximise sales revenue or cash flow without necessarily taking into consideration profitability. Cash flow considerations may become the primary financial concern of businesses at certain times during the operating cycle. An operator may, for example, be heavily reliant on the travel trade for a significant share of the organisation's business. Knowing that the travel trade may not pay its bills for 90 days or more, the operator may need to develop products that provide another source of quick cash to keep the business liquid. The alternative is to run a series of day trips that can be booked at short notice and for which the income is received at the time of purchase. In this way, the operator can retain a sufficient cash flow to service the higher-profit inbound market.

Survival

Finally, some businesses may be forced to adopt a survival pricing technique as a last-gasp option to keep the business alive. Profits are less important than survival. Survival pricing involves deep discounts or increased value-adding, sometimes to the extent that profits are traded off over the short term. Survival pricing is only recommended when the operation has an over-capacity problem, when there is intense competition or when macro-environmental factors have adversely affected the destination area.

The Seaview Air disaster, for example, had a dramatic impact on the viability of Lord Howe Island as a tourist destination. As a result of the crash and the loss of consumer confidence in small airlines, demand for visitation to the island slumped. Prior to the crash, Lord Howe had a vibrant tourism industry that appealed to the mid- to upper-scale traveller. The only way the operators could entice people to come to the island after the accident was to reduce prices to the point where Lord Howe was no more expensive than many coastal New South Wales destinations. As a result, prices declined to the level they were at in the mid-1980s, although costs have continued to rise. The operators are doing it tough, but this is what must be done to survive until the public confidence in small air carriers improves.

Price matching

A price matching policy is not recommended. In many cases, the prices charged may be similar among a number of operators, but this should only emerge if the operators have similar costs, offer similar products and are pursuing similar markets. There are a number of risks with a price matching policy. For a start, no two operators have the same costs; matching the prices of an operator with lower costs will only make the lower-cost operator stronger, as he or she can afford to add extra value and still maintain an acceptable margin. Price matching also leads to price wars, again giving advantage to the operator with the lower costs. It is advisable, instead, to develop a price that reflects the quality of the product, and if the price happens to be higher than those of competitors, ensure that added value is included to warrant the price differential.

Using price to influence market demand

Price is one of the tools that can be used to manipulate market demand. Different pricing strategies can be used to stimulate or dampen demand, to maximise profits during the high seasons and to generate repeat business. While one can manipulate prices, it is essential that this is done strategically and that overall the business achieves the right mix of prices to ensure that it remains viable.

Discounting versus value-adding

Discounting is a legitimate sales tactic, but it should be used only under certain market conditions and only as a short-term exercise. It can be an effective tool to stimulate demand and sell excess capacity or, if the region is suffering from an over-capacity problem, to retain existing business. Apart from these limited circumstances, however, discounting should be discouraged. Discounting during the high season can cause long-term damage to a business, for discounts suggest that the property is overpriced and that the price–value relationship is poor. Moreover, prolonged discounts can effectively re-establish the market price at a lower level.

Instead it is recommended that operators consider ways of adding value to the tourism experience. Value-adding is preferable to discounting, for it preserves the integrity of the price–value relationship and in doing so maintains the operator's desired position in the marketplace. Rather than offering the same for less, the operator offers more for the same price. The client benefits because the value of the experience is enhanced.

Off-season rates

Off-season rates are different from discounted rates. Off-season rates recognise the effect that fluctuating demand will have on the price. During the peak season, demand for tourism products is highest. At this time, prices can be adjusted upwards to reflect the scarcity value of the product being sold. During other seasons, when demand decreases, the scarcity value of the product declines, justifying a lower price. There is nothing wrong with publishing peak-season, shoulder-season and off-season rates. Indeed, this is standard practice. The principles of the customer mix still apply, though; the business can afford to reduce its rates in the off season if the peak season generates sufficient income. Indeed, if the operator manages the yield of the property effectively, off-season rates can be essentially profit-taking exercises.

Off-season rates are popular with tourist properties that have high fixed costs. While the operation may be seasonal, mortgage and loan repayments, insurance, rates, electricity and utilities and even some staff salaries continue all year. A number of smaller nature-based tourism businesses scale down their activities in the off season but still operate with the goal of covering fixed costs. Off-season rates can provide needed cash flow for the organisation.

Specials for repeat visitors

Regular clients can be rewarded in a variety of ways that are designed to retain their loyalty. Some operators choose to offer discounts to repeat visitors, especially if they are long-term customers. Others offer something akin to a frequent flyer program, whereby repeat visitors receive a free trip after they have purchased a specified number of trips. Others reward regular clients by adding something extra to the product. Valued clients can be given advance notice of the year's activities, priority booking rights, the best equipment or rooms and the like.

Indeed, the operator is aware of one nature-based tour operator who has created a 'gold class' for valued clients. These clients receive a special newsletter, are offered exclusive trips available only to other gold class members and have the first right of refusal on any trip offered. Another operator sells 'memberships' for his business which offer members discounted rates on trips, special members-only social nights, discounted shopping at retail outlets and even cinema entrance discounts.

These types of benefits can be justified on both economic and strategic marketing grounds. The marketing costs of attracting new clients are five to ten times higher than the costs of retaining existing clients. Astute operators realise that, with a little extra investment, established clients can keep coming back. Moreover, satisfied clients are the best form of advertising for most businesses. As such, developing programs to reward good clients can and should form an integral part of any promotional strategy.

Group rates

Whitewater rafting firms in eastern Canada have grown rich by focusing on group sales. The sales technique used is brilliant in its simplicity. Their approach to group sales is to offer one free trip to the person who organises the group. In doing so, the whitewater rafting business essentially converts one of its clients into a commissioned salesperson. The operators recognise that they spend, on average, about 10 per cent of their gross revenue on marketing. Giving the organiser a free trip is therefore costed as a marketing expense. However, the real cost to the operator is substantially lower than the retail value of the trip award. Indeed, the actual cost is the variable cost of the trip for the organiser, for the other clients have paid their share of the fixed costs.

The author used to work for the wilderness lodges in Northern Ontario. One of the lodge owners spent virtually nothing on promotional activities. Instead, he identified his market as people who went to a number of bars in the greater Chicago area. The deal he arranged with the owners of the bars was that, for every ten trips sold, the owner would receive one free trip. Over the course of the winter, bar staff sold the trips to their clients. The owner got a free trip and was able to reward his best staff with free trips too. Again, the clients sold the product for the operator, and again the only cost to the operator was the variable cost of the trip for the three or four people who earned a free vacation.

Many nature-based tourism businesses are ideally suited to group travel opportunities. This sector is typified by small, personalised group tours, often limited by the capacity of the transport vehicle or by the specifications of various licensing bodies. Moreover, groups represent a highly cost-effective market for many tour operators. Rather than having to persuade ten people to buy the trip individually, the operator must only convince one person of the merits of the trip and then have that person persuade his or her friends.

Trade rates

The commercial tourism distribution system, travel agents, wholesalers and inbound operators work as commissioned sales staff on behalf of the products they sell. The role that these operatives play in tourism and how nature-based operators can use them to their advantage will be discussed in greater detail in the next chapter. Suffice it to say, though, that the standard commission for travel agents is 10 per cent, for tour wholesalers 20 per cent (of which 10 per cent goes to the retail agent) and for inbound operators 30 per cent (10 per cent to the inbound operator, 10 per cent to the wholesaler and 10 per cent to the retail travel agent). In addition, operators may be expected to pay an additional 5 to 10 per cent commission to gain the status of 'preferred' suppliers. In a similar manner, hotel tour desks and local tourist information bureaux will expect a commission of anywhere from 5 to 15 per cent.

Introductory rates

Offering special introductory rates is useful when launching a new product line, or a product extension, but is not as useful when launching a new business. The idea of introductory offers works best with established businesses that have an established client base. Such businesses can reach their target markets in a cost-effective manner and, if the business has established a reliable reputation, may use existing clients effectively to launch new products. Introductory rates do not work as effectively for either new businesses or for businesses that have a very low repeat use rate.

Limited time offers

Limited time offers work well for large tourism ventures, but are often not very effective for small nature-based tourism businesses for two reasons. The first is that the lead time for purchasing peak demand seasonal tourism products may be quite long. Most ski lodges, for example, have a clear idea of how their winter will look as early as mid March, when the scramble to book accommodation begins. Operators also know that if a week in July has not sold by late June, it is unlikely to sell. The reason is that most people cannot organise a week's holiday in such a short time period. A limited time offer may not meet with great success.

By contrast, the purchase decision for short-duration nature-based tourism experiences is more spontaneous, especially if the nature-based experience represents a secondary activity to be undertaken at the destination. Many operators report that clients who travel to destination areas usually book their eco-experience one or two days in advance, well after they have arrived at the destination. A limited time offer represents value for clients, but may be of little value to the operator if potential clients only visit the area for short periods of time. This type of promotion works best when dealing with a local clientele.

1 Kotler & Turner, op. cit., p. 483.

2 Holloway & Robinson, op. cit.

3 A. V. Seaton & M. M. Bennett (1966) *Marketing Tourism Products, Concepts, Issues, Cases*, International Thomson Business Press, London.

4 E. Laws (1991) *Tourism Marketing: Service and Quality Management Perspectives*, Stanley Thornes, Cheltenham, UK.

5 Holloway & Robinson, op. cit., p. 90.

6 Kotler & Turner, op. cit.

7 R. Lawson, J. Gnoth & K. Paulin (1995) Tourists' awareness of prices for attractions and activities, *Journal of Travel Research*, 34(a), pp. 3–10.

8 D. Rodkin (1990) Wealthy attitude wins over healthy wallet, *Advertising Age*, 61(2), July, pp. S4, S6.

9 B. McKercher (1982) Accommodation preferences of Ottawa bound visitors, unpublished MA thesis, Carleton University, Ottawa, Canada.

10 M. Keane (1997) Quality and pricing in tourism destinations, *Annals of Tourism Research*, 23(1), pp. 117–30.

11 R. Grover (1992) Heartbreak Hotel for tourism, *Business Week*, Jan. 20, p. 36; B. Pritchard (1995), *Complex Marketing Made Simple*, Milner Books, Los Angeles.

12 Morrison, op. cit.

13 Richardson, op. cit.

The tourism distribution system

$t$he tourism distribution system is the network used by tour operators to get their products into the marketplace. In marketing jargon, distribution represents the third P of marketing, for it describes the Places where prospective customers gain access to the product.[1] Today, tour operators have the choice of literally hundreds of options for getting their product to the consumer. Many involve selling the product directly; others entail the use of retail intermediaries like local tour desks, tourist bureaux, state government tourist offices and motoring organisations. Still others involve the formal travel trade, which comprises retail travel agents, tour wholesalers and inbound tour operators.

Each has its merits and each has its deficiencies, but clearly some work better for different business situations. A small business offering a limited product range that targets one market may use a simple distribution system, while a larger business with various products targeting different markets may choose a more complex distribution system. The ultimate selection of distribution channels depends on how the market has been defined, which segments are targeted, the number of markets targeted, the goals of the business, its geographic location *vis-à-vis* its main markets, the type of business, the range of products offered, the life cycle stage of the product or business, the capacity of the business, the length of its operating season, the resources at the operator's disposal (both human and financial), the lead time required, the prevalence and appropriateness of intermediaries, the desired client mix, yield management principles, the knowledge and expertise of the operator and, finally, the operator's own creativity.

This chapter is designed to remove some of the confusion about tourism distribution systems. It will explain, in simple terms, the range of opportunities available to the nature-based tourism industry, identify various alternatives, discuss their costs and then describe the relative merits and deficiencies of each method. It begins by looking at a range of direct distribution channels and then examines a number of issues concerning the use of intermediaries.

Direct distribution versus using intermediaries

Nature-based tour operators have two broad options for linking their products with the consumer, as is shown in Figure 10.1. On the one hand, operators can choose to sell their products directly to the consumer. On the other hand, they can avail themselves of a variety of intermediaries who, for a commission, will endeavour to sell their product on their behalf. The number of intermediaries between the producer and the consumer is referred to as the number of steps in the tourism distribution system.

Figure 10.1   Tourism distribution systems

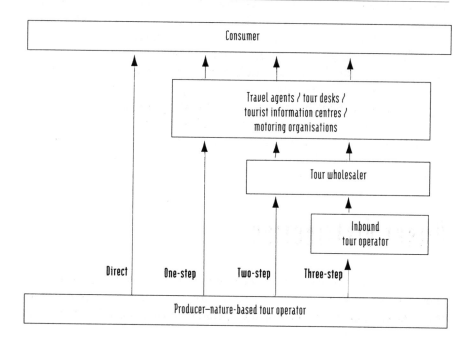

In the direct distribution system, producers sell their products directly to the consumer. Using a direct distribution method is the simplest way to reach prospective clients; however, it is also the most limiting and may constrain the ability of the business to grow.

A one-step distribution system involves the use of one intermediary to sell the product on behalf of the operator. Retail travel agents are the most common type of one-step distributors. Others include hotel tour desks, local tourist bureaux, state government tourist offices that have a retail arm and state motoring organisations. The standard fee or commission is around 10 per cent of the retail price. Travel agents may also package other component parts of the operator's product, such as transport and accommodation at either end of the trip, to create a new product.

A two-step distribution system involves the use of tour wholesalers who package the product for sale through retail travel agents—hence the two steps. The role of the tour wholesaler is akin to that of a small manufacturer, in that the wholesaler packages various components to create a new product to be sold. Most of the packaged tours available at travel agents have been assembled by tour wholesalers. Wholesalers differ from travel agents in that they rarely deal directly with the public. A two-step distribution system is used most effectively with inbound travel or with domestic travel where the clients must travel long distances.

The three-step distribution system represents a further refinement in the packaging of travel products and is used exclusively to bring international visitors to Australia. This system involves an inbound operator who packages the land content of a trip and then on-sells it to an overseas wholesaler who adds airfares and other components, thus creating a complete package for sale through overseas travel agents. This system has a number of advantages for small tour operators who wish to gain access to international markets.

In their early stages, most nature-based tour operators tend to use direct distribution systems almost exclusively. Many operators adopt the direct distribution approach, not because it is the most appropriate, but because they do not understand how the travel trade works. Many also are so fiercely independent that they are unwilling to pay a commission to anyone to help sell their product. As the business matures and as the operator begins to realise that in order to grow the business must reach new markets, resistance to using intermediaries diminishes.

Direct distribution

Direct distribution is the simplest means of reaching potential clients but, as shown above, is also the most restrictive, for the ability of the operator to reach the consumer is limited by the operator's own actions. In addition, it can also be a very costly option that provides few results, especially if the operator lacks the skills to use this system effectively. The success of direct distribution is closely linked to the consumer advertising and promotional strategies used by the operator, which will be discussed in the next chapter.

The advantages and disadvantages of this distribution method are summarised in Figure 10.2. The main advantages lie in its simplicity, the ability to target niche markets precisely and the opportunity it provides for operators to develop cost advantages by virtue of not having to pay commissions.

Figure 10.2   Advantages and disadvantages of using a direct distribution system

Advantages	Disadvantages
Simple to use	Limited reach: cannot reach the numbers of people that the travel trade can
No commissions, allowing operators to develop cost advantages	High up-front costs compared to the travel trade. The travel trade takes a commission on units sold; with direct distribution, the operator must invest money up-front to promote the product
Opportunity to target markets precisely	Often high distribution costs per client, especially if a non-targeted approach has been used
Ability to respond quickly to changing consumer tastes	Unless carefully planned as part of an overall strategic marketing strategy, the very real risk exists that the operator will adopt an ineffective shotgun approach, wasting scarce resources
Assurance that the product will get a high profile	If located in a regional area and targeting an urban audience, difficulty in gaining consumer awareness
Reluctance of many nature-based tour operators to use the travel trade	Difficulty in selecting media that are most appropriate
Ease in controlling inventory and releasing unneeded stock	Risk of no visibility in the marketplace because the operator cannot afford to maintain a high profile
Ability to target niche markets that the travel trade would not be interested in	Success depends on the skill level of the operator to clearly define products to satisfy viable target markets, to identify strategies to reach them and to deliver promotional campaigns that will produce desired results.
Ability to reinforce the brand through advertising and promotion	

Sources: various[2]

However, these benefits are offset by the limited reach of direct distribution systems and the high up-front costs of developing and delivering promotional campaigns. Often the greatest weakness in adopting direct distribution channels as the sole means of reaching clients lies not with this method, but with the skills of the person implementing various strategies.

Direct distribution can work effectively, provided the operator has developed products for clearly defined, viable market segments, has identified a cost-effective means of reaching these markets and has the resources available to do so. However, many businesses have not clearly defined their product markets and many nature-based tour operators lack marketing skills. As a result, operators often adopt a random approach to promotion, trying something here, something else there and eventually frittering away their scarce promotional budget. To work effectively, direct distribution must be targeted narrowly at desired markets. There is little room for error.

A wide variety of methods exist to reach the market directly. Some include displaying the business's brochures widely; operating a storefront business; conducting sales meetings; directly marketing from the business's database; advertising in newspapers, guidebooks, tourism promotion publications or the specialist magazines that will be read by the target audience; attending consumer shows; conducting direct promotions at shopping centres; and, increasingly, selling through the Internet. It is recommended that a wide variety of complementary direct distribution channels be established to create awareness of the product and to reinforce the message being sent.

A comment on the Internet

The Internet may revolutionise the tourism distribution system one day but, as with all new technologies, people are still trying to work out how to use it to their best advantage. While it may hold great promise in the future, at present it is little more than a toy that duplicates the telephone and the fax machine.[3] The great appeal of the Internet is the prospect of gaining global distribution for tourism products. Its great weakness, however, is that unless someone knows the specific URL (Universal Resource Locator) address of a site, it is unlikely they will stumble on it by accident.

Right now, using the Internet is like entering a great hall filled from floor to ceiling with millions of tourist brochures scattered randomly throughout. The hall is in total darkness and the searcher has only a pocket torch capable of illuminating one brochure at a time. Oh, yes, it also takes up to two minutes to find any brochure and over a minute to open any page in the pamphlet. In addition, the hall is being expanded in a geometric manner with seemingly millions of new brochures being added every month. In one search conducted in June 1997, over 666 600 ecotourism sites, 3 600 000 adventure tourism sites and 400 000 nature-based tourism sites were identified.

The current search engines are cumbersome and not very discriminating. Further, each search engine seems to use different criteria to highlight different sites. It is difficult to make the Internet work if the business does not appear in the top 20 sites in a search. Given the large number of sites, though, the odds of being identified are remote. No wonder recent studies indicate that fewer people are surfing the Net and, instead, are seeking the comfort of visiting known sites where they can get the information they seek. No wonder satisfaction levels of both users and site holders are declining.

Is the Internet a useful direct distribution tool? The answer is both yes and no. It can play an important communication role in support of other promotional activities and to inform regular customers of new products.[4] As well, if an operation can gain access to a high-profile site (such as state or Commonwealth sites or the sites of large Internet tourism providers), it may provide an opportunity for people who are familiar with the site to gather information about the specific product. But in and of itself, the author remains sceptical about the efficacy of directing a lot of effort to the Internet in the belief that substantial new business will emerge. That is why Internet service providers like to talk about hits, rather than sales that are generated from those hits because, while many sites will be visited, the jury is still out as to whether much tourism business is generated.

However, Internet sites can complement existing marketing activities and can play a useful role in supporting brands and providing additional information for clients.[5] Where the Net works best is where operators include their e-mail and URL addresses along with other contact details in their promotional tools. Clients wanting more information can contact the site day or night, 365 days a year to learn more about the business and the products it offers. It is also an effective tool for communicating information to existing clients, such as providing equipment lists, offering an on-line newsletter discussing the latest trips or, importantly, for notifying clients of last-minute openings for certain trips.

At the present time, e-mail provides the most exciting distribution innovations for tour operators. Many people believe that e-mail will make fax machines obsolete in the next 10 to 15 years as more and more people come on-line.[6] E-mail is a powerful and environmentally-friendly direct marketing tool that can be used to inform clients of new trips, specials or openings for existing trips. Also, depending on how well one manages one's client database, e-mail can provide a cost-effective means of targeting a business's most valued clients. The main caveat that must be remembered is that junk e-mail is starting to clutter people's computers. To be effective, e-mail, like any other direct marketing tool, must be used selectively.

The travel trade: using intermediaries

The travel trade intimidates many nature-based tour operators. Historically, this sector has been less willing to use the services of travel agents, tour wholesalers and inbound tour operators than other segments of the tourism industry. And, to be fair, the travel trade has also shown little interest in small tour operators. But that situation seems to be changing. Today, nature-based tour operators realise that if they are to extend the reach of their product they need to use the travel trade. In response, the number of specialist travel agents and tour wholesalers has increased, catering to the burgeoning market demand for non-mass tourism opportunities.

The travel trade works on the very simple premise of an incremental commission scale based on the number of steps involved. The more steps, the higher the commission. If a retail travel agent sells a nature-based tour operator's product, the standard commission is between 5 and 15 per cent. If a tour wholesaler packages the product with other components to create a 'new' product that the retail sector can sell, the standard commission is 20 to 25 per cent, half of which goes to the wholesaler and half to the retailer. By the same token, if an inbound tour operator packages the nature-based tour operator's product with other land content components in Australia and then distributes it to a wholesaler based overseas who adds airfares and other features which then create a new product for sale by the overseas travel retailer, then a commission of 30 to 40 per cent will be charged, again split evenly among the distributors. If no product is sold, no commission is charged. Simple!

However, where many small tour operators get into trouble is in not realising how commissions are costed into the products being sold. Commissions represent expenses that must be paid from normal retail price and not an extra cost to be added to accommodate the needs of the travel trade. As a result, the net returns to the operator are less if using the travel trade than if selling direct. However, this becomes an attractive option if the operator believes that the net benefits to the business offset any possible loss in revenue.

The net returns to the operator from a tour that might be sold directly for $700 would be $630 if sold through a travel agent, $560 if sold through a tour wholesaler and $490 if sold through an inbound tour operator. There is a mistaken belief that commissions can be added on top of the retail price (thus charging a price of $770 for a one-step distribution system, $840 for a two-step and $910 for a three-step) but no travel agent, tour wholesaler or inbound operator would consider selling the product at such an inflated price, for it would simply not be price-competitive.

Retailers

The retail arm of the travel trade has direct contact with the consumer. Retailers comprise mostly travel agents, but may also include tour desks at hotels, motoring organisations like the RACV or the NRMA who sell products to their members, and local or state tourist information centres that have a retail arm. Best estimates suggest that about 3500 retail travel agents operate throughout Australia. Some are owned independently, while most these days are affiliated with national or transnational chains.

At their core, travel agents act as distributors that endeavour to sell travel products in exchange for a fee or commission. Commissions can vary from 6 to 20 per cent of the retail sales price depending on the product, the volume of sales, the price and the arrangement made with the supplier, but usually average at about 10 per cent. More than that, though, agents are brokers of information.[7] Their stock-in-trade is what they know and the information they can find out. Their success ultimately depends on providing products that will satisfy the needs of their clients.

Travel agents provide a number of opportunities for the nature-based tourism industry to expand the reach of their product. In particular, retail travel agents, tour desks and tourist bureaux:

- provide access to new markets and greater penetration of existing markets in a cost-effective manner
- create a wider range of distribution outlets for the product
- assume the promotional costs of selling the product and the risks of promotion
- put a face to the product being purchased
- can be used to develop selected high-value domestic and overseas markets
- can reduce marketing costs, as the costs of commissions can be significantly less than the costs of using direct distribution channels in new markets
- can reduce operating costs: if there is no sale, there is no commission charged.

However, the tourism industry must also be aware of the limitations inherent in using retail agents, including:

- the limited reach of individual travel agents; to achieve broader market coverage, the operator must either use many travel agents or work with a wholesaler or inbound operator

- the potential high costs of commissions, especially if the business did not consider commissions in setting its prices or miscalculated its client mix (as often happens)
- loss of control over the product
- the risk of being given low-priority status by travel agents, either because the agent does not feel there will be much demand for the product, or because other operators are more profitable for the agent, either through higher commissions or easier booking procedures
- allegations of corruption and kickbacks among tour desk outlets located in hotels and resorts, where clients are directed to 'preferred' clients on the basis of a higher commission or other monetary perks.

While travel agencies have high cash flows, traditionally they work on notoriously tight margins.[8] With a standard commission rate of 10 per cent, an agency grossing one million dollars a year will net only $100 000, from which all operating costs, salaries and marketing expenses must be paid. Moreover, the typical travel agency has running costs of at least $50 an hour for each consultant. The consultant must, therefore, generate about one dollar in commission for every minute he or she works for the agency in order to be profitable. Thus, a key operational consideration, from the perspective of the travel agent, is the need to maintain high productivity levels among staff. If it takes a travel agent a total of two hours to sell an $800 product that produces $80 in commission—from initial enquiry to consultation, to lodging the booking, to receiving confirmation to providing the travel documents and all the other seemingly insignificant but time-consuming tasks involved in serving clients—the agent has lost money on the transaction.

For this reason, travel agents prefer to deal with suppliers that can provide them with enough information up-front (in the form of brochures or trip notes) and sufficient back-up service to answer client questions, get a commitment from the client and make the booking. The higher the return to the travel agent, the more prepared they are to spend more time with clients. For a travel agent to be prepared to sell a $100 day trip which produces a $10 commission, the agent must be able to complete the entire transaction—from the moment when clients walk through the door to when they walk out again—in less than 10 minutes. If the commission is higher, the travel agent will be prepared to commit proportionately more time.

Using the retail travel trade: issues to consider

Simplicity of booking

Nature-based tour operators who are planning to use the retail sector as an alternative distribution system must have a simple and sure booking procedure. If the tourism business's internal booking procedures are inefficient, it will cost the retail sector time and therefore money.

Regular office hours, or an acceptable alternative

A vital part of processing enquiries efficiently is ensuring that the tourism business maintains regular office hours to field phone calls from travel agents. This is absolutely vital if the operator is running day trips from a destination area.

If the operator is running trips that have a longer lead time, alternative systems can be developed that, while not as efficient as maintaining regular office hours, may prove acceptable to the agents. Phones and fax machines have been used in the past, on the proviso that the operator confirms bookings the next business day. E-mail and the development of a travel trade specific web site outlining booking procedures and availabilities of trips may also provide an alternative as more travel agents come on line. Again, the key to making this system work is to respond promptly to requests.

Hidden costs

Before electing to use the travel trade, operators must work out the real costs associated with these services. Nature-based tour operators may have to produce a special run of brochures for the retail sector. As well, if they are sufficiently large, they may have to consider investing in one of the computerised global distribution systems, or as a minimum consider a toll-free telephone service.

Some tourist bureaux and local tour desks charge for the privilege of allowing a business to display its brochures, on top of the commissions they charge for selling products. Depending on the size of the tourist bureau and the amount of traffic it attracts, the costs can range from a few tens of dollars to a couple of hundred dollars. The cost of displaying brochures widely may outweigh the business generated from such a distribution channel.

If the price of the product is relatively low, operators may have to consider paying a higher commission. Travel insurance, for example, is a relatively low-cost item. To make it attractive to travel agents, the standard commission rates are 40 per cent. Alternatively, if the marketplace is crowded with a number of businesses offering similar products at similar prices, the operator may consider increasing the commission or return to the travel agent to make his or her product more appealing. In the past, Air New Zealand has been able to compete effectively against Qantas partly because its commission structure is twice as high. By contrast, one of the many things that killed Compass Airlines was its insistence on paying a 5 per cent commission on domestic flights when industry norms were around 10 per cent.

Pricing the product

In establishing the price for the product being offered, nature-based tour operators must consider whether or not they wish to use the travel trade. As mentioned earlier, the margin between costs and price are often so small that the operator is precluded from using any form of intermediary. The type of distribution system to be used must be considered very carefully during the product development phase and not after the product has been launched. If the operator desires to use the travel trade at some point, then margins must be built into the price at the start to allow for this contingency.

Controlling yield and managing the client mix

In Chapter 9, the importance of getting the right mix of customers at the right mix of prices for the right mix of products being offered to achieve the business's goals was discussed. The same philosophy applies to the mix between clients booking directly and those using the travel trade. Astute operators strive to manage the client mix between direct bookings and those made through intermediaries, just as they strive to manage the client mix on trips. Again, the desired ratio must be determined during the financial planning exercise at the start of each financial year.

The suitability of the business for the travel trade

The travel trade is certainly not interested in working with all nature-based tourism businesses. At the same time, not all nature-based tourism businesses will benefit by using the travel trade. The industry is most interested in those businesses with a strong track record of delivering advertised trips and businesses that are of a sufficiently large size and have a sufficiently large volume that they can sell the product profitably. For the most part, they are leery about dealing with new businesses, preferring to wait a few years to see if they will survive. By the same token, few real benefits may accrue from using the travel trade if the operator has an established clientele, strong direct distribution channels and a high occupancy rate.

A strategic business decision

Regardless, the decision to use the travel trade, or any other distribution system, must be made for strategic business purposes. As with all distribution channels available to nature-based tour operators, using the retail travel trade has a number of pluses and minuses. An operator may identify the travel trade as a means of expanding into new markets, as a means of extending the season or as a means of launching new products. If the business does not need to expand, or if growth can be achieved in other ways, the operator may not need to use travel agents.

Wholesalers

Tour wholesalers act as intermediaries between the retail travel sector and the producers of the travel product. By gathering component parts of the product together, they create a new, comprehensive travel product that can then be sold to the public by travel agents. Tour wholesalers are the businesses that create packaged holidays. Packaged holidays are standardised, repeatable offers comprising two or more elements of transport, accommodation, food, destination, destination attractions and other facilities and services. The product is then offered for sale to the public at a published inclusive price, in which the costs of the product components cannot be separately identified.[9]

The great appeal of wholesalers is their ability to broaden the market base through a wider distribution network or through the packaging of the nature-based experience with other components to produce a new product that appeals to different market segments. Wholesalers have a large network of retail travel agents through which they sell their product. Using wholesalers is attractive to nature-based tour operators for a number of other reasons. Wholesalers:

- can provide access to more domestic and international markets in a cost-effective manner
- can lengthen operating seasons by attracting a different type of clientele, such as seniors who are not constrained by school holidays or clients from different countries where holiday patterns are different from those in Australia
- can create much greater consumer awareness
- can reduce the risks in developing new markets. Wholesalers, like travel agents, work on a commission basis; if there are no sales, no commissions are charged
- can provide a highly cost-effective method of diversifying and expanding a business
- can simplify many aspects of the business. People on a package have paid a fixed price for a predetermined array of services. This also helps the operator to develop efficient systems to cater for clients
- can assist an operator in maximising the per person returns from a business by ensuring that additional services are included in the package. A diversified operator may negotiate meals, accommodation and entries to attractions, thus using his or her facilities to their greatest potential.

However, using wholesalers is not without its drawbacks. Clearly, not all businesses are suited to this type of operation. By their very nature, tour wholesalers tend to deal with high-volume product. Many small operators may simply not have the capacity to be attractive to wholesalers. The standard commission rate is 20 per cent, but can increase to 25 per cent for 'preferred' suppliers. This fee may be too steep for many operators.

Because of the nature of their businesses, the need to produce brochures and the need to get product to the retail trade, wholesalers have extremely long lead times. It is not uncommon for tour operators to demand confirmed prices and to make block bookings six to twelve months prior to the departure date. Indeed, some demand this information two years before departure. Many operators will have no idea of the dates of their trips, the capacity they wish to offer the wholesaler, or costs this far in advance. For this reason, wholesalers generally prefer to deal with established businesses that have a proven track record.

There are also a number of other factors that must be considered before deciding to use wholesalers:

- Wholesalers have been known to exert significant price pressure on suppliers that they know are dependent on them for a substantial part of their business. The result is that suppliers may find themselves in a profitless volume situation, where the margins are so low that the only way they can survive is by taking large numbers of people.

- The tour wholesaling business is highly volatile, with a number of large organisations collapsing in recent years. Before committing to a wholesaler, make sure that their track record is strong.

- Because of the long lead times, wholesalers cannot respond quickly to changes in consumer tastes.

- Wholesalers have been known in the past to become increasingly demanding of suppliers, asking for a variety of extras but being unwilling to pay for them.

- Fluctuating exchange rates can play havoc with operators who are reliant on overseas tour wholesalers. The competitive appeal of the product can be affected adversely should the Australian dollar appreciate, should the local currency depreciate or should the currencies of competing destinations (like New Zealand) depreciate.

- There can be significant cash-flow implications as wholesalers typically take 60 or more days to process payment, with one study showing that 15 per cent took more than 90 days.[10]

Inbound tour operators

Inbound tour operators, or IBOs, have a specialist function in the travel trade. They are generally, though not always, involved in providing the Australian land content of a trip for overseas tour wholesalers. The typical land content may include tours, accommodation, transport (air or bus), entries, meals, attractions and local guides or trip leaders. The wholesaler then adds international airfares and other features at the beginning and the end of the trip to create the product, which is then sold through travel agents. IBOs have become an essential player in the inbound tourism industry. Recent industry figures reveal that inbound operators serve about 70 per cent of all inbound tourists, with almost 90 per cent of visitors from Asia using their services.

IBOs provide a number of advantages for nature-based tour operators:

- They provide the most cost-effective means for small and not-so-small players to enter the international tourism marketplace.
- Because their head offices are in Australia, communications between the tour operator and the inbound market are easier.
- IBOs are flexible in the type of product they offer, creating opportunities for specialist products and tours that would not otherwise be attractive to the mainstream international travel trade. As a result, more opportunities for niche players exist through IBOs than through traditional wholesalers.

The main disadvantage of this type of distribution system is, again, cost. As the IBO represents an additional step in the distribution system, higher costs must be expected. Like the other members of the travel trade, they work on commissions. Nature-based tour operators using IBOs can be expected to pay at least 30 per cent commission, divided between the IBO, the wholesaler and the retailer. The same caveats that apply to wholesalers also apply to inbound tour operators.

[1] Middleton (1994) op. cit.

[2] Sources, in part: Anon. (1985) Firm discovers marketing tool in alternative capital, *Marketing News*, 19(23), p. 12; R. Coyne (1995) The reservation revolution, *Hotel and Motel Management*, 210(12), pp. 54–7; D. Dawson (1989) Direct marketing: Home sweet home, *Marketing*, October, pp. 55–6; Gilbert, op. cit.; J. Lawrence (1991) Travel marketing: Data base opening doors, *Advertising Age*, 62(47), p. S6; C. Sambrook (1991) Travel's double agent, *Marketing*, Oct., pp. 19–20; C. Wolff (1996) Tapping into the travel bazaar, *Lodging Hospitality*, 52(3), p. 43.

[3] J. Murphy, E. J. Forrest, C. E. Wotring & R. A. Brymer (1996) Hotel management and marketing on the Internet, *Cornell Hotel and Restaurant Administration Quarterly*, 37(3), pp. 70–7.

[4] ibid.

[5] A. H. Walle (1996) Tourism and the Internet: Opportunities for direct marketing, *Journal of Travel Research*, Summer, pp. 72–7.

[6] I. Jarrett (1996) Travel agents have doubts about the Net, *Asian Business*, 32(9), p. 66.

[7] J. Case & J. Useem (1996) Six characters in search of a strategy, *Inc*, 18(3), pp. 46–55.

[8] ibid.

[9] V. T. C. Middleton (1988) *Marketing in Travel and Tourism*, Heinemann, London, p. 273.

[10] Sources, in part: T. Allen (1985) Marketing by a small tour operator in a market dominated by big operators, *European Journal of Marketing*, 19(5), pp. 83–90; T. Baum & R. Mudambi (1994) A Richardian analysis of the fully inclusive tour industry, *Service Industries Journal*, 14(1), pp. 85–93; W. C. Gartner & T. Bachri (1994) Tour operators' role in the tourism distribution system: An Indonesian case study, *Journal of Comparative International Consumer Marketing*, 6(3,4), pp. 161–79; D. C. Gilbert & S. Soni (1991) UK tour operators and consumer responsiveness, *Service Industries Journal*, 11(4), pp. 413–24; S. E. Kimes & D. C. Lord (1994) Wholesalers and Caribbean resort hotels, *Cornell Hotel and Restaurant Administration Quarterly*, 35(3), pp. 70–5; C. Morley (1994) Discrete choice analysis of the impacts of tourism prices, *Journal of Travel Research*, 33(2), pp. 8–14.

Chapter 11

Promotion

*t*he promotional mix is the set of tools available to convey the message of the product to target markets. These come in four types: advertising, personal selling, sales promotions, and public relations and publicity. Sometimes public relations and publicity are treated as separate entities. Each is designed to prompt people into positive action after they have received information about the product or service on offer.[1] The promotional mix can be used to reinforce positive images among existing clients, create new attitudes and behaviours among non-clients, or help overcome negative associations with a product or service.[2]

Promotions can be used to influence demand in a number of ways:

- to create awareness where no demand existed previously
- to convert latent demand into sales
- to revive demand when interest falters
- to maintain the status quo
- to dampen demand (especially if promotion is removed)
- to shift demand from peak periods to shoulder seasons
- to lessen the perceived risk of participation, and in doing so to overcome psychological barriers to participation
- to limit unwholesome demand for tourism activities that may be socially unacceptable or physically dangerous (like sex tourism)
- to turn around negative destination images.[3]

This chapter examines the use of promotions as part of an integrated business and marketing strategy. It begins by reviewing some general principles of promotion, its role in marketing and business strategies and some of the key considerations in making promotions work for the business. The chapter then discusses the four major types of promotional activities a business can use. It also deals with brochures: a critical promotional tool, but one that is often misused by small tour operators.

Principles

The buying process: AIDA

The buying process has been given the acronym AIDA for Awareness, Interest, Desire and Action. The role of promotion is to stimulate potential clients at one or more of these levels and direct them to purchasing a tourism product.[4] The AIDA process acknowledges that the purchasing decision follows a temporal sequence from creating the initial awareness of the product to closing the sale. Because consumers use different information for different purposes before, during and after making the tourism purchasing decision, different messages will need to be bundled at different times along the temporal sequence to achieve the desired goals.[5]

The first stage—creating *awareness* of the existence of the product—is the greatest challenge facing new tour operators. Obviously, before anyone will buy a nature-based tourism product, he or she must be aware of it. However, the challenge of creating awareness is extremely difficult, as tour operators must strive to be seen in a crowd of 3000 other nature-based tourism businesses, 45 000 tourism businesses and literally millions of non-tourism products. The operator must both let the travelling public know the product exists and convince them that it is better than competitors' products. The task can be made easier if promotion is used as one aspect of an overall tactical marketing plan. A clear sign of a lack of tactical planning is an unfocused, or shotgun, approach to promotion. This approach is adopted by those who believe that, if they spread the message widely enough, the desired clients are bound to find out about the product. In reality, this results in vast wastage of often limited marketing resources. Astute operators, on the other hand, adopt a focused promotional strategy that is reinforced through repeated messages.

While creating awareness is the first stage in attracting clients, awareness of a product does not guarantee use. Most people are aware of SBS television, for example, but the ratings suggest than only two to four per cent of the viewing audience watch it. The second challenge, then, is to translate awareness into *interest*. The third step is to stimulate the public to *desire* that product above all others by convincing them that it is the most appropriate product to satisfy their needs. The interest and desire stages of the AIDA process are therefore concerned with positioning the product favourably in the consumers' minds. Finally, the last stage, *action*, is the pay-off stage, where prospective clients are stimulated to buy the product. Heightened awareness or interest mean little if the sale cannot be closed. A variety of tactics can be used to close sales.

Promoting benefits and reinforcing the message

Two rules apply to promotions, regardless of which stage in the AIDA process promotions are targeted from, or which of the four elements of the promotional mix are used. They are:

1 Promote the benefits of the product, not its features.
2 Reinforce the message.

As marketing guru Bob Pritchard states:

> It is not sufficient to advertise the features or attributes of a product. People do not respond to features, they only respond to benefits. One of the biggest obstacles facing many marketers is the lack of understanding of the 'product' they are selling. Often they use advertising to promote the elements that have the most personal appeal, frequently related directly to the intricacies of the product. This may not motivate the consumer.[6]

Elsewhere Pritchard adds:

> No business can make a profit unless your customer profits from the product . . . Throw out your current promotional material and replace it with customer friendly brochures that focus on applications and solutions that will help your customers. Technical jargon is the kiss of death, 90% of clients, unless you are in a technical business, do not understand it. It puts people off.[7]

In addition, the promotional campaign must reinforce the core message or core benefits being sold. Sending conflicting messages will serve only to confuse consumers, weaken the desired position in the marketplace and open the door for competitors to steal clients. Observe the television for a few days and watch how the major advertisers have each carved a position in the marketplace and defend it fiercely with ads that reinforce that position. Over time the position is moved, but each time it does the new position is reinforced. Books on marketing mistakes, like Robert Hartley's text *Marketing Mistakes* or Michael Gersham's *Getting it Right the Second Time*, are full of stories of businesses that failed to create or defend a strong position.[8]

Conversion rates

One of the frustrating things for marketers is that even highly effective promotional campaigns may yield relatively meagre results. A particularly successful direct mail advertising campaign, for example, will generate a response rate of between three and seven per cent. (This high non-response rate creates an interesting ethical issue for nature-based tour operators who are committed to ecologically sustainable practices. Can they justify direct mail when 97 per cent of the material sent out will go straight into the bin?) Classified ads in nature magazines with circulations of many thousands may only generate a dozen enquiries. Display ads may generate 50 or 60. A tourism operator would be ecstatic with 100 bookings from a consumer show that attracts perhaps 100 000 visitors. Badly targeted promotions may result in no response at all. In short, promotion is a gamble with long odds. Poor promotions will lengthen the odds of success even more. But given that most nature-based tour operators are looking to attract between 200 and 500 clients a year, the odds may be acceptable.

Tracking

The only way to determine if promotions work is to track the response rate from each activity. Yet surprisingly few tour operators monitor the performance of their promotions, which makes it impossible for them to plan future promotions effectively. A number of simple techniques can be used to track the success of promotions:

- Ask every person who telephones for information where they heard about the business or the product being offered.
- Include something distinctive in each ad. It is common, for example, for people to include a letter after a post office box number (PO Box 123a, PO Box 123b) or ask people to write to different staff members (Peter Sportsman, Amy) in different ads.
- Punch a hole in, or tear off a corner of, a coupon when attending different travel shows. This way, when mail is received, it is possible to determine where the client received the information.
- If a business has more than one telephone line, use different phone numbers in different ads.

Proper media mix

The proper mix of media must be used to achieve the desired marketing results.[9] Tour operators are confronted with literally hundreds of outlets where they can promote their products. Some of them will be extremely effective, but most will prove to be virtually useless. The realities of limited budgets allow operators little room for error. Many outlets will offer to promote products for a fee. They may offer enticements that make their vehicle sound like the best thing since sliced bread. But remember, the main reason they want to promote any operator's product is to sell their own ad space and not to sell the operator's product. The decision about the media mix must be based on how the media chosen will achieve the organisation's objectives and how well each of those media is performing.

Print is the most popular medium for nature-based tour operators, as most cannot afford television or radio advertising. Quite frankly, these electronic media are not cost-effective for anyone but the largest players. Tour operators have the choice of a wide variety of print media, including daily and weekly newspapers, specialist tourist newspapers, regional tourism promotion magazines, generalist magazines, specialist environmental magazines, the Yellow Pages and, increasingly, trade journals.

Selecting the right medium is difficult, for each produces different results. Research in America, for example, has shown that visitors attracted by newspaper ads spent more than those lured by magazine ads. Black and white newspaper ads were more cost-effective than black and white magazine ads.[10] For some, ads in magazines with a high editorial-to-ad ratio work well, while for others advertorial magazines perform acceptably. One rule to observe, though, is to ensure that the total editorial content of the magazine is consistent with the product being offered.[11] Regardless of any of this, however, there are a number of simple factors to consider:

- the fit with the business's overall marketing and business objectives
- the fit between the product and the target market
- the fit between the quality perception of the publication and the quality image of the business
- the volume of copies produced
- the frequency of publication (a weekly magazine has a short life, a monthly magazine a longer life and a quarterly magazine an even longer life)
- how long the medium is retained (some are read and thrown away, others are kept for longer periods)
- the presence or absence of competitors' ads—this can be beneficial or detrimental
- the geographic reach of the medium
- the lead time required to place an ad
- how long the magazine will be out before departure dates
- the cover price of the publication
- the level of support the publication can offer in design and layout
- the location of the advertisement in the magazine and the operator's ability to influence location

- the ability of the magazine to provide detailed circulation figures and other relevant research data
- how well established the magazine is
- the publisher
- costs associated with advertising.

The challenge with any promotional campaign is to rise above the clutter of other products. One of the best ways of doing this is to advertise in places that are complementary to the organisation's goals, but where few competitors currently advertise. The standard print outlets, like most outdoor or environmental magazines, regional tourism promotional newspapers and local tourist information pamphlets, are so cluttered with ads that it is difficult to gain much visibility. Choosing alternative media like trade journals produced by professional bodies (such as the Australian Society of Certified Practising Accountants, the Australia Medical Association and many others) may yield positive results. These media have been found to be very effective in developing business in the hotel sector, especially during recessions.[12]

Hints for small operators

Small tour operators cannot hope to compete like the major players. However, they can compete against them effectively by narrowing their focus and guarding their own clientele.[13] A recent study of small restaurants revealed that those that were able to compete well against chains targeted their markets very effectively and developed programs to retain customer loyalty. Markets with the highest potential received a greater share of promotional effort than low-potential markets.[14] As well, good operators ensured their most valuable markets were secure before they embarked on programs to expand their market base.

Advertising

Advertising seeks to inform prospective buyers and persuade them to use a product, service or organisation. Its goal is to influence buyer behaviour and manipulate demand.[15] Many people confuse advertising with marketing. While advertising is a vital element of marketing, it is merely the end product of the marketing process. A number of excellent books have been written by industry practitioners detailing the specifics of developing and implementing advertising campaigns. The reader is encouraged to seek these books for more information.

Advertising has many uses in the tourism industry. As Middleton summarises, it can be used to:

- create awareness of a product or service
- inform people about special services (such as frequent flyer programs)
- create a corporate image
- communicate a special offer
- directly sell a product or service
- solicit consumer information with the use of incentive questionnaires
- develop and reinforce brands
- improve distribution
- overcome negative attitudes
- reach new target audiences
- inform people of new uses for products (former country inns can now become health spas)
- announce, launch or relaunch various products or services
- reinforce awareness
- contribute to partnerships and co-operative advertising ventures.[16]

Much of the advertising done by the travel and tourism industry is ineffective. A few years ago, a panel of experts analysed many travel ads and found them to be largely deficient. The weaknesses they identified included a lack of targeting, poor production quality, a lack of distinctiveness, campaigns devoid of a clearly defined strategy, poor recall, a lack of catchlines and a lack of professionalism in copy and layout.[17] In short, few ads seemed capable of overcoming the psychological barriers that cause resistance to new images.[18] This can be achieved only if the advertisement sells the benefits of the product and not its features, keeps the message simple and appeals to the emotions rather than the intellect.[19] Martyn Forrester, in his excellent and humorous little book *Everything You Always Suspected Was True About Advertising,* sums up this sentiment best when he writes:

> Holidays aren't holidays—they're opportunities for [the] nuclear family to seek individual and group fulfilment on a sunlit beach. Write your ad accordingly.[20]

Maximising success

The success of any advertising campaign starts with a clear definition of the goals and objectives of the campaign, the identification of the target audience, the identification of the most appropriate media for reaching that audience and a thorough and realistic assessment of the financial and creative resources available. The ad itself must satisfy a number of criteria. It must be interesting enough to read or listen to. It must be persuasive enough to fulfil its selling function. It must communicate instantly, effortlessly and with utmost clarity the desired message. It must be based on the truth.[21] And it must also position the product uniquely in the mind of the consumer.

Headlines make or break ads

The headline is the single most important factor in determining the success or failure of an advertisement. It must attract the attention of readers, appeal to them and entice them to read further. If the headline does not cause them to stop and take notice, the ad will not be read. It is as simple as that. Headlines should be positive and should use words that stimulate the interest of the reader. In addition, they should offer the reader the prospect of a personal benefit. As such, they are the most difficult part of an ad to write. One suggestion is to identify the competitive advantages the business has and then craft a number of headlines around them. Another alternative is to write the ad copy and keep deleting extraneous words until the headline appears. It is always useful to have others review the headline to ensure that the message being received is the one intended.

Colour and images

The use of colour and images can add dramatically to the effectiveness of an advertisement. Full colour ads are generally more attractive, but are more expensive. If cost is an issue, the use of just one or two colours can have a dramatic effect. Psychologists and advertising executives have spent years assessing the emotional impact of colours. Hard colours suggest vitality and vibrancy, while soft colours suggest a subdued, quiet mood. Red implies power and authority (which explains why so many politicians wear red ties), while green reflects an environmental conscience. It is important to consider the quality of the paper stock and the background colour of the paper, if using colour. Ads on newsprint work best with basic, clear colours, while ads on better quality paper can be in more subtle shades.

Photographs can set the mood of a product or service, enhance the message being sent and also serve to break up the copy.[22] Action photos, pictures of happy people doing happy things or photos that create romantic, exotic or even erotic moods can all make an ad more appealing. In spite of attempts to create a non-sexist 1990s, research shows that sex still sells among all demographic groups and especially among 'generation Xers'. The best way to express the sexual excitement of a trip is through photos.[23] However, poor photos can destroy an advertisement or brochure just as much as good photos can enhance it. Poor-quality photos, pictures of people looking bored, cold or unhappy or old photos all send negative messages. Likewise, colour photos often do not reproduce well in black and white ads. In many instances, drawings would be more effective.

The ad copy and layout

The ad copy must always give the reader a reason to purchase the product and not an excuse to reject it. Apart from providing needed information about the name and contact details, ads must be informative, positive and engrossing. The ad must sell benefits and must highlight the competitive difference of the organisation. Short, punchy sentences will keep the consumer's attention. If the location is unfamiliar, the ad copy may have to sell the region as well as the product. Above all else, ads must include a call to action. Attaching a coupon or offering an enticement to act will enhance its response rate.

The copy must be factual and honest. It should also be consistent with the overall positioning of the product and the overall theme of the current marketing campaign. The amount of detail depends on the size of the ad and how much open space is desired. A classified ad of a few column centimetres may only include a headline, a few words of description and contact details. Larger ads can include more detail. The type of medium selected will influence the size and layout of the ad. Ads in 'throwaway' media will need to be able to be read quickly and should, therefore, have plenty of open space. Ads in media that are read in depth can afford to have more copy and less open space.

Odd shapes, swirls or curved lines will attract the reader's attention and will help make the ad stand out. Other layout principles include:

- making the copy an integral part of the layout (it must integrate with the other aspects of the ad)
- having something dominate the ad, be it a headline or a graphic
- ensuring the ad is well proportioned (the rule of thumb is that a vertical 5 x 3 ad is more attractive than a horizontal 3 x 5 ad)
- making the ad read from left to right and ensuring that it is large enough.[24]

A comment on brochures

Brochures are one of the most important forms of advertising, yet are also one of the most poorly used promotional tools. The brochure itself can be a stand-alone advertising instrument or a supplement to other material. However, few tourist brochures work as effectively as they could. The layout, colour selection, choice of paper stock, graphics, photos and ad copy are often poor. In addition, there is little evidence of any strategic marketing evident in most brochures, and the result is an undifferentiated product that is easily forgotten. Consequently, the wastage rate for brochures is well over 90 per cent.[25] Remember, people pay nothing for brochures and, as such, they often have little value for the reader. Further, we are all deluged with thousands of brochures and leaflets a year. Unless the product advertised is seen to provide a real benefit to the reader, the brochure will be ignored.

The biggest problem with poor brochures is that they tend to stress the features of the product and not its benefits. Few people will be interested in a four wheel driving tour where the participants will travel 70 kilometres a day on rough dirt tracks, eat tinned food and sleep in rough tents. They will be more interested in a trip that gets them off the beaten track, sends them on an adventure of a lifetime, allows them to eat heartily and then lets them fall asleep under the stars. The following questions must be considered when designing a brochure:

- What is the headline of the brochure?
- What is the core product?
- Who is the target audience?
- What messages are being sent?
- What are the legal requirements?
- What is the desired print run?
- What image is desired (this will influence the layout, use of colours, size and style of the brochure)?
- What budget is available and what can be delivered for that budget?
- What is the expected lifespan of the brochure?[26]

As with all promotional material, it is best to employ a professional to help design the brochure. Sometimes the printer can offer creative advice; but remember, printers specialise in printing the product, not in designing it! If the decision is made to design it in-house, then the following suggestions will be useful. Photographs and graphics must be relevant to the ad copy, the print must be legible (both font size and typeface) and it must be easy to identify the prices for each product. Best use should be made of all the space available. A crammed brochure full of small print is unattractive to the reader. The use of colours depends on the overall image desired and the budget. One- or two-colour brochures can be very effective, but four-colour brochures can have the greatest impact.

Personal selling

Personal selling, as the name implies, involves direct contact between the prospective client and the representative of the organisation. The goal of personal selling is to influence people to make positive buying decisions. It is generally accepted that there is a selling sequence involving prospecting for and qualifying clients, planning and delivering sales presentations, overcoming objections, closing the sale and countering any post-purchase dissonance that may occur.[27] Personal selling comprises all aspects of the sales relationship between the operator and the client or intermediary and includes such features as responding to telephone calls, face-to-face contact with clients, dealing directly with third parties, imparting information, responding to complaints and the like.

For the most part, nature-based tour operators will be involved in three types of direct sales activities: dealing directly with the consumer, either at the place of business or over the phone; selling the product to intermediaries, including retail and wholesale agents; and direct selling at consumer travel shows. Indeed, for some businesses, direct selling will be the main promotional activity. Effective direct selling is complemented by sales staff who know the value of the product being sold, can promote its benefits and, most importantly, can close the sale. Again, research indicates that far too many tour operators do not perform this aspect of the job as well as they could.[28] Not everyone is suited to be a salesperson. If the operator lacks sales skills, then it is in the best interest of the business to hire sales staff.

Sales promotions

Sales promotions are short-term, non-regular programs designed to stimulate demand for a good or service. The tourism industry often needs to embark on promotions because of the perishable and non-replaceable nature of its product.[29] If a product goes unsold, the opportunity to sell that product is lost for ever. Sales promotions can be targeted at a variety of audiences including the public, the travel trade network and a business's own employees. Sales promotions aimed at the public are used to sell excess capacity, to shift the timing of the purchase, to attract or reward regular customers or to counter competitors' strategies. Promotions targeting the distribution network are designed to foster loyalty among distributors to secure their support, to support distributors' own merchandising activities and to improve dealers' awareness of the product. Internal promotions are usually aimed at motivating the sales force to sell more product, to sell slow-moving product lines or to generate sales for shoulder season activities. They can also be designed to identify and reward a business's star employees.[30]

A variety of sales promotion techniques can be used. Some of them include:

- incentive programs for travel agents
- incentives at shows, like offering discounts if the client purchases the product at the show
- special prices or special deals
- competitions and sweepstakes
- vouchers and coupons
- gifts and premiums
- volume discounts
- cash refunds
- self-liquidating promotions, especially if incentive travel is involved
- point-of-purchase displays
- cause-related promotions, such as giving away a free trip as part of a promotional campaign by an environmental organisation
- sponsorship
- merchandising, give-aways and the like.[31]

Publicity and public relations

Businesses are always looking for alternative ways to get their message to the consumer. One such way is through publicity; the other is through a public relations program. Publicity aims to promote the product through the media by creating a newsworthy item about one aspect of the business. Almost anything can become a news story, if it is packaged properly and aimed at the right media. A new product or service, the hiring of new staff, the negotiation of a new distribution network, the development of a scientific tour, the expansion into overseas markets, major capital investment and the like can qualify as newsworthy stories. If a news story cannot be created, there are certainly almost unlimited opportunities for the nature-based tourism sector to create photo opportunities. If the photo opportunity is unique, it may be possible to gain national and international media exposure.

The goal of public relations is quite different from that of publicity. PR programs are designed less to generate free publicity and more to reinforce or enhance the image of a business. PR activities can include the issue of press releases and the organising of familiarisation tours, lunches and receptions, staged events and product visits for the media. As Bob Pritchard, one of Australia's leading advertising executives, states:

> Public relations builds an image in terms of credibility and recognition, creating a favourable attitude to the activity or the product by means that are not seen to be hard sell. Advertising is self praise and is expected to be complimentary, while public relations reflects what others are saying and therefore carries more weight with the public.[32]

Nature-based tourism lends itself particularly well to publicity and pubic relations programs because so much of the subject matter is, by its very nature, newsworthy. People have a strong interest in the outdoors and in the environment. They want to see, or at least become aware of, rare and unique experiences. The excitement offered by adventure tourism, be it in the form of a whitewater rafting tour, hang-gliding, abseiling or even a sedate bicycle ride through the countryside, is appealing. Moreover, the genuine commitment of many ecotourism operators to protecting the environment creates an ideal opportunity to develop productive, cost-effective public relations campaigns.

Developing databases

Marketing activities can be enhanced by the development of databases that provide complete details about clients and prospects. Clients and prospects are the most valuable resource any business has. It costs a business about ten times as much to entice a new client as it does to persuade a current client to become a repeat buyer. Once people have made the initial purchase decision, the likelihood is that they will become repeat customers. If they buy a second time, they are even more likely to become loyal customers. Nurturing existing clients and developing prospects is, therefore, a most cost-effective way of doing business.

A number of excellent database software packages are available at a relatively low cost; however, any word processing or spreadsheet package can be used. Depending on the level of sophistication required, the database can include such material as information about the demographic, psychographic and socio-economic profile of their clients, their interests, buying patterns and special needs, the last time they purchased a product and how much they have spent on the organisation's product.[33]

The best databases recognise that not all clients are of equal value to a business. A five-tiered system works best, whereby clients are classified according to their frequency of purchase and expenditure. Category 1 clients are those who are frequent, high-value customers. Category 2 clients are occasional buyers who spend modest amounts. Category 3 clients are those who are infrequent or new users, whose value to the organisation is undetermined. Category 4 represents those people who are prospects but who have not purchased a product yet. Category 5 represents inactive clients.

Different promotional strategies can be developed for each tier in the database that roughly relate to the client's or prospect's stage in the AIDA continuum. Category 1 and 2 clients are clearly the most valued customers and need to be nurtured. These people are already very familiar and presumably satisfied with the organisation and its products. As such, they respond best to promotions that are designed to motivate them to further action, such as sales promotions, incentives, reward programs and the like. Category 3 clients have shown some desire to buy the product. The challenge is to convert them from occasional users to frequent users. Different promotional strategies are needed that highlight the range of personal benefits they will receive. Prospects (Category 4) have some interest in the organisation and its products. Promotional tactics for this group must be aimed at overcoming any resistance they may have to buying the product. Finally, it is important to understand why former clients have stopped buying the product and to determine if they can become active clients again. It may be that they are simply one-off users. However, their decision to abandon the business may also reflect a level of dissatisfaction with the business and its product that will need to be addressed.

[1] Richardson, op. cit.

[2] Seaton & Bennett, op. cit.

[3] Kotler, summarised in Seaton & Bennett, op. cit.

[4] B. McKercher & I. Coghlan (1994) *Tourism Marketing Short Course*, Charles Sturt University, Albury.

[5] Seaton & Bennett, op. cit.

[6] Pritchard, op. cit., p. 23.

[7] ibid., p. 11.

[8] R. Hartley (1992) *Marketing Mistakes*, 5th edn, John Wiley & Sons, Brisbane; M. Gersham (1990) *Getting it Right the Second Time*, Addison-Wesley, NY.

[9] R. T. Reilly (1988) *Travel and Tourism Marketing Techniques*, 2nd edn, Delmar Publishing, Albany, NY.

[10] G. R. Yochum (1985) The economics of travel advertising revisited, *Journal of Travel Research*, 24(2), pp. 9–12.

[11] G. Ricketts (1986) Magazines: Adding in edit, *Marketing and Media Decisions*, 21(10), pp. 88–90.

[12] P. Warren & N. W. Ostergren (1986) Trade advertising: A crucial element in hotel marketing, *Cornell Hotel and Restaurant Administration Quarterly*, 27(1), pp. 56–62.

[13] T. Howard (1995) Study to small operators: Use homefield advantage in marketing, *Nation's Restaurant News*, 29(21), p. 38.

[14] R. R. Perdue (1985) Segmenting state travel information inquiries by timing of the destination decision and previous, *Journal of Travel Research*, 23(3), pp. 6–11.

[15] Richardson, op. cit.; Middleton (1994) op. cit.

[16] Middleton (1994) op. cit.

[17] G. Upton (1985) Travel ads miss the boat, *Marketing*, 20(2), pp. 22–5.

[18] Middleton (1994) op. cit., p. 164.

[19] Pritchard, op. cit.

[20] M. Forrester (1988) *Everything You Always Suspected Was True About Advertising: But Were Too Legal, Decent and Honest to Ask*, Fontana Paperbacks.

[21] Smith, op. cit.

[22] H. A. Laskey, B. Seaton & J. A. F. Nicholls (1994) Effects of strategy and pictures in travel agent advertising, *Journal of Travel Research*, 34(4), pp. 13–19.

[23] A. Pritchard & N. J. Morgan (1996) Sex still sells to generation X: Promotional practice and the youth package holiday market, *Journal of Vacation Marketing*, 3(1), pp. 69–80.

[24] Reilly, op. cit.

[25] P. Hodgson (1993) Tour operator brochure design research revisited, *Journal of Travel Research*, 32(1), pp. 50–2.

[26] Source: in part Smith, op. cit.

[27] Seaton & Bennett, op. cit.

[28] A. Pizam (1990) Evaluating the effectiveness of travel trade shows and other tourism sales-promotion techniques, *Journal of Travel Research*, 29(1), pp. 3–8.

[29] Middleton (1994) op. cit.

[30] ibid.

[31] Sources: in part Anon. (1994) A new tool for the single market, *Business Europe*, 34(34), pp. 2–3; Pritchard, op. cit.; Richardson, op. cit.; Seaton & Bennett, op. cit.

[32] Pritchard, op. cit.

[33] P. A. Francese & L. M. Reneghan (1990) Data-base marketing: Building consumer profiles, *Cornell Hotel and Restaurant Administration Quarterly*, 31(1), pp. 60–3.

Chapter 12

Product development, itineraries and route planning

*t*he role of the tour operator is to satisfy intangible tourism needs by creating tangible 'product' to be consumed by the client. This task is accomplished through packaging the various component parts of a trip and then adding value to create a new product for sale. Packaging has been defined as:

> the presentation of several products and services that would normally be purchased separately by travellers, but which, in a package, are offered as a single product at a single price . . . Basically, the concept is to provide a comprehensive experience for customers, accompanied by the various tourist services they will require.[1]

This chapter examines a range of issues to do with assembling tourism products. It begins with a discussion of the benefits of packaging. The practicalities of route planning are then reviewed and some of the logistical considerations are discussed.

The benefits of packaging

Packaged tour products are all around us. Club Med, Contiki Tours, AAT King's, Qantas Jetabout, Jetset Travel and others all sell packaged tours. Most of these packages target the mass tourist. Most nature-based tour operators are also involved in packaging to some degree, be it through the development of their own tours or by offering their products as a component of packages developed by other tour operators. Packaging provides a number of benefits to consumers and the industry alike. Consumer benefits include:

- a new product
- a product with appeal to specific markets
- better value for the consumer dollar
- ease of purchase in being able to buy one product, rather than having to assemble the components oneself
- a standardised and commoditised product that ensures a consistent quality of tourism experience.

Benefits to the operator include:

- a specialist product that appeals to specific markets
- a product that is easier for the consumer to purchase
- value-adding, which permits a higher price to be charged
- a standardised and commoditised product that ensures the provision of tourist services of a consistent quality
- cost savings
- access to new markets
- ease of access to new distribution channels, especially to the travel trade
- increased marketability of the product through piggybacking on other products in the region
- opportunities for attracting new marketing partners and participating in co-operative marketing ventures.[2]

The decision to package components into a new product, or to include the operator's product in someone else's package, may be made for a number of reasons, including:

- the desire to make the business grow
- the desire to enhance customer service
- the need to outsource goods and services
- the recognition that other suppliers may be able to provide goods and services at a higher quality and a lower price
- the opportunity to purchase the expertise of others
- the real cost benefits associated with leasing services rather than buying them (for example, leasing 200 bed-nights at a hotel rather than buying the hotel)

- being able to generate business based on the goodwill and positive reputation of your suppliers.

It must also be recognised that one of the main reasons why consumers purchase packaged nature-based tourism is the ease with which such an experience can be organised. Packaging converts an adventure experience from a high-involvement purchasing decision to a low-involvement one. By making one phone call, customers can have everything organised, including travel partners. If they organised the trip themselves, they would have to select a route, find partners, acquire the equipment, arrange pick-up and drop-off points, purchase food and more. All of these require some cost, either financial or temporal. Packaging helps reduce these costs.

Importantly, too, packaging helps reduce the strangeness or perceived risk of the nature-based tourism experience to an acceptable level. Most people want to experience some change when they travel, but they are prepared to experience it only to the extent that they are not personally threatened by the change.[3] In other words, people want to experience change, but from the security of their own environmental bubble. The environmental bubble is that personal security blanket that allows them to experience the thrill of strangeness without the fear of being overwhelmed by it.

Different people can tolerate different amounts of strangeness when they travel. Some tourists can tolerate only limited change and will, therefore, demand tourism products that provide them with an experience that is as similar to their home environment as possible. This unease at things strange explains why mass tourism destinations like Bali have evolved to provide Western-style hotels with Western-style beds and amenities, English-speaking hotel staff and Western menus. People who travel to Bali want the thrill of visiting an exotic land, but are only comfortable doing so if they can experience it from the safety of their own social and cultural norms.

Others, though, have a greater capacity to enjoy strangeness, and indeed deliberately seek tourist experiences that force them to explore outside their normal comfort zone. But even these people are only willing to participate in tourism to the extent that the strangeness is non-threatening. The process of packaging nature-based tourism products is really a process of reducing the amount of strangeness to an acceptable level. The provision of guides, expertise, equipment and transport will allow the person who would not otherwise be physically or psychologically able to participate to enjoy a challenging tourism experience.

An example will illustrate how packaging can reduce the level of strangeness in a trip, and in doing so expand the market base for tour operators. Female clients of Victorian adventure tour operators were asked to describe the type of person they felt could participate independently in the type of experience they had just consumed. The responses were quite remarkable. None of the clients interviewed said that they would consider going without a commercial operator. They described that type of person as someone who would have a higher skill level, more experience in the outdoors, a greater knowledge of the area visited and more self-confidence than themselves. The tour operator played the role of facilitator, mentor and sounding-board to the clients. This modest level of support reduced the risk and strangeness of the adventure to an acceptable level.

Importantly, from a tourist industry perspective, packaging allows operators to standardise, commoditise and modify the product being offered to facilitate ease of consumption. This process enables the operator to ensure that a consistent quality of experience is delivered on each trip offered. In addition, it allows the operator to reduce risk, develop efficiencies in the delivery of products, process clients more efficiently and build systems that will facilitate growth of the business. Packaging allows the tourist's experience to be ordered, predictable and controllable, as much as possible, while still ensuring that that experience is authentic. The commoditisation of the tourism product enables tourists to take in the novelty of the area with limited physical or emotional discomfort.

A further benefit to the industry is that packaging allows the operator to expand the business's market base to attract a more mainstream clientele. How many people own abseiling equipment? The answer is very few, and most of them would not be interested in using a commercial operator. Packaging abseiling by providing the equipment, a trip leader and instruction opens up an entirely different, and substantially larger, market who would never consider abseiling on their own.

Itinerary development

As with everything else about tourism, there are few hard and fast rules about setting itineraries. In fact, little research has been done on itinerary development.[4] However, there are a number of principles that tour operators must consider relating to the objectives of the package, the theme of the tour, the component parts to be included and the ability of the operator to personalise the tour and make it special in the eyes of the consumer.

Icons or demand generators

Every successful tourism product, organisation or destination area must have some unique attraction that draws people to it. In tourism parlance, these are called primary attractions. In marketing jargon, they are called demand generators. If there is one rule about packaging, it is that without a strong enough attraction or demand generator, a successful package cannot be created.

Demand generators are what give the customer a reason to buy the package, give the package its theme and dictate how the product can be positioned competitively in the marketplace. The features of a demand generator should be of a high-quality, experiential character—a unique, exciting, one-of-a-kind experience that appeals to the target market.[5] Icons can include experiences, activities or the opportunity to visit unique places or cultures.

The greater the distance clients are expected to travel to consume the product, the more distinctive and unusual the demand generator must be. An operator running day trips from Melbourne aimed at the Melbourne market may identify demand generators that have local significance. It is unlikely, though, that such attractions will appeal to inbound tourists who may not be aware of their existence. By the same token, an alpine ecotour may appeal to a wider domestic market because of the nationally unique nature of the Australian Alps. However, the Victorian Alps will probably have little international appeal because, by world standards, the high country is little known. However, Uluru, Kakadu and the Great Barrier Reef have the ability to attract visitors from around the world.

The role played by the components

The component parts of a package can serve a number of purposes. In some cases packaging is a necessary, yet secondary, aspect of the 'product'. An ecotourism operator, for example, may want to offer a six-day flora and fauna interpretative tour of the Australian alpine environment. In order to develop that 'product', it will probably be necessary to include accommodation and transport. In this case, the component parts are needed to deliver the product, but do not form the core feature of the trip.

In other cases, the component parts will be integral to the product. The day trips taken to Victoria's Phillip Island to view the fairy penguins, the koala and kangaroo reserves and the giant worm attraction are an example of such a package. The success of the product in the marketplace relies on the ability of the operator to package a variety of experiences into one product.

In other cases still, the component parts can serve both purposes. The author used to guide for an adventure tourism business that ran packaged bicycle tours through the American State of Vermont. The tours included five-day bike rides, stopping at historic inns each night. The inns represented both a needed secondary component of the trip (enabling the route to be created) as well as an integral aspect of the experience being sold (the rural, historic, relaxed country atmosphere of Vermont).

A key issue, then, is the role that the component parts will play in the development of the product. If the components are an integral aspect of the trip, it will be necessary to ensure that they reflect the overall image and message being sent. The quality of an inn-to-inn bicycle tour would be diminished by a stay in a modern high-rise hotel. By the same token, the integrity of a Phillip Island ecotourism experience would be damaged if the trip included a day ticket to the Phillip Island Motorcycle Grand Prix. If, on the other hand, the component parts represent a secondary aspect of the trip, then the operator has more flexibility in the types of services or facilities that can be included. An alpine flora and fauna tour could be run effectively out of a ski lodge in one of the resort villages without damaging the credibility of the program.

Packaging is a two-way street. There will be times when an operator may be the packager and other times when the operator's product may be included in others' packages. There are a number of benefits in allowing one's product to become a component in someone else's package, the most notable being the ability of the business to broaden its market base at a relatively low cost. However, there are also some considerations that must be taken into account before embarking on this path, particularly relating to bookings, deposits and payment schedules.

Route and itinerary planning

Developing suitable itineraries is largely an iterative process. The guiding principle is to remember always that the package is being designed to satisfy the needs, wants and desires of the target client group, and for no other reason. It has been stated before, but it is worth repeating, that the product must always be developed from the perspective of the consumers, their interests and their abilities. Thus the theme of the product, the component parts to be assembled, how it is positioned and how it is promoted must be developed with the target clientele in mind.[6]

Theming the package is essential in developing a strong positioning strategy for the product, for it will express the image of the type of experience being offered. The theme should appeal to the requirements of the clients, be they for adventure, heritage, escape, learning or the exotic. Successful themes can be incorporated directly into the organisation's name or the title of the tour. Organisations with names such as 'Ecosummer Expeditions', 'Auswalk', 'Eldertreks—Exotic Adventures for the Young at Heart', 'Quest Nature Tours' and 'River Ventures' all convey a clear theme to the consumer. Similarly, such specific tour names as 'Belize—in the path of the Maya' (Ecosummer), 'At the edge of the Andes' (Quest), 'Sulawesi—Tribal Relics in the Rainforest' (Eldertreks) and 'Expeditions in Luxury' (River Journeys) position the product in the consumer's mind. How the product is positioned will, in turn, determine the type of client it attracts. Moreover, how the product is positioned will tell the client how it differs from the array of other nature-based tourism products they may be considering.

Practicalities, components and logistics

Practicalities

There are a number of practicalities that must be considered when developing a product. Tourism Canada suggests that elements to be included must:

- be consistent with the positioning (high-quality goods and services should accompany high-end experiences)
- be appropriate to the expectations of the market (an expensive, exclusive product will not succeed if the clients are accommodated in a backpackers' hostel)
- contribute to the product and reflect value to the consumer
- add to the quality of the experience.[7]

Components

Some items that may or may not be included in the package include:

- Accommodation: usually for extended tours some form of accommodation is included. Depending on the quality of the experience offered, the price and its overall theme, the accommodation component may range from do-it-yourself camping to five-star quality accommodation.
- Food: typical plans include the American Plan (AP three meals a day), Modified American Plan (MAP two meals a day) and the European Plan (EP no meals or a light breakfast). Unless the trip is a camping trip, or unless the lodging used normally includes meals in its tariff, meals are generally not included in most tours. The exception may be lunch stops.
- Transport: transport usually includes transfers to and from convenient pick-up points and may in some instances include inter-city transport. Transfers for day trips make the purchase decision just that much simpler. For longer trips, a convenient, safe parking lot will reduce the concerns clients may have about the safety of their possessions while they are on tour.
- Entrance fees: these charges can include the admission fees to attractions along the tour route. The inclusion of entrance fees adds value to the product being purchased and, again, makes it easier for the

consumer to purchase. Moreover, one-price tours are more attractive to clients who may be on fixed budgets.

- Taxes and tips: some packages include local taxes or gratuities.
- Equipment: adventure and outdoor operators can gain a substantial marketing edge by providing equipment for activities that people would normally not be expected to have equipment for. Horse riding operations have done it for years, providing the horse, saddle and safety gear. Similarly, whitewater rafting firms provide rafts, paddles and life vests.
- Guides and lessons: recent American research reported by Tourism Victoria shows that 32 per cent of all travellers want to learn a new activity or become educated about different lifestyles and cultures while on vacation.[8] The provision of qualified guides, interpreters and instructors will help achieve this objective.

The decision to include or exclude various component parts will vary depending on the level of service being offered, the desired price of the trip, whether people will or will not have equipment and the availability of alternatives for the client. The more the operator includes in the package, the more control he or she can exert over the total experience offered. However, the more that is included, the higher the price will be. The likelihood that people will own equipment will also determine the need to package aspects of the trip. 'Tag-along' four wheel drive tours assume that clients have their own four wheel drive vehicle. Extended wilderness ski treks, on the other hand, usually offer full equipment from skis and boots to winter gear, tents and sleeping bags. In a similar manner, most Great Barrier Reef tour operators offer masks, snorkels and flippers for their guests.

Therefore, when deciding what to include or exclude, these two maxims should be kept in mind:

- Nothing that customers are sure to require and that they cannot logically be expected to provide should be left out.
- The component parts must be compatible and of a consistent quality standard.

Logistics

The logistics involved in organising and operating tours will vary for each type of experience offered and will be influenced by the time of year the tour is offered, the duration of the tour and the amount of travel required to get to the start of the tour. Figure 12.1 (page 168) lists a number of logistical issues that must be considered when tour itineraries are being established.

Figure 12.1　Logistical considerations in developing tour itineraries

- Having a sufficient number and variety of activities to keep clients occupied and entertained
- The amount of time required to experience or consume each activity (the more standardised and commoditised the activity, the more rapidly it can be consumed; more activities can be included in the itinerary)
- Travel time to and from the main destination
- Daily starting and finishing times—realistic for the clients and suitable for the needs of the trip
- Transit times between sites
- The number and timing of breaks—clients get bored after more than an hour in a bus
- The need to break up the trip if a long drive is involved
- Linking breaks and activities—can activities be logically and conveniently linked with planned breaks?
- Avoiding bottlenecks and meeting deadlines
- Route selection considerations—logical, aesthetically attractive, safe, quick access
- Desired level of contact with non-trip participants—type and frequency of contact
- Selecting appropriate lunch and tea spots
- Logistics involved in camping—arriving at the campsite before dark, getting set up and preparing meals
- Sufficient time for staff to prepare themselves for the next day's activities
- Safety considerations—escape routes
- Seasonal or climatic variability—hours of daylight, temperature, likelihood of adverse weather
- The speed of the group and its ability to travel long distances—how far and how fast it can go are determined by the slowest member
- Spare time to allow for unplanned delays

The number and variety of activities incorporated in a trip will depend ultimately on the time required to experience each activity fully, the travel time required to reach the main destination of the trip and the transit time involved in travelling between secondary destinations. The more standardised, modified and commoditised the activities are and the closer they are to each other, the easier they are for tourists to do. For example, it is possible for bus ecotourists to Phillip Island to visit half a dozen or more purpose-built eco-attractions in a day. Some of the attractions can be experienced in as little as 20 minutes if the tourism experience is well stage managed. On the other hand, because the outer Great Barrier Reef is still presented in a non-commoditised way, clients will want to spend three or four hours snorkelling around its wonders. Thus, the more natural the experience, the longer the operator must allow for that experience to be fully appreciated. As a result, fewer activities can be planned. In some instances only one activity may be needed in an itinerary, especially if it is an activity like bushwalking or four wheel driving.

The duration of the tour will be determined by the location of the demand generator and the ease with which it can be reached. If the destination is local, the trip can start at almost any time. If the demand generator is located some distance from the point of origin, then clearly it will take longer to deliver the product. The more distant the demand generator, the greater the opportunity and need to include ancillary activities to complement the trip. Half-day Aboriginal cultural tours can be run easily out of Alice Springs because the location of the tourist experience is on the edge of town. By contrast, trips to Uluru involve an overnight stay. To make the journey more enjoyable, these tours will visit cattle stations and road houses and stop at scenic spots along the way.

Breaks form an integral part of any trip. They allow clients to rest, stretch their legs, eat, have a drink and go to the bathroom. Breaks serve an even more important role for the tour operator, for they provide an excellent opportunity to add value. Choosing the right time to stop and the right place to stop takes on added importance. Generally, on the outbound portion of a trip, people like to have a break at least once an hour and often more frequently. This applies whether they are bushwalking, riding a horse or sitting in a bus, but does not apply if the trip commences early in the morning.

The need for breaks allows the operator to include tea, shopping and photo opportunities as part of the tour itinerary. Further, it justifies taking people to complementary secondary attractions. A one-stop price that includes entry into many attractions is seen as offering good value to guests. Moreover, the choice of the location of the break allows the guide to demonstrate his or her local knowledge by selecting the best spot. Clients will appreciate walking an extra 300 metres if they can find a magnificent view at the end of it. On the other hand, if the guests have just spent their break in a mosquito-infested swamp only to find a spectacular view just down the track, they will not be impressed.

Social interaction is a fundamental feature of any packaged tourism experience. The interaction can occur both within and outside the group.[9] To a large extent, in most organised tour activities some type of bonding is encouraged among trip participants, while efforts are made to exclude others from entering the group. The type, nature and frequency of contact with others must be a prime consideration when establishing the itinerary. Clients want to feel that they have purchased an exclusive experience, especially if they have paid a handsome price for their trip. Part of that exclusivity comes from limited social contact with anyone outside the immediate travel party, unless the clients or the guides themselves invite that person to join them. Lunch, tea and camping spots that are exclusive or imply exclusivity will be appreciated by most clients.

Climatic or seasonal considerations may also play a role in choosing a suitable itinerary. Factors such as the hours of daylight available, extreme heat or cold or the likelihood of adverse weather will influence route selection. The longer summer days in southern Australia permit more activities to be offered than in the winter. Shorter winter days, however, enable more people to participate in dawn, dusk or night-time fauna spotting activities. In summer, itineraries will have to be adjusted to keep people out of the extreme heat of the day. Wet or snow seasons will permit some activities and preclude others.

In self-propelled nature-based tourism activities, such as bushwalking, bicycle touring, sea kayaking or cross-country skiing, the group will only be able to move as fast as the slowest person. The likelihood is that commercial clients will be less fit, and therefore less able to travel long distances than recreational users. Moreover, they will regard the activity as fun first and as a means of getting fit second. They will want to take lots of breaks. Setting lunch spots or campsites that are unrealistically far for clients will turn an otherwise enjoyable trip into something to be endured. Ten kilometres with a full pack represents a full day, as does 15 to 18 kilometres with a day pack or 80 kilometres on a bicycle.

Finally, there are a number of safety issues to consider when establishing itineraries. Escape routes must be identified so that people can be evacuated in the event of an accident. If the group is camping, each day's activities must be planned in such a way that the camp site is reached well before dark to enable people to set up their tents, eat and relax before going to bed. Itineraries must include access to water and should also be set so that clients do not become exhausted trying to reach unattainable objectives. There must be sufficient time for staff to prepare themselves for the next day's activities. And lastly, some spare time must be built into the schedule to plan for unexpected eventualities, be they a flat tire, a thunderstorm, a missing tour member or simply a slow walker.

[1] Economic Planning Group of Canada (1995) *Packaging For and Selling To the United States Pleasure Travel Market,* EPCG for Tourism Canada, p. 33.

[2] ibid.

[3] E. Cohen (1979) A phenomenology of tourist experiences, *Sociology,* 13, pp. 170–201; (1988) Traditions in the qualitative sociology of tourism, *Annals of Tourism Research,* 15, pp. 29–46.

[4] M. Opperman (1995) A model of travel itineraries, *Journal of Travel Research*, Spring, pp. 57–61.

[5] EPCG, op. cit.

[6] ibid.

[7] ibid.

[8] TV (1997) op. cit.

[9] J. Urry (1990a) The consumption of tourism, *Sociology*, 24(1), pp. 23–35; (1990b) *The Tourist Gaze*, SAGE Publications, London.

Chapter 13

Systems, on-site operations and self-management

*E*ffective business people work smarter and not harder. Virtually everybody endorses this principle, but few practise it. In the nature-based tourism industry, working smarter means developing a series of operating and administrative systems that will allow the operator and his or her staff to work at maximum efficiency. Meredith states: 'Systems are essential for management to control operations. The absence of systems increases the probability of business failure through growth and expansion being out of control.'[1] He also suggests, in an earlier work, that a lack of systems is one of the major causes of business failure.[2] For nature-based tourism businesses, systems are also essential to control the quality of tourism experience offered, to ensure that the business operates in an ecologically sustainable manner and to help the owner maintain a balance between work and non-work.

So far, this book has discussed systems from a financial management and business planning perspective. This chapter examines systems from an operational and personal perspective. In particular, it discusses a number of administrative procedures that can be put in place, on-site operational systems and risk minimisation systems. It concludes by offering a few ideas about how operators can set up personal systems to ensure that they do not become consumed by their business. After all, there must be life after work!

Why systems?

There are many reasons why businesses should develop formal systems or operating guidelines. Among other things, systems enable a business to:

- control and manage the day-to-day operations of the organisation
- ensure that all staff know exactly what is expected of them
- control inventory
- control costs
- ensure that the quality of the product is consistent, regardless of who delivers it
- control and reduce exposure to risks
- allow the operator to manage and lead the organisation, while delegating duties to staff
- ensure that all aspects of the product are as ecologically sustainable as possible
- plan for and adapt to staff turnover or the sudden, unexpected loss of the owner through illness or misadventure
- be professional
- set benchmarks to make the running of the business more efficient.[3]

Developing and implementing systems involves commitment and rigour. It may also entail letting a degree of bureaucracy slip into the organisation and relinquishing some day-to-day control on the part of the operator. Consequently, many people are unwilling to formalise a set of systems, even though most businesses have a wide array of informal systems. Rather than being recognised as systems, though, they tend to be regarded as 'the way the organisation does business'. The guides know what is expected of them; the business has a booking and cancellation procedure; some books and records are kept; the insurer has told them what their risk exposure is; the trips are run in a certain way. However, the lack of formal systems means that most businesses do not run as efficiently as they could. The result is lower profits, an inconsistent product offering and lower client satisfaction.

Because of this, the Australian Tourism Operators Network (ATON) requires operators to write an operating systems manual before they can be accredited. Written systems formalise the steps to be taken for a wide variety of activities to ensure consistency of program delivery and optimisation of service quality. While systems standardise the procedures involved in running a business, putting them in place does not mean that the authenticity of the tourism experience needs to be compromised in any way. In fact, quite the opposite is true. Systems can enhance the business by ensuring a consistently high-quality experience for all clients. Indeed, tour operators should emulate the approach to systems developed by the franchised fast food industry. These types of businesses have perfected their systems to the extent that anyone with a modicum of training can run a business profitably. The result is that they are among the most efficient and successful businesses around.

The systems needed in nature-based tourism

The accreditation document of the Australian Tourism Operators Network provides a good overview of some of the types of systems required by nature-based tourism businesses.[4]

Enquiry and booking systems

Responding to enquiries starts a relationship between the client and the tour operator that will hopefully culminate in many repeat visits. Its importance to the overall performance of the business, therefore, cannot be overstated. If the initial enquiry is handled well, it will help close the sale. If handled poorly, it will drive prospective clients away for ever. Prospective clients will have heard about the business, picked up a brochure in a shop or seen an advertisement in some magazine, but will have no actual contact with the business until they call or write for information. The person on the end of the line must convince the prospective client that the business is professional, that the trips are well organised and that the operator will provide a safe and enjoyable experience.

It is essential, therefore, that all staff who answer phones are knowledge-able about the product, have a helpful telephone manner and know how to close a sale. It is amazing how many times a product is un-sold over the phone. Staff who cannot answer basic questions about equipment needs, departure dates and prices, who offer 'humorous' anecdotes about clients getting lost and suffering from hypothermia, or are simply rude or dismissive will send a clear message to prospective clients to stay away. There is also nothing more frustrating than calling an organisation, leaving a message on an answering machine and then never receiving a reply. It is the same when people write requesting information, only to have their letters go unanswered or to receive inappropriate material.

It is vital when responding to client enquiries to remember always that the client is doing the operator a favour by buying the product, not the other way around!

The next step in developing a positive client–guest relationship occurs when the booking is taken. The client's name, address and other contact details, the product they wish to buy, the price and the method of payment must all be confirmed. At this point it is also useful to ask if the client has any special requirements (dietary, medical or other safety needs). It is always best to have this information prior to the departure. This also provides an opportunity to give that extra bit of service that will engender faith in the client. Clients should be given all the information they need about the trip and be advised of the organisation's cancellation policy. It is worthwhile at this point to suggest they purchase travel insurance.

Once the booking has been confirmed, it is always advisable (time permitting) to send a confirmation notice. This action further reinforces the relationship with the client, as well as providing the opportunity to include useful additional information about the organisation, the product, equipment and clothing requirements, departure times, return times and the like. One point is worth mentioning: if additional information is being sent, it should be consistent with the overall quality image the business is trying to project. A photocopy of a photocopy of a faded fax may undermine the quality image. It is better to invest $50 and have extra information sheets printed professionally.

The following tenets must be adopted as basic to any enquiry and booking system:

- Standard practices must be in place to ensure the office is attended regularly, phones are answered in a consistent and courteous manner and enquiries are processed efficiently.
- Confirmations of bookings should sent with any additional relevant material.
- The business must have a documented cancellation policy.
- Requests for further information should be handled promptly and efficiently.
- A system should be established for handling and processing deposits and full payments.

It is useful to develop a quality management program to ensure that prospective clients are greeted in the manner desired and that booking procedures serve the needs of the guests. An easy method, if the operator has salaried staff, is to have a friend go through the booking procedure and make a report on the quality of the service offered. A more expensive method is to hire a consultant to review the procedures. This action may be worthwhile if the conversion rate of enquiries into bookings is unsatisfactory. Alternatively, the operator could contact competitors and pose as a prospective client. A great deal can be learned from what competitors do extremely well and what they do extremely poorly.

Inventory

Conventional wisdom has it that the tourism industry does not have inventory control problems like other businesses. This maxim certainly applies to the accommodation sector, where if a room is not sold it cannot be stored for future sale. But it does not apply to tour operators who package components to create new products. They have almost the same inventory problems as other small manufacturers. Their inventory control task is twofold: first, to ensure that enough product is inventoried to meet consumer demand; and secondly, to ensure that unused products are released back to suppliers at little or no cost to the operator. Operators store product by putting deposits on items like accommodation, entrances and the like. Suppliers will demand that tentative bookings be confirmed as early as 60 days prior to the trip taking place. If the operator fails to release the product in time, the business may be liable for the full cost of the goods, even though they are not used.

However, the operator may not be able to provide accurate numbers for the product so far in advance. Some clients may have put deposits down, but will want to cancel. Others will want to book a trip much closer to the departure date. If the operator releases the stock too soon, he or she may be unable to cater to the needs of late booking guests. On the other hand, if the operator holds on to the stock in anticipation of late bookings which do not materialise, he or she could be liable for substantial sums of money.

The key for many operators is to develop acceptable booking and cancellation policies for both suppliers and clients that satisfy all parties as much as possible. A booking control system for suppliers must be able to anticipate demand accurately and release un-needed stock prior to the date when full payment is due. By the same token, if the operator's product is being packaged by someone else, the operator needs a similar inventory system to ensure that reserved bookings are paid for in full, or cancelled in time to allow them to be resold.

Developing cancellation policies for clients is also a fundamental part of any inventory control system. From the clients' perspective, cancellation policies dictate the relevant terms and conditions if they wish to withdraw from a confirmed booking, and their financial obligations if they cancel at the last moment. From the operator's perspective, the main function of cancellation policies is to minimise the risk of exposure to debt. Usually, if sufficient advance notification is given for the operator to cancel the booking without suffering a financial penalty, the client will receive most or all of the deposit moneys. A small administration fee may be applied to pay for the internal office work. If, on the other hand, cancellations are made after the operator has incurred non-refundable expenses, the client will be liable for such expenses. Clients are advised to purchase travel insurance to protect against this eventuality if the reason for cancellation is medical or due to a family crisis.

Thus, inventory challenge becomes one of:

- determining the quantities of 'stock' necessary, such as rooms, meals and transport to ensure the smooth delivery of the product
- establishing a system to clearly define needs for specific trips well in advance
- establishing a system to release un-needed stock back to the supplier in time to ensure no costs are applied to it
- establishing a clearly-defined cancellation policy for guests
- determining future needs.

Buildings, equipment and transport

Operationally, the business must ensure that it has a suitable amount of equipment and stock for its clients' use. Further, all buildings, equipment and transport must be of an acceptable standard and maintained at an adequate level to allow clients to use them safely. Staff who are using equipment must be familiar with it and, if necessary, qualified to use it. One of the problems facing seasonal tour operators is that, during the peak season, equipment may be used almost continuously. A trip may end late one night and another trip begin early the next morning. As a result, equipment may not be cleaned, let alone well maintained. Dirty equipment may result in inconvenience to a client. Failure to maintain equipment may cause serious injury or death and a nasty lawsuit.

To avoid this, the following principles must be considered when establishing systems for the use and maintenance of gear:

- Personnel must be qualified and experienced to use equipment and perform basic maintenance.
- An inventory system should be created for equipment used and a regular replacement program should be adhered to.
- The business should have adequate supplies of appropriate equipment for its needs.
- Plans should be developed to use excess capacity equipment.
- Equipment and technology used should be continuously upgraded to meet the changing standards of the sector and changing consumer needs.
- Proper equipment must be carried on all trips and maintained in good working order.
- Equipment should be replaced when its 'use by' date approaches.

Personnel: specialist skills

Insurers are insisting increasingly that all staff working in specialist areas of the nature-based tourism sector must be fully qualified in their specialist area. In addition, they are insisting that as many staff as possible possess suitable first aid skills. The following suggestions made by ATON are vital for any nature-based tourism business:

- The basic skills needed for each activity should be outlined and the business should ensure that personnel have those skills.
- Staff should have basic skills such as first aid and other specialist skills that may be required for their activity (for example, radio operations, swimming skills and the like).
- Opportunities should be provided for staff to acquire new skills or to upgrade their existing skills.
- Personnel should be able verify any formal qualifications they claim to have.
- Qualifications should be current and systems should be established to ensure that staff keep their qualifications current.
- Qualifications should come from accredited organisations.
- Staff should have the opportunity to become multi-skilled.
- Staff must follow accepted safety standards (for example, bicycle tour guides must wear helmets).
- Staff performing specialist duties should have appropriate specialist skills that meet acknowledged industry standards, including drivers' licences and guiding programs.
- Staff must have specialist first aid and safety qualifications where required (for example, Bronze Medallion for swimming).[5]

Risk management

Tour operators and their staff have a moral and legal responsibility to ensure that their products are offered in as safe a manner as possible. At the same time, they also have an obligation to notify clients of any potential risks that may be associated with participating in the experience offered and may want to request that the clients themselves act in an appropriate manner. The entire issue of risk management is becoming increasingly important as Australia follows the litigious example set by the United States. The questions of risk minimisation and liability insurance are becoming daunting as premiums rise, the incidence of claims increases and the size of settlements grows geometrically. In the last few years, premiums for certain types of activities have tripled and the number of insurers providing coverage has dwindled.

For these reasons, the insurance industry is playing a more active role in helping tour operators minimise their risk and in so doing to reduce their potential exposure to liability claims. It is worthwhile asking insurance agents to conduct inspections of the business to identify likely risk areas and to suggest modifications to operations that could be implemented. Adopting risk-averse operating policies need not limit the quality of the experience. Indeed, if done correctly, it can be presented as an added benefit to the client that enhances the experience. An insurer was concerned that a horse-riding operator allowed his clients to wander through the paddock where the horses were tied up. He felt the risk of a horse kicking a client was increased by this action. The operator stopped allowing clients into the paddocks and now escorts his guests around the periphery, introducing them to the horses and helping them select the one they want. The operator then brings the horse to the client. Everyone benefits from this situation: the client receives a more personalised service, while the operator has reduced his or her risk exposure.

One way to minimise risk is to ensure that all clients read and sign a waiver of liability. The waiver of liability is one of the most effective tools available to inform clients of potential risks and to notify them that their own negligent actions may result in personal injury. While the jury is still out, literally, as to whether liability waiver forms are actually legally binding, insurers report that the incidence of claims is much lower when waivers are completed. Importantly, the liability waiver gives the operator a chance to talk to each client individually about the risks associated with the product and about the systems the business has established to minimise the risks. It also gives the operator a chance to talk to each of the staff about the same issues.

Discussions with tourism industry insurance specialists reveal that it takes, on average, four or more years for notification of personal injury claims to be recorded. The reason is that the impact of an injury, especially if the person is young, is not noted for many years. A client might have slipped while bushwalking and jarred his back. At the time he might have thought little of it, but as time progressed his back failed to get better. Three years later, his doctor diagnoses a permanent back injury and asks how he might have injured himself. Bingo, a potential insurance claim has been launched! In all likelihood, the owner of the business does not remember what happened in the business three weeks ago, let alone three years ago, especially if the incident appeared to be trivial at the time.

Once a claim is lodged, though, the onus shifts to the operator to disprove the injury (which is difficult) or to disprove negligence that might have led to the injury. As a former claims representative (in a previous life many years ago), the author can attest that simple negligence is one of the easiest things to prove, especially if it is the word of an injured party who remembers the incident against that of a business operator who has no recollection of it. Did the operator have a fully qualified guide on the trip who had first aid training? No! Then the operator was negligent. Was the guide over 18? No. Then sorry, out of luck. Did anyone offer assistance to the injured client? No. Why not? Negligence! Could the operator have foreseen that there was some level of risk? Did the operator notify the client? No? Negligence! Was the trail slippery or muddy? Did the operator advise the client to be cautious or to select an alternative route? Why not? A lawyer would argue, justifiably, that this was evidence of negligence.

As well, as a former claims representative, the author can stress that it is often in the insurer's best financial interests to reach an out-of-court settlement, even if the operator's case is strong. The reasons are threefold. One is that, even if the operator's case is strong, there is always a risk that he or she will lose and that the insurer will be liable for a huge payout. The second is that the costs of initiating litigation and commencing the long and cumbersome process of building a defence are usually higher than the size of the out-of-court settlement. Third, it is widely recognised in the insurance sector that once a claimant retains a lawyer, the cost of the settlement will usually be higher than if the claimant acted on his or her own behalf. Settling quickly will reduce the amount the insurer will have to pay.

Most industry bodies have devised incident report forms as a means of recording all accidents, regardless of how trivial they appeared at the time. That way, the operator and the insurer have a permanent account of what happened, who was working that day, what the conditions were, who the guide was and even who other participants in the trip were. Even if a claim is lodged ten years after the fact, there is a record of what happened and what actions were taken to mitigate the injury. A typical incident report form is shown in Figure 13.1.

How the incident is managed will influence whether a liability claim will be launched and the extent of the payout, if a claim is proven. The first rule of crisis management is to ensure that all other clients are safe. One person slipping and falling represents an incident. If others go to help and injure themselves, then there is a major crisis. The author's best friend died in just such circumstances. If the injury is severe or if it appears that the location where the injury occurred is unstable, the rest of the party should be removed from the scene and given something to do to keep their minds occupied. The party should not be split up, unless the tour leader is convinced that the people sent ahead (or back) are familiar with the surroundings and have the skills to travel on their own. It is important not to allow the rest of the party to panic. If this is managed satisfactorily, it will be much easier to take care of the person who is injured.

After the rest of the party has been seen to, attention can be directed to the client and his or her injuries. The client should be examined, the extent of the injury assessed and, if necessary, the appropriate first aid administered.

Figure 13.1 An incident report form

ACCIDENT / ILLNESS REPORT

ACCIDENT DETAILS

Date _____ Time _____

Name of _____

Business _____

Guide _____

Patient _____

Age _____

GENERAL CONDITIONS

☐ Good ☐ Fair ☐ Serious ☐ Fatal

Main Problem _____
_____
_____
_____
_____
_____
_____

Cause of Problem _____
_____
_____
_____
_____
_____
_____

Allergies _____

Medication _____

Exam. Findings _____

Witness _____

Signature _____

EVACUATION DETAILS

Need to evacuate _____

Exact Location _____

use map or chart also _____

Terrain _____

Weather ____ Temp ____ Precip. ____

Wind ____ Clouds ____ Vis. ____

CONDITION OF GROUP

☐ Poor ☐ Good

IMMEDIATE NEEDS

Stretcher ____ Doctor ____

Personnel ____ First Aid Supplies ____

Food ____ Boat ____

Clothing ____ Vehicle ____

Shelter ____ Air Evac. ____

Other ____

Senior Medical Person _____

Time Evacuation Requested _____

Time Evacuation Occurred _____

Facility or Hospital _____
_____
_____
_____

Phone at Present Location _____

Address _____
_____
_____

TO BE COMPLETED BACK AT OFFICE

Trip started from _____ to be completed at _____

No. in Party _____ No. of Guides _____ Activity time Lost _____

Enclosed are ☐ Signed waiver ☐ Photos ☐ Statement from Witnesses

---

DESCRIPTION: DRAW IN TYPE AND LOCATION OF INJURIES

Head injuries | Puncture
Laceration | Gunshot

Anterior view | Posterior view

Abrasion | Amputation
Fracture | Asphyxia
Sprain/strain | Burn
Crushing | Electrocution
Other(specify)

Treatment given
_____
_____
_____

Medication given
_____
_____

Dosage 1 ____ 2 ____
Time 1 ____ 2 ____

Location of injury
Number each injury site above and describe below

1 _____
2 _____
3 _____

Form completed by
Was this re-injury of previous injury? Yes ☐ No ☐

VITAL SIGNS FLOW SHEET
Remember to repeat exam and vital signs every 15 minutes, until stable, then hourly.

Time	Pulse	B/P	Resp	Airway	Consciousness	Skin	Temp	Pupils

If no first aid is needed, the tour leader should remain with the client until it is established that they can continue. It may be necessary to organise the evacuation of the client; if hospitalisation is required, an ambulance should be called. Legally, owners and staff have a duty of care that is commensurate with their knowledge and skills. Thus, a first aid trained guide would be expected only to conduct him- or herself at a level appropriate to someone who knows basic first aid.

Morally, however, the business may have a greater responsibility to the client. Indeed, for minor injuries, good customer service practices play as important a role as medical care. The ability to make the injured party feel comfortable and to convince them that they are in capable hands will reduce the level of trauma they may feel, ease the stress of the situation and may lessen the amount of shock. It will also mitigate any self-consciousness or embarrassment the client may feel if the injury happened through self-negligence, or in an innocuous situation where an injury would not normally be expected. Bushwalkers turn ankles walking along trails; skiers often break their wrists if they fall from a standing position; people may slip while crossing a stream. All these types of accidents can cause acute embarrassment as well as pain.

Paying special attention to and reassuring the client, providing that extra bit of care on site and making follow-up calls will show genuine concern about the well-being of the client. At the least, it will make the client feel better and will demonstrate to other guests that the operator cares about his or her clients. At the most, providing strong customer service has been shown to lessen the likelihood that a liability claim will be launched and to reduce the amount of the settlement.

The Australian Tourism Operators Network identifies a number of risk management systems that need to be established. These include:

- **risk management plans** outlining the actions to be taken in the event of an emergency
- **workplace health and safety systems** to ensure the workplace is safe for staff and clients
- **emergency procedure manuals** to ensure that the business has adequate equipment to cope with an emergency, that staff are qualified to deal with an emergency, and that relevant people are notified. In addition, these procedures should be practised regularly
- **first aid training** of a suitable standard for the activity; also making sure that at least one qualified person is on every trip
- **a first aid kit**, well stocked, current and suitable for the activity being undertaken.

Ecologically sustainable systems

In addition to ethics of care to their clients, nature-based tour operators also have an equally strong ethic of care to ensure that their operations are conducted in an ecologically sustainable manner. While this theme is explored in greater detail in the next chapter, it is important to recognise here that operating systems must be developed to minimise the potential adverse social and physical environmental impacts of nature-based tourism activities.

The Australian Tourism Operators Network and the Ecotourism Association of Australia identify the need to:

- establish guidelines and inform staff of appropriate procedures to minimise environmental impacts
- establish a system for reporting impacts and environmental accidents
- establish environmental performance criteria
- establish guidelines and develop programs to rehabilitate degraded areas
- develop systems and policies for water use, noise, air quality, wildlife disturbance, waste minimisation and minimal impact activities
- consult with the local community
- advise clients of their responsibilities when visiting sensitive areas.

Again, such systems need not impose an onerous workload on the operator or interfere in any way with the product being offered. Indeed, if observed correctly, the ethical standards that the operator has identified may be a source of sustainable competitive advantage and may actually help the business increase its sales.

Personal systems: managing oneself

Finally, all people working in the tourism industry must develop a series of systems for themselves to manage the workload they assume and their stress levels and to ensure that their non-business lives remain in balance with their business lives. As mentioned at the start of this book, many people enter the nature-based tourism sector for lifestyle reasons. While it may seem an attractive lifestyle for some, the reality of operating a small business is that it can consume the individual totally. Cotterill and others have identified the risk of personal burnout as a major issue for the industry.[6] The nature of the business is that many trips are taken on weekends, but that suppliers and potential clients feel the operator should also be available during the week for enquiries and deliveries. The owner-operator does all the administration, bookings and office work, leads trips, cleans the vehicle after the trip and prepares for the next one. As a result, the nature-based tourism business is often a twelve-hours-a-day, seven-days-a-week business. Other facets of one's life are traded off in pursuit of the perceived needs of the business.

The challenge, then, becomes one of controlling the number of hours worked, reducing the amount of stress the operator is placed under and ensuring that enough time in the day is allocated to the social and personal side of life. Some address this situation by operating seasonal businesses and by using the off season as a chance to catch up with the rest of their lives. Some sacrifice part of their own income to hire staff. Others develop personal systems that allow them to work as efficiently as possible. In many instances, the development and application of the range of business and operational systems discussed in this chapter facilitates this balance. However, a number of other personal issues may need to be addressed to help that process even more.

A number of self-help books have been written on this topic. Any bookstore can direct you to a seemingly endless array of books on the subject and most business planning seminars devote at least one session to balancing one's life. Most, though, say pretty much the same thing. One of the more interesting books is written by Sally Matheson, who is a successful Australian businesswoman. Her short book, titled *Secrets: A Personal Survival Plan for Success in Small Business*, offers a number of good ideas. Some of the suggestions made by Ms Matheson include:

- establishing and following good habits, like always answering mail and enquiries on the day they arrive
- setting aside 'quiet' times when the phone or fax isn't ringing to do concentrated work—she suggests early mornings
- establishing a list of priorities each day and doing them in order of priority
- establishing business and operating systems so that everyone knows what to do and only has to be told once
- not overwhelming oneself with tasks—she suggests listing no more than six things to do in a day and then doing them
- eliminating meetings as much as possible or, if they cannot be avoided, setting a time limit (say 30 minutes) and ending the meeting at that time
- keeping accurate records and updating them regularly
- delegating tasks to others
- hiring staff—a clerical person is probably more cost-effective than the opportunity costs associated with the owner's doing clerical work
- planning the entire year ahead

- managing one's time: ensuring that there is enough to spend with family and friends. This may mean leaving tasks unfinished, going on holidays or closing the office for a day.[7]

Operators who do not develop systems fear that, if they leave the business for even one moment, it will cease to run. Good operators, on the other hand, know that they can and must take time off to refresh themselves. One of the most popular ways is a self-reward system of taking the occasional 'mental health' holiday after an especially heavy work period. For the same reason, it is a good idea to take at least one day off a week during the peak season. The only days available may be Mondays or Tuesdays. That is fine. For someone running an accommodation house it may be impossible to take a full day off, but it should be possible to arrange at least half a day a week off to do something—anything—that is not work related.

As well, it is vital to strike a balance between work and non-work activities. The author has observed that the amount of time it takes to do a task is directly proportional to the amount of time available. If an operator is used to working twelve-hour days, it will take twelve hours to do a day's work. If the operator has other things to do outside normal work hours, it is amazing how he or she can get things done in a normal eight-hour day. Working excessively long hours is a sure recipe for burnout. It is so easy to have the job overwhelm the person, especially if that person is the owner of the business. It can become all-absorbing and very isolating.

It is vital to the ongoing emotional health of operators to develop the ability to put the business in a compartment along with all the other aspects of their lives. When it is time to do work, it is time to open that compartment and become totally absorbed with the tasks in hand. When it comes time to do other things, the work can be put back in its box and left there until it is time to work again. When on a tour, all energies should be directed to delivering that tour. If the operator frets about other business issues, the clients will know and the quality of the experience will suffer. Basically, the best advice for a busy operator is to eat well, sleep well, exercise well, relax well, have the odd treat, and remember that it is only a job; it's not a life!

---

[1] Meredith (1993) p. 265.

[2] Meredith (1988) op. cit.

[3] Source: in part Meredith (1995) op. cit.

[4] ATOA (1995) op. cit.

[5] ATON (1995).

[6] Cotterill, op. cit.

[7] S. Matheson (1993) *Secrets: A Personal Survival Plan for Success in Small Business*, The Business Library, Melbourne, chapters 17 & 18, pp. 121–36.

Chapter 14

Some ethical considerations

*b*usiness ethics have been defined as the application of morality by individuals with respect to the management of business decisions.[1] Acting in an ethically responsible manner must be the underlying tenet for the nature-based tourism sector for, by its very nature, acting in anything less than an exemplary manner will lead to the downfall of the industry. Nature-based tour operators have multi-dimensional ethical concerns, ranging from ensuring continued access to and maintenance of the integrity of natural ecosystems for their ongoing livelihood, to developing and maintaining productive links with traditional land owners, to controlling the actions of their clients. Ethical practice is good business that can be a source of sustainable competitive advantage. Indeed, ethics are so important to this sector that this chapter could just as easily have been placed at the beginning of this book.

An ethical business enterprise, according to the Ethical Enterprise Network, is committed to:

- creating and sharing sustainable prosperity
- sustaining the environment with which it interacts
- equity and justice in trading
- respect for both people and the environment
- responsibility, accountability and disclosure.[2]

Further, ethical tourism respects the interests of other stakeholders.

In the past, some members of the tourist industry have failed to satisfy these objectives. The literature is full of stories condemning tourism for an array of practices that have resulted in adverse social and environmental consequences. The industry has been chastised for its promotional practices[3] and tourism has been castigated as a trivialiser of cultures and as a destroyer of traditional ways of life. Moreover, research conducted on attitudes to tourism in national parks reveals that there is a great deal of antipathy towards tourism. Some of the complaints are legitimate; in other instances, tourism has been a convenient scapegoat.

None the less, a clear message has been sent by government agencies and peak industry bodies that some practices can no longer be tolerated. The predecessor of Tourism Council Australia, the Australian Tourism Operators Network and the Ecotourism Association of Australia have all developed 'codes of practice'.[4] While these are noble in intent, some commentators argue that, although the codes are carefully written, exacting and commendable, they are of little practical benefit because participation is voluntary and enforcement is often non-existent.[5]

This chapter will discuss some of the ethical issues that all nature-based tour operators must consider. It begins by describing the ethical business and makes some recommendations about sound business practice. A discussion of ecological sustainability, dealing with host communities and being responsible for the actions of tourists follows. The chapter concludes by reviewing some of the easy and not-so-easy considerations that tour operators must make to work in an ethical manner.

The ethical business

Let us make no mistake about it, businesses are established for commercial reasons. They provide goods and services for exchange with a view to making a profit. This recognised objective is, however, complementary to the objective of running an ethical business, for the survival of any business depends on two factors: developing a solid relationship with customers based on honesty and goodwill, and treating employees and suppliers in a just manner. Vallance identifies common decency in dealing and justice as the two critical factors in running an ethical business.[6] Similarly, Payne and Dimanche name four key values for ethical tourism businesses: justice, integrity, competence and utility. Justice relates to the idea of fairness and good faith in all transactions. Integrity relates to the concept of honesty, sincerity, candour and respect for the self and others. Competence reflects the ability of the organisation to deliver the services promised and utility encompasses the practical concept of efficacy and the philosophical concept of providing the greatest amount of good.[7] Ethical business practices, therefore, involve more than simple compliance with the letter of the law. The truly ethical business acknowledges that it has a greater moral obligation to deal fairly and equitably with all people, businesses and organisations it contacts.

Ethics is being seen increasingly as a strategic tool to be used by businesses as part of their total quality management system. Viewed in this way, ethical principles can be used to determine the direction of a business and to implement actions to improve its performance.[8] Businesses have used ethical activities, such as the development of environmental programs, to foster pride among employees.[9] Importantly, many clients of nature-based tour operators develop such an affinity with a business that they begin to feel a part of that business. The actions of the business can create a sense of pride in the client and are seen as a reflection of the client's own value system.

Business practices

Business ethics are more than just a ideology. To be truly effective, they must filter through the entire business to the point where they become part of the organisation's culture. A number of suggestions for achieving such a culture are listed below.

Business goals and business decisions:

- Commit to the principle of best practice by eliminating practices that are damaging to trade or consumers.
- Develop and display a code of ethics for the business.
- Incorporate social and environmental goals into the business's goals.
- Strive to maximise the quality of the experience for clients.
- Prevent accidental or deliberate actions that can cause environmental damage.
- Pay bills on time—good business practices help other businesses to survive and thrive.
- If encountering financial difficulties, notify suppliers immediately.
- Meet community obligations by paying appropriate taxes.
- Provide a safe workplace.

Staff:

- Support training for guides and managers.
- Employ staff who are qualified, or ensure that staff gain the necessary qualifications.
- Employ staff who are well versed in and respectful of local culture and environments.

- Keep employees informed of alterations to their services.
- Where possible, strive to encourage multi-skilling among staff and to develop career paths for staff.
- Remunerate staff fairly, depending on responsibilities undertaken.
- Adopt an equal opportunity staffing policy.
- Commit to industrial democracy through an increase in employee decision-making.
- Respect people's personal space and privacy.

Relationship with peers and other service providers:

- Always deal fairly with other businesses.
- Support suppliers that have a conservation ethic and purchase goods only from suppliers that do not engage in exploitative personnel or environmental practices.
- Offer opinions about other businesses with professional integrity and courtesy.
- Do not tolerate illegal or unethical actions by others. Prior to notifying regulatory bodies, however, proof of indiscretions must be obtained.
- Communicate honestly and openly with staff and encourage them to do so with you.

Dealing with complaints:

- If a complaint is lodged, take immediate steps to deal with it amicably.
- If the complaint cannot be resolved, seek mediation.
- Demonstrate respect for those people who may lodge complaints.
- Communicate honestly and openly.

Using local goods and services:

- Share the prosperity of the business with the region where the trips occur.
- Use locally produced goods and shop locally, if possible.

Equity and justice:

- Donate a share of business profits to causes that are complementary to the goals of the business (conservation, wetlands protection and the like).
- Support equitable employment policies.[10]

Marketing

The ethical standards of tourism marketing have been called into question by some commentators. The industry has been accused of creating images that do not reflect the reality of the destination, of reinforcing clichéd, stereotypical and racist views, of running sexist advertisements, of misleading the travelling public, of exploiting locals and of making claims that cannot be justified. Some operators who claim their products contribute to environmental causes have been found to be misleading the public. In addition, the term 'ecotourism' has been so misused by tourism marketers that it is becoming increasingly difficult for legitimate ecotourism businesses to gain the credibility they deserve.

The Trade Practices Act, discussed in Chapter 4, stipulates a number of rules regarding misleading advertising. Ethical nature-based tourism marketing practices must go beyond the letter of the law and could consider:

- ensuring that the image presented is consistent with the reality of the product offered
- wherever possible, avoiding stereotypical, clichéd or sexist promotional tactics
- communicating the fragility of the destination being visited
- showing the client that the operator has a long-term interest in the region being visited
- being factual and accurate in all promotional material
- informing all staff of their ethical obligations
- setting and stating limits on the number of clients to be taken
- being careful to use the right labels (for instance, using the terms 'ecotourism', 'accredited' and so only where appropriate)
- stating all relevant conditions clearly
- showing respect for clients and supporting the rights of consumers
- engaging in sales approaches that allow clients to purchase goods of their own free will.[11]

Operating an ecologically sustainable business

The environment is the stock-in-trade of the nature-based tourist industry. Without continued access to it and the maintenance of the ecological integrity of natural areas, this sector would cease to exist. If a business by its own actions, complicity or complacency, destroys the environment or allows it to be destroyed by someone else, it destroys its own future. It is axiomatic, then, that operating in an ecologically sustainable manner lies at the heart of any ethical nature-based tourist business. The Commonwealth Government issued its overarching policy document on ecologically sustainable tourism development in 1991.[12] Most state governments have followed suit, along with a number of regions. Today, most tourism organisations in Australia have produced their own ecologically sustainable codes of practice.

Sustainability was defined in the late 1980s by the World Commission on Environment and Development as 'development that meets the needs of the present without compromising the ability of future generations to meet their own needs'.[13] This definition led to much confusion, as both pro- and anti-conservationist stakeholders used the word to support their own agendas. Anti-conservationists argued a platform of constant wealth, whereby the driving force was economic growth. According to this view, natural resources could be consumed, provided they generated wealth. In other words, the status quo should be maintained. This argument was rebutted widely by conservationists as well as by many industry leaders.[14] These argued on behalf of a 'constant natural capital' approach to sustainability, according to which the absolute stock of natural resources of air, water, minerals, plants and animals must not be allowed to be depleted any more than it has and, indeed, should grow over time. Ultimately, this view of ecologically sustainable development, or ESD as it is known today, was accepted.

ESD poses a number of opportunities and threats to the tourism industry. On the positive side, maintenance of natural resources will ensure that the primary attraction for the nature-based sector is preserved. On the negative side, one of the management tools used to conserve and expand natural and near-natural areas is to exclude those activities that may threaten their ecological integrity. Tourism is one such activity that has been identified by some groups.[15]

Principles of ecologically sustainable development

A review of the principles of ESD offers valuable insights into how the tourism industry must act in relatively undisturbed areas. Underlying the entire ESD philosophy is a commitment to operate within the social and biophysical limits of the natural environment. To abide by this tenet, tour operators may have to trade off economic gain for ecological sustainability and, indeed, will have to accept that there are some places where tourism should be excluded.

Improving material and non-material well-being

This principle relates to a fundamental shift in the way economic progress is measured. Traditionally, development has been measured in economic terms (gross domestic product, sales, export revenue and so on). Under ESD, however, a more complete measurement of growth must be carried out that includes a range of non-monetary benefits. To be sustainable, tourism must help improve the quality of life for local residents, strive to narrow disparities between the richest and poorest residents of a community and involve local residents in any decision-making processes. Nature-based tourism has a unique opportunity to maximise local benefits while minimising costs.

Intergenerational equity

The concept of intergenerational equity maintains that the range of activities available to future generations should be at least as broad as the range available to the current generation. While the actual location of the activity may change, the range and opportunities cannot decrease. This ethos emerges out of the recognition that the biological rate of change the earth is undergoing is faster than at any other time in its known existence, except during periods of mass extinctions. The fear is that, unless this rate can be slowed, within 20 years the planet's biodiversity will be irreversible damaged.

This principle has many implications for the tourism industry from an ecological, sociological and experiential nature. New tourism development in natural or near-natural areas may be restricted if the impacts of that development are seen to damage natural processes. By the same token, tourism activity that may diminish the opportunity for others to enjoy an area, either through the granting of preferential rights to tourism, or through a changed experience that makes an area less attractive, would be regarded as undesirable. It is possible that some tourism activities will be relocated from areas where it is deemed to be unacceptable.

Dealing cautiously with risk and irreversibilities

Ecological sustainability principles advise people to proceed cautiously in situations where the consequences of actions are unknown, or where the potential exists for adverse impacts. Indeed, the preferred option may be to abandon the project if the impacts cannot be determined. This principle is seen by developers and some bureaucrats alike as adversely affecting their ability to initiate projects in a timely and cost-effective manner. However, tour operators have an obligation to ensure that the consequences of their activities are known in advance and to develop strategies to mitigate impacts.[16]

Protecting biological diversity and ecological integrity

The tourism industry has great potential to exert a number of adverse impacts on the environments it uses. The reality is that any type of nature-based tourism, regardless of how sympathetic, involves some permanent restructuring of the environment, the introduction of more people or the potential for adverse impacts to be felt. Often, the introduction of weeds or other pests that can out-compete natives is done innocently. An examination of one of the car parks at Kosciusko National Park found 27 weed species that are not known to occur in the Alpine area.[17] Apple trees, plum trees and raspberry canes have found their way into sub-alpine woodlands through seeds either carelessly discarded by visitors or in human faeces. Plants that were introduced into gardens in resort villages have now spread beyond the gardens and are becoming a problem.

It is often the most rare and fragile habitats that hold the greatest allure for nature-based tourism. Hard questions need to be asked about the acceptability of tourism in these areas. One of the greatest flaws of most ecotourism policies is that they never question the legitimacy of tourism as a land use. In a number of cases, tourism may be counter-productive to the best interests of the environment. The industry as a whole will have to accept that it will and should be excluded from some areas in order to ensure that ecological processes are maintained.

Pricing environmental values

A large part of the environmental crisis facing the earth today is caused by the fact that users of natural resources have never been charged the full cost of the use of that resource. Through years of formal government policy, developed under the belief that economic growth can occur most quickly through the exploitation of natural resources, an industrial attitude has developed that focuses on production with scant regard for the disposal of waste. As a consequence, use levels of natural resources have exceeded the resources' ability to assimilate waste and to renew themselves to the point that the biological integrity of much of our resource base has been compromised.

While it is easy to point the finger at traditional consumptive industries like logging, mining and fisheries, tourism is no different. Tour operators using protected areas have never had to pay a resource rent that is a true reflection of the value of the resource they use. Sure, many pay modest licensing fees to state governments for the privilege to operate in parks. Some may even pay a modest per capita fee for the opportunity to take people to the Great Barrier Reef or onto Aboriginal land. But the amount charged is usually only a token sum that does not reflect the full cost of managing the resource. A few years ago, the total licence revenue paid by commercial tour operators using Victoria's national parks, for example, did not even cover the cost of the person administering the licences, let alone go to assist park management activities.

Operational issues

Most operators have a genuine desire to operate in a clean, green and sustainable manner. If they fail to do so, it is often more out of ignorance than out of a malicious disregard for the environment. The Commonwealth government has produced a number of excellent guides for the industry to encourage best practice in tourism operations.[18] In addition, most state government tourism and conservation departments have developed guidelines on environmentally sensitive operations. These deal with waste minimisation, recycling, conserving energy and the like.

Easy actions to achieve sustainability

Many of the operational issues involved in developing a sustainable product can be addressed very effectively at little cost to the operator. To begin with, many operators may choose to conduct an environmental audit of their business. Details of the types of information to seek are available from most national conservation organisations or state environment departments. Usually, the operator will discover that it is relatively easy to establish environmental operating systems. Waste reduction and recycling programs are among the easiest to implement.[19] The benefit is that, while such programs will help the environment, they may also be very cost-effective for the operator, potentially saving thousands of dollars. Importantly, these actions create goodwill in the host community and with clients. Briefing sessions about the fragility of environments being visited and instructions about how they are expected to act in these environments will foster a sense of stewardship among clients. Most people will want to do the right thing, but may know little about what is right and what is wrong.

Not-so-easy actions to achieve sustainability

A true commitment to ecological sustainability, however, may involve making a number of difficult decisions about the business, business practices and the areas in which the business operates. Some of the decisions may result in accepting less revenue in exchange for maintaining the state of the environment. Ideologically, this trade-off is easy; but realistically, it may be very difficult, especially if the business is marginal. Every operator is faced with short seasons, the threat of inclement weather, the likelihood that not all trips offered will run, the reality that not all trips that do run will be full, financial pressures that extend throughout the year and a very real desire to make their business successful. In addition, some operators may feel that artificial limits placed on their business by licensing organisations are unfair.

What can be done? The temptation to ignore licensing requirements, to add just a few more people to a trip, to continue to visit fragile areas when the operator knows the visits may damage the area, to visit areas where they know they should not go or to continue with construction projects in sensitive areas after the agreed-upon completion date to ensure the project is operational by the next season can be overwhelming. One person contacted for this book indicated that he had set up a separate expense account for the fines he will pay for violating his licence. His rationale was that, for his business to be viable, he had to violate the conditions set on his licence. It was cheaper to pay a fine than to forgo needed revenue.

Many of these ethical predicaments are a result of the operator's running a marginally viable business. The root cause of the problem lies in the fact that the business probably should not exist at all, and not in the desperate actions taken to try to keep it afloat. Adopting the business planning principles discussed throughout this book is the best way of ensuring that the groundwork can be laid for the operation of an ethical business. If a sound business opportunity has been recognised, if the operator has identified a large enough target market, if an appropriate product has been developed to satisfy the needs of this market and if the operator has sufficient resources to run the business, then there should be no financial need to run an unethical, unsustainable business. Planning the business with ecologically sustainable development ideals in mind from the outset should mean that operators will not have to face these dilemmas.

Dealings with host communities

Host communities are at risk of being the recipients of the adverse effects of tourism, while gaining few benefits. For these reasons, ethical tour operators try to distribute some of the wealth generated from the trip in the community where the tourism experience occurs. It is suggested that, where possible, operators buy goods and services locally and encourage their clients to do so. Such practices provide the ideal win-win situation for all parties. The community benefits directly by sharing in the wealth generated by tourism, and the operator benefits by developing strong relationships with local businesses that may be useful if an emergency occurs.

The opportunity also exists to encourage meaningful input from the local community into the development and delivery of nature-based tourism products.[20] One of the complaints about tourism is that it is often seen to be imposed on communities without any consultation. The literature on this subject is extensive. Studies on the impacts of tourism have shown that negative attitudes towards tourism are influenced by the perceived threat of tourism to existing lifestyles and a feeling of disempowerment.[21] Building productive relationships with the community is the single most important act that an operator can initiate to foster a positive attitude to tourism. In some instances local involvement is mandatory, such as to negotiate access to Aboriginal lands, heritage sites or private land. In other instances, local knowledge can be useful in helping the operator develop a better product.

Operators have an obligation to advise guests about local cultures and traditions and to inform them of acceptable behaviour in the areas visited. Clients can offend locals through their own innocent and ignorant (in its true Latin sense of unknowing) actions. It is important for the operator to inform guests of what is appropriate and to explain why certain actions are inappropriate. People are far less likely to climb Uluru once they are informed that it is a site of cultural significance to the local Aboriginal owners. Others will remove their shoes or try not to disturb people in temples if they are made aware of how their actions can disturb people at prayer. A polite request and information work better than a big stick.

Other stakeholders

The country's national and state park system is becoming an increasingly popular venue for nature-based tourism. So too is the potential for conflict between the tourism industry and other legitimate stakeholders.[22] Operators must remember that, while parks provide a wide variety of tourism opportunities, most were established initially to cater to non-tourism values. Indeed, it is fair to say that there is a significant degree of antipathy to tourism and suspicion about the merits among a large cohort of park users. Why? The answer is fear—fear that tourism will lead to their expulsion from the park. Displacement could occur overtly, through the granting of exclusive or priority use areas to tour operators, or it could occur insidiously through a subtle changing of the park experience that reduces satisfaction levels to the point where people choose to stop visiting.

Underlying this fear are the beliefs that tourism is an activity that is fundamentally different from recreation and that basic attitudinal and value differences exist between tourists and recreationists. There is a widely-held philosophical perception among many people that recreation is an acceptable and desired park use, but that commercial uses, such as tourism, are not.[23] It is often intellectually difficult for many people to acknowledge that they are really non-fee-paying tourists when they visit a park. By denying that they are tourists, they are also denying that they are part of the park management problem associated with overuse. More than that, though, tourism and tourists are seen to be part of an alien and threatening culture for many stakeholders. Any tour operator visiting national parks must be aware of these sentiments.

The emergence of tourism as a significant protected area activity has transformed permanently the traditional use culture of many areas by introducing a new player who is both alien and hostile to the traditional users. Tourism has a clear commercial focus, which is at odds with the overtly anti-commercial focus held by most conservation and recreation-oriented stakeholders. Tourism is seen as an exploiter of the park that consumes resources for commercial gain, often at an unacceptable environmental cost. Non-commercial users universally see their own actions as contributing to the well-being of the resource, be they conservationists, bushwalkers, skiers, four wheel drivers, horse riders or shooters.

Tourism is also a highly resource-competitive activity[24] and, when supported by formal government policy, can be a voracious competitor. It is common for other stakeholders to feel that tourism has been granted preferential treatment and that tourism interests are driving national park policy decisions. The current political climate favouring the expansion of tourism in parks serves only to heighten these concerns. The result has been a fundamental alteration of the traditional power relationships in park management, with disaffected parties feeling disempowered.

Research conducted by the author on attitudes to tourism in the Victorian Alps has shown that the perceived effect of tourism on various stakeholders will vary depending on the stakeholders' interests.[25] Antipathy to commercial bushwalks felt by bushwalkers' clubs is driven by the belief that commercial clients are somehow less legitimate park users. Encounters with these 'undesirables' are thought to diminish the experience sought by the 'true' bushwalker. Antipathy to four-wheel-drive tourism from the four-wheel-drive fraternity is influenced again by a feeling that tour operators are less legitimate users who do not share the same conservation ethic. In addition, they are afraid that the tourism industry will be granted exclusive use areas, which will result in a further restriction on four wheel driving. Conservationists fear that ecotourism has the potential to be destructive, regardless of how environmentally sound the operator intends to be. Their concerns have more to do with how frequently and intensively an area will be used to satisfy the commercial needs of the operator, and less to do with the activity itself.

Overcoming antipathy

How can tour operators overcome this antipathy? For a start, all tour operators must appreciate that, regardless of how environmentally friendly their operations are, a portion of park users will object to their presence in any park. The opposition is based partly on differences in attitude to the role and purpose of parks, partly on observed transgressions of other tour operators and partly on an emotional, irrational belief that the actions of the operator or the client are incompatible with their achieving their own goals.

Overcoming negative attitudes rests solely with the operators themselves. The task is daunting, but ethical operators have the greatest chance of being the vehicle for change. They must first convince other park users that they are partners rather than competitors in park use debates. Part of this task can be achieved by convincing leaders of other organisations that their goals are compatible and that their clients are looking for similar experiences.

Further, nature-based tourism must reinforce its place as a legitimate park activity. The industry provides a public good by exposing new people to the park who will then take the conservation message home with them. Most importantly, legitimacy in the eyes of many park visitors comes from developing a sense of stewardship toward the park. Operators must become visibly involved in managing the areas they visit. They must do more than make a financial contribution to green organisations or pay a nominal licence fee. High-profile actions like maintaining a hut or providing interpretation workshops for clubs will create goodwill between the industry and other users. Importantly, the financial cost of these actions need not be high.

Finally, the industry must be diligent in ensuring that it and its clients operate to the highest ethical standards possible. The onus is placed on individual operators to strive for excellence in all aspects of their operations. It also places a moral obligation on operators to tolerate nothing less than the same commitment from the entire industry. The nature-based tourism industry cannot tolerate any operator who is not committed to best practice.

[1] M. J. Segon (1993) Ethics, in Collins, C. (ed.), *Effective Management*, CCH International, Sydney, pp. 521–51.

[2] Ethical Enterprises Network (1997) *Guide to Ethical Enterprise: In Business for a Better World*, EEN, Melbourne.

[3] M. Wheeler (1995) Tourism Marketing ethics: An introduction, *International Marketing Review*, 12(4), pp. 38–49.

[4] Australian Tourism Industry Association (1990) *Code of Environmental Practice*, ATIA, Canberra; Victorian Tourism Operators Association (1996b) *Members' Code of Ethics*, VTOA, Melbourne; Ecotourism Association of Australia (1996b) *Ecotourism Association of Australia Code of Practice*, EAA, Brisbane.

[5] S. Sims (1994) Responsible travel, *Successful Meetings*, 43(6), p. 24.

[6] E. Vallance (1995) *Business Ethics at Work*, Cambridge University Press, Cambridge.

[7] D. Payne & F. Dimanche (1996) Towards a code of ethics for the tourism industry: An ethics model, *Journal of Business Ethics*, 15(9), pp. 997–1007.

[8] Vallance, op. cit.

[9] L. D'Amore (1993) A code of ethics for socially and environmentally responsible tourism, *Journal of Travel Research*, 31(3), pp. 64–6.

[10] Sources: in part EAA (1996b) *Ecotourism Association of Australia Code of Practice*, Brisbane; VTOA (1995c) op. cit.; EEN (1997) op. cit.

[11] Sources: in part Payne & Dimanche, op. cit.; Vallance, op. cit.; VTOA (1995c) op. cit.; Wheeler, op. cit.

[12] Ecologically Sustainable Development Working Groups (1991) *Ecologically Sustainable Development Working Groups Final Report: Tourism*, Government of Australia, Canberra.

[13] World Commission on Environment and Development (1987) *Our Common Future*, WCED, Oxford University Press, Melbourne.

[14] D. Pearce, A. Markandya & E. Barbier (1989) *Blueprint for a Green Economy*, Earthscan Publishing, London; M. Hare (1990) (ed.) *Ecologically Sustainable Development: A Submission*, Australian Conservation Foundation, Greenpeace (Australia), The Wilderness Society, World Wide Fund for Nature—Australia, for example.

[15] B. McKercher (1993a) The unrecognised threat to tourism: Can tourism survive sustainabililty? *Tourism Management*, 14(2), pp. 131–6; (1993b) Tourism in parks: The perspective of Australia's national parks and conservation organisations, *GeoJournal*, 29(3), pp. 307–13.

[16] D. Ing (1995) Sustainable tourism charter issues, *Hotel and Motel Management*, 210(100), pp. 4, 36.

[17] K. McDougall (1996) Weeds in Victorian alpine areas, in *Alpine Ecology Course Notes*, Dept of Natural Resources and Environment, Melbourne.

[18] Commonwealth Department of Tourism (1995), *Best Practice Ecotourism: A Guide to Energy and Waste Minimisation*, DOT, Canberra; Commonwealth Department of Industry, Science and Tourism (1996) *Tourism Switched On: Sustainable Energy Technologies for the Australian Tourism Industry*, DIST & Tourism Council Australia, Canberra; and others.

[19] W. Hart (1993) The Three R's, *Cornell Hotel and Restaurant Administration Quarterly*, 34(5), pp. 18–19.

[20] Anon. (1995) Ecotourism—ethical profits, *African Business*, 199, pp. 36–9.

[21] A. Milman & A. Pizam (1988) Social impacts of tourism on Central Florida, *Annals of Tourism Research*, 15, pp. 191–204; R. R. Perdue, P. Long & L. Allen (1990) Resident support for tourism development, *Annals of Tourism Research*, 17, pp. 586–99; D. Getz (1993) Impacts of tourism on residents; leisure: Concepts, and a longitudinal case study of Spey Valley, Scotland, *Journal of Tourism Studies*, 4(2), pp. 33–44; (1994) Residents' attitudes towards tourism: A longitudinal case study of Spey Valley, Scotland, *Tourism Management*, 15(4), 247–58; B. King, A. Pizam & A. Milman (1993) Social impacts of tourism: Host perceptions, *Annals of Tourism Research*, 20, pp. 650–65; R. Madrigal (1993) A tale of tourism in two cities, *Annals of Tourism Research*, 20, pp. 336–53.

[22] McKercher (1993a,b) op. cit.; (1996b) Understanding attitudes to tourism in protected areas, in Richins, Richardson & Crabtree, op. cit.; (1997) Benefits and costs

of tourism in Victoria's Alpine National Park: Comparing the attitudes of tour operators, management staff and public interest group leaders, in Hall, C. M., Jenkins, J. & Kearsley, G. (eds), *Tourism Planning and Policy in Australia and New Zealand*. Irwin, Sydney, pp. 99–100.

[23] A. Landals (1986) The bloody tourists are ruining the park, in *Tourism and the Environment*, Canadian Society of Environmental Biologists, Edmonton, pp. 89–99; J. D. Hunt (1990) Linking tourism, wilderness and economic development, in Lime, D. (ed.), *Managing America's Enduring Wilderness Resource*, University of Minnesota, St Paul, pp. 570–6.

[24] McKercher (1993b) op. cit.

[25] McKercher (1997) op. cit.

The future of nature-based tourism

*I*n spite of the fact that nature-based tourism has been around in one form or another for many years, in many ways it is still a 'new' tourism phenomenon that is in the early stages of its life cycle. Like all new phenomena, it is still defining itself and the array of products it offers. In addition, industry leaders who will provide the direction for the future growth of the sector are now just beginning to emerge. The inevitable progression of nature-based tourism through its life cycle will lead to a markedly different sector than the one that exists today, just as the modern aeroplane bears little resemblance to the pioneering aircraft seen at the start of the twentieth century. The seeds of change have been sown in the recent past. How the sector changes, though, will depend on how effective many of these initiatives are. In this epilogue, the author would like to discuss some of the factors that he thinks will shape nature-based tourism over the next ten years and speculate on their possible impact. As it is a personal view, the reader may choose to agree, disagree or ignore these observations.

Nature-based tourism is now in the rapid growth phase of its life cycle. Consumer demand is strong, with growth rates significantly higher than the background rate for tourism. Typically, periods of rapid growth provide the best opportunities for new businesses to enter a sector.. As with any product or product category, though, the period of rapid growth is transitory. Growth rates inevitably must slow, if for no other reason than that it becomes increasingly difficult to find enough new users to maintain the same rate of growth as the absolute number of users increases. Ten per cent growth for a sector attracting 100 000 visitors, for example, requires 10 000 new users; ten per cent growth for a sector attracting 1 000 000 users requires an additional 100 000 new users.

As nature-based tourism moves into the maturity phase of its life cycle over the next decade or so, four or five significant things are likely to occur.

First, competition will intensify. At present, the rapid expansion of the nature-based tourism market means that both new and existing businesses can grow by attracting some of the clients who are trying the products for the first time. As the absolute expansion of the market slows, new entrants can survive and existing businesses can grow only if they steal clients (market share) from other established businesses. Price discounting is one means used to try to steal share, as is focusing more on the point of differentiation. To survive, then, businesses must ensure that they protect their own client bases, as well as maintain operational efficiencies to enable them to withstand price wars.

Second, as competition intensifies, businesses will have to differentiate their products more precisely to ensure that they have achieved and can defend the right position in the marketplace. Those businesses that will thrive will adopt a strategic marketing management approach to nature-based tourism, positioning their products uniquely as discrete, well-defined products. 'Me too' operators, or operators who do not understand the subtleties of marketing, will find that demand for their products will decline.

Third, the barriers to entry for new players will be much higher than they are today. Within the next decade or so, clear market leaders will emerge both nationally and regionally. These well-known, well-respected, well-resourced and well-connected businesses will have an established clientele that is satisfied with the range of products on offer. To compete effectively, new businesses will have to be at least as well resourced as the established businesses. Gone will be the days when someone with $10 000 could enter the marketplace and hope to compete on an equal footing with established operators. This trend is already noticeable in many areas of the tourism industry. The failures of Compass marks I and II can be attributed to the fact that the barriers to entry for a new domestic airline were so high that even with almost $100 million, in retrospect it seemed doomed to failure. It is happening to a lesser extent today in Cairns, where new entrants wanting to offer reef cruises must compete with well-established and well-financed businesses offering 300-seater wave-piercing catamarans. Competition is so intense and the cost of entry into this market is so high that few new entrants have appeared in the past few years.

Fourth, the maturation process will also see a broadening of the market base away from allocentric tourists to a more midcentric tourist. This type of traveller has markedly different needs and, as a result, desires significantly different tourist experiences. We are already seeing that trend appearing today with the emergence of hard and soft ecotourists. As the market base broadens, soft ecotourists, looking for a more relaxing, less intense holiday experience, will become increasingly important to the industry. Some operators may find that they have to modify their product to satisfy this market. Others will find the idea abhorrent and will steadfastly refuse to change their product.

By the same token, the market is already showing signs of becoming more sophisticated and discriminating in its purchasing patterns. Knowledgeable consumers are more demanding about the products and services they want, and are also more willing to complain if the products do not suit their needs. Of course, this means that the sector will have to evolve to a new standard of professionalism. In particular, the ethical and operational standards of the industry will continue to improve. Some of this improvement will be driven by knowledgeable clients demanding better service, some by government agencies establishing more stringent guidelines for operations in protected areas, some by traditional land owners demanding meaningful involvement in new nature-based tourism developments, some by insurers demanding safer practices, some by banks demanding higher business standards and some by industry leaders promoting various accreditation programs.

In the last three years, both the Australian Tourism Operators Network and the Ecotourism Association of Australia have developed accreditation programs. In addition, the Inbound Tour Operators Association is energetically marketing its Australian Guide Qualification Program, which is designed to set high standards for guides working in all sectors of the tourism industry. It remains to be seen, however, how strong the take-up rate of these programs will be, so long as participation remains voluntary. Industry associations feel that their programs will both raise industry standards and provide participants with a distinct competitive advantage over non-accredited businesses. But this will only occur if being accredited is seen to be a meaningful indicator of quality by both the travel trade and the consumer. To gain widespread market acceptance, though, accreditation must be embraced widely by industry. If only a small number of operators choose to participate, the program will fade. The failure to set standards will make it difficult for reputable businesses to gain the credibility they deserve.

The one major threat facing this sector is that its popularity may prove to be a fad. The risk is that a trendy moniker will be applied to a certain type of activity, but when the next trend emerges, as it will, the old trend will be abandoned. The reader will note that the author has steadfastly refused to use the term 'ecotourism' throughout this book for that very reason. He feels that ecotourism reflects only a small segment of the entire nature-based tourism paradigm, and also reflects the least sustainable name for the array of activities encompassed by this book. Ecotourism has gained such a high profile that it has come to mean almost any form of non-urban tourism. The term has been hijacked by marketers who do not understand its concepts, by destinations that are clearly not ecotourism destinations and by businesses that are capitalising on a trend. His advice to operators is, if they wish to label their products as ecotourism products, to make sure that they can be accredited as such—alternatively, when the backlash hits, to be prepared to reposition the products quickly.

Overall, however, the future looks positive for nature-based tourism, although without a doubt the type, scale and professionalism of the sector will change dramatically over the next few years. To thrive, the industry will have to ensure that it continues to provide products that satisfy the needs, wants and desires of its clients. The types of products offered will have to evolve as the needs, wants and desires of the clientele change. Those operators who act in a proactive manner are best suited to survive and thrive into the next century. This task can be best achieved by adopting a strategic business planning and marketing focus to the development and operation of nature-based tourism.

References

Aaker, D. (1995). *Strategic Marketing Management*, 4th edn. John Wiley & Sons, Brisbane.

Allen, T. (1985). Marketing by a small tour operator in a market dominated by big operators, *European Journal of Marketing*, 19(5), pp. 83–90.

Anon. (1985). Firm discovers marketing tool in alternative capital, *Marketing News*, 19(23), p. 12.

Anon. (1994). A new tool for the single market, *Business Europe*, 34(34), pp. 2–3.

Anon. (1995). Ecotourism—ethical profits, *African Business*, 199, pp. 36–9.

Australia and New Zealand Banking Corporation (1990). *Summary of Small Business in Australia*.

Australian Bankers' Association and Department of Tourism (1993). *The Business of Tourism: A Financial Management Guide for Tourism Related Businesses*. ABA & DOT, Canberra, pp. 127–34.

Australian Tourism Industry Association (1990). Code of Environmental Practice. ATIA, Canberra.

Australian Tourism Operators Association (1995). *ATOA Accreditation Program*. ATOA, Melbourne.

Australian Tourist Commission (n.d.). *Asia, Europe, Japan, Market Segmentation Studies, Executive Summary*. ATC, Sydney.

Baum, T. & Mudambi, R. (1994). A Richardian analysis of the fully inclusive tour industry, *Service Industries Journal*, 14(1), pp. 85–93.

Berry, A. & Jarvis, R. (1994). *Accounting in a Business Context*. Chapman & Hall, London.

Bharadwaj, S. G., Varadarajan, P. R. & Fahy, J. (1993). Sustainable competitive advantage in service industries: A conceptual model and research propositions, *Journal of Marketing*, 57(4), pp. 83–99.

Blamey, R. (1995). The nature of ecotourism. Occasional paper no. 21. Bureau of Tourism Research, Canberra.

—— (1996a). *The Elusive Market Profile: Operationalising Ecotourism*. BTR, Canberra.

—— (1996b). Profiling the ecotourism market. In Richins, H., Richardson, J. & Crabtree, A. (eds), *Taking the Next Steps*. Ecotourism Association of Australia, Brisbane, pp. 1–9.

Boritz, J. E. (1990). *Approaches to Dealing with Risk and Uncertainty*. Canadian Institute of Chartered Accountants, Toronto.

Brandt, S. C. (1982). *Entrepreneuring: The Ten Commandments for Building a Growth Company*. Mentor Books, Scarborough, Canada.

Bransgrove, C. (1992). *Tour Operators Business Guidebook*. Small Business Development Corporation, Victorian Tourism Commission, Melbourne.

Brown, L. (1995). *Competitive Marketing Strategy*, 2nd edn. Thomas Nelson, South Melbourne.

Bull, A. (1989). *The Economics of Travel and Tourism*. Pitman, Melbourne.

Case, J. & Useem, J. (1996). Six characters in search of a strategy, *Inc*, 18(3), pp. 46–55.

Cha, S., McCleary, K. W., & Usyal, M. (1995). Travel motivations of Japanese overseas visitors: A factor-cluster segmentation approach, *Journal of Travel Research*, Summer, 34(1), pp. 33–9.

Cherasky, S. M. (1992). Total quality for sustainable competitive advantage, *Quality*, 31(8), Q4, Q6–7.

Clarke, J. (1995). The effective marketing of small scale tourism enterprises through national structures: Lessons from a two way comparative study of farm tourist accommodation in the United Kingdom and New Zealand, *Journal of Vacation Marketing*, 1(2), pp. 137–53.

Cohen, E. (1979). A phenomenology of tourist experiences, *Sociology*, 13, pp. 170–201.

—— (1988). Traditions in the qualitative sociology of tourism, *Annals of Tourism Research*, 15, pp. 29–46.

Collins, R. (ed.) (1993). *Effective Management*, CCH Publications, North Ryde, Sydney.

Commonwealth Department of Industry, Science and Tourism (1996). *Tourism Switched On: Sustainable Energy Technologies for the Australian Tourism Industry*. DIST & Tourism Council Australia, Canberra.

Commonwealth Department of Tourism (1995). *Best Practice Ecotourism: A Guide to Energy and Waste Minimisation*. DOT, Canberra.

Cotterill, D. (1996). Developing a sustainable ecotourism business. In Richins, H., Richardson, J. & Crabtree, A. (eds), *Taking the Next Steps*. Ecotourism Association of Australia, Brisbane, pp. 135–40.

Coyne, R. (1995). The reservation revolution, *Hotel and Motel Management*, 210(12), pp. 54–7.

D'Amore, L. (1993). A code of ethics for socially and environmentally responsible tourism, *Journal of Travel Research*, 31(3), pp. 64–6.

Dawson, D. (1989). Direct marketing: Home sweet home, *Marketing*, October, pp. 55–6.

Dibb, S. & Simkin, L. (1993). The strength of branding and positioning in services, *International Journal of Services Industry Management*, 4(1), pp. 25–35.

Donaghy, K. & McMahon, U. (1996). Managing yield: A marketing perspective, *Journal of Vacation Marketing*, 2(1), pp. 55–62.

Donoho, R. (1996). Broadening their horizons, *Sales and Marketing Management*, 148(3), pp. 126–8.

Eagles, P. (1992). The motivations of Canadian ecotourists. In Harper, G. & Weiler, B. (eds), *Ecotourism*. Bureau of Tourism Research, pp. 12–20.

Eccles, G. (1995). Marketing, sustainable development and international tourism, *International Journal of Contemporary Hospitality Management*, 7(7), pp. 20–6.

Ecologically Sustainable Development Working Groups (1991). *Ecologically Sustainable Development Working Groups Final Report: Tourism*. Government of Australia, Canberra.

Economic Planning Group of Canada (1995). *Packaging For and Selling To the United States Pleasure Travel Market*. EPGC, for Tourism Canada.

Ecotourism Association of Australia (1996a). Ecotourism accreditation program. EAA, Brisbane.

—— (1996b). Ecotourism Association of Australia Code of Practice. EAA, Brisbane.

Edgar, D. A., Littlejohn, D. L. & Allardyce, M. L. (1994). Strategic clusters and strategic space: The case of the short break market, *International Journal of Contemporary Hospitality Management*, 6(5), pp. 20–6.

English, J. W. (1990). *Small Business Financial Management in Australia*. Allen & Unwin, London.

—— (1995). *How to Organise and Operate a Small Business in Australia*, 6th edn. Allen & Unwin, Sydney.

Ethical Enterprises Network (1997). *Guide to Ethical Enterprise: In Business for a Better World*. EEN, Melbourne.

Evans, M. R., Fox, J. B. & Johnson, R. B. (1995). Identifying competitive strategies for successful tourism destination development, *Journal of Hospitality and Leisure Marketing*, 3(1), pp. 37–45.

Forrester, M. (1988). *Everything You Always Suspected Was True About Advertising: But Were Too Legal, Decent and Honest to Ask*. Fontana Paperbacks.

Francese, P. A. & Renaghan, L. M. (1990). Data-base marketing: Building consumer profiles, *Cornell Hotel and Restaurant Administration Quarterly*, 31(1), pp. 60–3.

Gaffikin, M. (1993). *Principles of Accounting*, 3rd edn. Harcourt Brace, Sydney.

Gartner, W. C. & Bachri, T. (1994). Tour operators' role in the tourism distribution system: An Indonesian case study, *Journal of Comparative International Consumer Marketing*, 6(3,4), pp. 161–79.

Gersham, M. (1990). *Getting it Right the Second Time*. Addison-Wesley, NY.

Getz, D. (1993). Impacts of tourism on residents' leisure: Concepts, and a longitudinal case study of Spey Valley, Scotland, *Journal of Tourism Studies*, 4(2), pp. 33–44.

—— (1994). Residents' attitudes towards tourism: A longitudinal case study of Spey Valley, Scotland, *Tourism Management*, 15(4), 247–58.

Gilbert, D. C. (1996). Relationship marketing and airline loyalty schemes, *Tourism Management*, 17(8), pp. 575–82.

—— & Soni, S. (1991). UK tour operators and consumer responsiveness, *Service Industries Journal*, 11(4), pp. 413–24.

Goway Travel (1995). *Goway Canadian Vacations*. Goway Travel, Melbourne.

Greenley, G. E. & Matcham, A. S. (1986). Marketing orientation in the service of incoming tourism, *European Journal of Marketing*, 20(7), pp. 64–73.

—— & —— (1990). Marketing orientation in the service of incoming tourism, *Marketing Intelligence and Planning*, 8(2), pp. 35–9.

Greer, T. & Wall, G. (1979). Recreational hinterlands: A theoretical and empirical analysis. In Wall, G. (ed.), *Recreational Land Use in Southern Ontario*, Dept of Geography Publication Series no. 14, Waterloo University, Waterloo, Canada, pp. 227–46.

Grover, R. (1992). Heartbreak Hotel for tourism, *Business Week*, Jan. 20, p. 36.

Hare, M. (ed.) (1990). *Ecologically Sustainable Development: A Submission*. Australian Conservation Foundation, Greenpeace (Australia), The Wilderness Society, World Wide Fund for Nature—Australia.

Hart, W. (1993). The Three R's, *Cornell Hotel and Restaurant Administration Quarterly*, 34(5), pp. 18–19.

Hartley, R. (1992). *Marketing Mistakes*, 5th edn. John Wiley & Sons, Brisbane.

Hawkins, D. E. (1994). Ecotourism: Opportunities for developing countries. In Theobald, W. (ed.), *Global Tourism: The Next Decade*. Butterworth Heinemann, Melbourne, pp. 261–73.

Herity, J. (1990). Globe '90 policy making for tourism and sustainable development: The role of environmental impact assessment. Paper presented at Globe '90, Vancouver.

Hey-Cunningham, D. (1993). *Financial Statements Demystified*. Allen & Unwin, St Leonards.

Hiam, A. (1990). *The Vest Pocket CEO: Decision Making Tools for Executives*. Prentice Hall, Englewood Cliffs, NJ.

Higham, J. (1997). Sustainable wilderness tourism: Motivations and wilderness perceptions held by international visitors to New Zealand's Backcountry Conservation Estate. In Hall, C. M., Jenkins, J. & Kearsley, G. (eds), *Tourism Planning and Policy in Australia and New Zealand: Cases, Issues and Practice*. Irwin, Sydney, pp. 75–86.

Hill, N. (1989). How to arrive at your marcom budget, *Industrial Marketing Digest*, 14(1), pp. 65–77.

Hill, T. & Shaw, R. (1995). Co-marketing tourism internationally: Bases for strategic alliances, *Journal of Travel Research*, 34(1), pp. 25–32.

Hodgson, P. (1993). Tour operator brochure design research revisited, *Journal of Travel Research*, 32(1), pp. 50–2.

Holloway, J. C. (1989). *The Business of Tourism*, 3rd edn. Pitman, London.

—— & Robinson, C. (1995). *Marketing for Tourism*, 3rd edn. Longman, Harlow.

Hopkins, L. (1993). *Cash Flow and How to Improve It*. Wrightbooks, North Brighton, Vic.

Howard, T. (1995). Study to small operators: Use homefield advantage in marketing, *Nation's Restaurant News*, 29(21), p. 38.

Hunt, J. D. (1990). Linking tourism, wilderness and economic development. In Lime, D. (ed.), *Managing America's Enduring Wilderness Resource*. University of Minnesota, St Paul, pp. 570–6.

Ing, D. (1995). Sustainable Tourism Charter issues, *Hotel and Motel Management*, 210(100), pp. 4, 36.

Jarrett, I. (1996). Travel agents have doubts about the Net, *Asian Business*, 32(9), p. 66.

Keane, M. (1997). Quality and pricing in tourism destinations, *Annals of Tourism Research*, 23(1), pp. 117–30.

Keasey, K. & Watson, R. (1993). *Small Firm Management, Ownership, Finance and Performance*. Blackwell, Oxford.

Kimes, S. E. & Lord, D. C. (1994). Wholesalers and Caribbean resort hotels, *Cornell Hotel and Restaurant Administration Quarterly*, 35(3), pp. 70–5.

King, B., Pizam, A. & Milman, A. (1993). Social impacts of tourism: Host perceptions, *Annals of Tourism Research*, 20, pp. 650–65.

Kotler, P. & Turner, R. E. (1989). *Marketing Management*. Prentice Hall, Scarborough.

Landals, A. (1986). The bloody tourists are ruining the park. In *Tourism and the Environment*. Canadian Society of Environmental Biologists, Edmonton, pp. 89–99.

Lang, C. T., O'Leary, J. T. & Morrison, A. M. (1996). Trip driven attributes of Australian outbound nature travellers. In Prosser, G. (ed.), *Tourism and Hospitality Research: Australian and International Perspectives*. Bureau of Tourism Research, pp. 361–77.

Laskey, H. A., Seaton, B. & Nicholls, J. A. F. (1994). Effects of strategy and pictures in travel agent advertising, *Journal of Travel Research*, 34(4), pp. 13–19.

Lawrence, J. (1991). Travel marketing: Data base opening doors, *Advertising Age*, 62(47), p. S6.

Laws, E. (1991). *Tourism Marketing: Service and Quality Management Perspectives*. Stanley Thornes, Cheltenham, UK.

Lawson, R., Gnoth, J. & Paulin, K. (1995). Tourists' awareness of prices for attractions and activities, *Journal of Travel Research*, 34(1), pp. 3–10.

Lindberg, K. (1991). *Policies for Maximising Nature Tourism's Ecological and Economic Benefits*. World Resources Institute, February.

Litvin, S. W. (1996). Ecotourism: A study of purchase proclivity, *Journal of Vacation Marketing*, 3(1), pp. 43–54.

Madrigal, R. (1993). A tale of tourism in two cities, *Annals of Tourism Research*, 20, 336–53.

Maitland, I. (1994). *The Business Planner*, Butterworth Heinemann, Oxford.

Manning, R. E. (1990). Opportunities for linking wilderness and tourism. In Lime, D. (ed.), *Managing America's Enduring Wilderness Resource*. University of Minnesota, St Paul, pp. 629–33.

Matheson, S. (1993). *Secrets: A Personal Survival Plan for Success in Small Business*. The Business Library, Melbourne.

McDougall, K. (1997). Weeds in Victorian alpine areas. In *Alpine Ecology Course Notes*. Dept of Natural Resources and Environment, Melbourne.

McIntosh, R. W. & Goeldner, C. (1990). *Tourism: Principles, Practices, Philosophies*. John Wiley & Sons, Brisbane.

McKercher, B. (1982). Accommodation preferences of Ottawa bound visitors. Unpublished MA thesis, Carleton University, Ottawa, Canada.

—— (1993a). The unrecognised threat to tourism: Can tourism survive sustainability? *Tourism Management*, 14(2), pp. 131–6.

—— (1993b). Tourism in parks: The perspective of Australia's national parks and conservation organisations, *GeoJournal*, 29(3), pp. 307–13.

—— (1996a). Attitudes to tourism in Victoria's Alpine National Park. PhD dissertation, University of Melbourne.

—— (1996b). Understanding attitudes to tourism in protected areas. In Richins, H., Richardson, J. & Crabtree, A. (eds), *Taking the Next Steps*. Ecotourism Association of Australia, Brisbane.

—— (1996c). Perceived differences between 'tourism' and 'recreation' in parks, *Annals of Tourism Research*, 23(3), pp. 563–76.

—— (1997). Benefits and costs of tourism in Victoria's Alpine National Park: Comparing the attitudes of tour operators, management staff and public interest group leaders. In Hall, C. M., Jenkins, J. & Kearsley, G. (eds), *Tourism Planning and Policy in Australia and New Zealand*. Irwin, Sydney, pp. 99–110.

—— & Coghlan, I. (1994). *Tourism Marketing Short Course*. Charles Sturt University, Albury.

—— & Davidson, P. (1995). Women and commercial adventure tourism: Does the industry understand its dominant market? In Faulkner, B., Fagence, M., Davidson, M. & Craig-Smith, S. (eds), *Tourism Research and Education in Australia*. Bureau of Tourism Research, Canberra, pp. 129–40.

Mercer, D. (1991). *A Question of Balance: Natural Resource Conflict Issues in Australia*. The Federation Press, Leichhardt, NSW.

Meredith, G. (1988). *Small Business Management in Australia*, 3rd edn. McGraw-Hill, Sydney.

—— (1993). *Small Business Management in Australia*, 4th edn. McGraw-Hill, Sydney.

—— (1995). *Small Business Management in Australia*, 5th edn. McGraw-Hill, Sydney.

Middleton, V. T. C. (1988). *Marketing in Travel and Tourism*. Heinemann, London.

—— (1994). *Marketing in Travel and Tourism*, 2nd edn. Butterworth Heinemann, Sydney.

Mill, R. C. (1996). Societal marketing: Implications for tourism destinations, *Journal of Vacation Marketing*, 2(3), pp. 215–21.

—— & Morrison, A. M. (1985). *The Tourism System: An Introductory Text*. Prentice Hall International, London.

Milman, A. & Pizam, A. (1988). Social impacts of tourism on Central Florida, *Annals of Tourism Research*, 15, pp. 191–204.

Morley, C. (1994). Discrete choice analysis of the impacts of tourism prices, *Journal of Travel Research*, 33(2), pp. 8–14.

Morrison, A. M. (1996). *Hospitality and Travel Marketing*, 2nd edn. Delmar Publishers, Albany, NY.

Murphy, J., Forrest, E. J., Wotring, C. E. & Brymer, R. A. (1996). Hotel management and marketing on the Internet, *Cornell Hotel and Restaurant Administration Quarterly*, 37(3), pp. 70–7.

Nash, B. & Zullo, A. (1988). *The Misfortune 500*. Pocket Books, Sydney.

National Executive of Small Business Agencies (1990). *Cash Flow: Cash Management*. Managing the Small Business Series no. 23, NESBA, AGPS, Canberra.

—— (1991). *Checklist for Starting a Business*. Managing the Small Business Series no. 1, NESBA, AGPS, Canberra.

—— (1993). *Costing and Pricing*. Managing the Small Business Series no. 42, NESBA, AGPS, Canberra.

—— (1995). *Sources of Finance for Small Business*. Managing the Small Business Series no. 2, NESBA, AGPS, Canberra.

National Parks Service (1983a). *National Parks Service Policy on Tourism*. NPS, Melbourne.

—— (1983b). *Bogong National Park: Proposed Interim Management Plan*. NPS, Melbourne.

Newell, M. (1995). *Secrets of Small Business Success*. Stirling Press, Old Noarlunga, SA.

O'Brien, V. (1996). *The Fast Forward MBA in Business*. John Wiley & Sons, NY.

Opperman, M. (1995). A model of travel itineraries, *Journal of Travel Research*, Spring, pp. 57–61.

Palmer, A. J. & Mayer, R. (1996). Relationship marketing: A new paradigm for the travel and tourism sector? *Journal of Vacation Marketing*, 2(4), pp. 326–33.

Payne, D. & Dimanche, F. (1996). Towards a code of ethics for the tourism industry: An ethics model, *Journal of Business Ethics*, 15(9), pp. 997–1007.

Peacock, R. W. (1993). *Small Business Success: Your Home Based Business*. McGraw-Hill, Roseville.

Pearce, D. (1989). *Tourist Development*, 2nd edn. Longman Scientific, Harlow, UK.

Pearce, D., Markandya, A. & Barbier, E. B. (1989). *Blueprint for a Green Economy*. Earthscan Publishing, London.

—— & Wilson, P. M. (1995). Wildlife viewing tourists in New Zealand, *Journal of Travel Research*, Fall, pp. 19–26.

Pearce, P. L. & Moscardo, G. M. (1985). The relationship between travellers' career levels and the concept of authenticity, *Australian Journal of Psychology*, 37(2), pp. 157–74.

Perdue, R. R. (1985). Segmenting state travel information inquiries by timing of the destination decision and previous, *Journal of Travel Research*, 23(3), pp. 6–11.

—— (1996). Target market selection and marketing strategy: The Colorado downhill skiing industry, *Journal of Travel Research*, Spring, pp. 39–46.

——, Long, P. & Allen, L. (1990). Resident support for tourism development, *Annals of Tourism Research*, 17, pp. 586–99.

Pizam, A. (1990). Evaluating the effectiveness of travel trade shows and other tourism sales-promotion techniques, *Journal of Travel Research*, 29(1), pp. 3–8.

Plog, S. (1974). Why tourist destination areas rise and fall in popularity, *Cornell Hotel and Restaurant Administration Quarterly*, 1(4), pp. 55–8.

Porter, M. (1991). Know your place, *Inc*, 13(9), pp. 90–5.

Pritchard, A. & Morgan, N. J. (1996). Sex still sells to generation X: Promotional practice and the youth package holiday market, *Journal of Vacation Marketing*, 3(1), pp. 69–80.

Pritchard, B. (1995). *Complex Marketing Made Simple*. Milner Books, Los Angeles.

Qantas (1996). *Qantas Vacations Brochure*. Qantas, Sydney.

Ratnatunga, J. & Dixon, J. (1993). *Australian Small Business Manual*, 3rd edn. CCH Publishing, Sydney.

Reilly, M. D. & Millikin, N. L. (1995). *Starting a Small Business: The Feasibility Analysis*. Montguide, Montana State University, Bozeman, Montana.

Reilly, R. T. (1988). *Travel and Tourism Marketing Techniques*, 2nd edn. Delmar Publishing, Albany, NY.

Reynolds, W., Savage, W. & Williams, A. (1994). *Your Own Business: A Practical Guide to Success*. Thomas Nelson, Melbourne, pp. 29–35.

Richards, G. & Friends, K. (1995). The UK ski market, *Journal of Vacation Marketing*, 1(3), pp. 259–64.

Richardson, J. I. (1996). *Marketing Australian Travel and Tourism: Principles and Practice*. Hospitality Press, Melbourne.

Ricketts, G. (1986). Magazines: Adding in edit, *Marketing and Media Decisions*, 21(10), pp. 88–90.

Ries, A. & Trout, J. (1986). *Positioning: The Battle for Your Mind*. Warner Books, NY.

—— & —— (1993). *The 22 Immutable Laws of Marketing*. Harper Collins, London.

Rita, P. & Moutinho, L. (1992). Allocating a promotion budget, *International Journal of Contemporary Hospitality*, 4(3), pp. 3–8.

Rodkin, D. (1990). Wealthy attitude wins over healthy wallet, *Advertising Age*, 61(2), July, pp. S4, S6.

Rowe, M. (1996). Beyond heads in beds, *Lodging Hospitality*, 52(1), pp. 42–4.

Sambrook, C. (1991). Travel's double agent, *Marketing*, Oct., pp. 19–20.

Samson, D. (1994). *Preparing a Business Plan*. AusIndustry, Canberra.

Saxon, R. & Allan-Kamil, C. (1996). *A Woman's Guide to Starting a Small Business in Australia*. Allen & Unwin, St Leonards.

Seaton, A. V. & Bennett, M. M. (1996). *Marketing Tourism Products, Concepts, Issues, Cases*. International Thomson Business Press, London.

Segon, M. J. (1993). Ethics. In Collins, C. (ed.), *Effective Management*. CCH International, Sydney, pp. 521–51.

Siegel, E., Schultz, L., Ford, B. & Carney, D. (1987). *The Arthur Young Business Plan Guide*. John Wiley & Sons, Brisbane.

Sims, S. (1994). Responsible travel, *Successful Meetings*, 43(6), p. 24.

Smith, G. (1996). *Do-It-Yourself Marketing: Practical Hints and Tips for Marketing in Australia*. Prentice Hall, Sydney.

Sorensen, L. (1993). The special interest travel market, *Cornell Hotel and Restaurant Administration Quarterly*, 34(3), pp. 24–8.

Stanley, P. (1994). *Accounting for Non Accountants: The Plain English Guide to Accounting*. Business Library, Melbourne.

Taylor, H. (1996). How to develop a strong hotel brand strategy with a weak branding budget, *Journal of Vacation Marketing*, 2(1), pp. 63–7.

Temple, P. (1989). Prosperity without profit, *Accountancy*, 104(1151), pp. 86–90.

Timmons, J. A. (1989). *New Venture Creation: Entrepreneurship in the 1990s*, 3rd edn. Irwin, Boston.

Tourism Canada (1988). *Adventure Travel in Western Canada*. MacLaren Plansearch, TC, Ottawa.
—— (1990). *Adventure Travel in Eastern Canada*. Tourism Research Group, TC, Ottawa.
Tourism Victoria (1993). *Tourism Victoria: Strategic Business Plan*. TV, Melbourne.
—— (1995). *Tourism Victoria: International Markets Update*, TV, Melbourne.
—— (1997). *Tourism Victoria: Strategic Business Plan 1997–2001: Building Partnerships*. TV, Melbourne.
Tracy, J. A. (1994). *How to Read a Financial Report*, 4th edn. John Wiley & Sons., Brisbane.
Trade Practices Commission (1993a). *Unconscionable Conduct in Consumer Transactions*. TPC, AGPS, Canberra.
—— (1993b). *Unconscionable Conduct in Commercial Dealings*. TPC, AGPS, Canberra.
Upton, G. (1985). Travel ads miss the boat, *Marketing*, 20(2), pp. 22–5.
Urry, J. (1990a). The consumption of tourism, *Sociology*, 24(1), pp. 23–35.
—— (1990b). *The Tourist Gaze*. SAGE Publications, London.
Vallance, E. (1995). *Business Ethics at Work*. Cambridge University Press, Cambridge.
Victorian Department of Conservation and Environment (1992a). *Ecotourism: A Natural Strength for Victoria—Australia*. DCE, Melbourne.
—— (1992b). *Alpine National Park: Bogong Unit Management Plan*. DCE, Melbourne.
Victorian Department of Conservation and Natural Resources (1995). Tourism guidelines. Internal DCNR document forming part of the *National Parks Service Guidelines and Procedures Manual*.
Victorian Department of Conservation, Forests and Lands (1989). *Alpine Area Bogong Planning Unit Proposed Management Plan February 1989*. CFL, Melbourne.
—— (1990). *Presenting Victoria: CFL's Tourism Policy*. CFL, Melbourne.
Victorian Tourism Operators Association, (1995a). 1995 membership renewal survey. Internal document. VTOA, Melbourne.
—— (1995b). New member survey. Internal document. VTOA, Melbourne.
—— (1995c). *Tourism Accreditation Program: Tour Operators and Attractions*. VTOA, Melbourne.
—— (1996a). 1996 member survey. Internal document. VTOA, Melbourne.
—— (1996b). *Members' Code of Ethics*. VTOA, Melbourne.
Vogelaar, D. M. (1994). *How to Write a Business Plan*. Australian Business Library, Melbourne.
Walle, A. H. (1996). Tourism and the Internet: Opportunities for direct marketing, *Journal of Travel Research, Summer,* pp. 72–7.
Warren, P. & Ostergen, N. W. (1986). Trade advertising: A crucial element in hotel marketing, *Cornell Hotel and Restaurant Administration Quarterly*, 27(1), pp. 56–62.
Weaver, D., Glenn, C. & Rounds, R. (1996). Private ecotourism operations in Manitoba, Canada, *Journal of Sustainable Tourism*, 4(3), pp. 135–46.
Weiland, R. (1995). Market trends, *Successful Meetings*, 44(5), p. 54.
Weiler, B., Richins, H. & Markwell, K. (1993). Barriers to travel: A study of participants and non-participants in Earthwatch Australia programs. In Hooper, P. (ed.), *Building a Research Base in Tourism. Proceedings of the National Conference on Tourism Research*. Bureau of Tourism Research, pp. 151–61.
Wheeler, M. (1995). Tourism marketing ethics: An introduction, *International Marketing Review*, 12(4), pp. 38–49.

Wight, P. (1996a). North American ecotourists: Market profile and trip characteristics, *Journal of Travel Research*, Spring, pp. 2–10.

—— (1996b). North American ecotourism markets: Motivations, preferences and destinations, *Journal of Travel Research*, Summer, pp. 3–10.

Wild, C. (1996). The North American ecotourism industry. In Richins, H., Richardson, J. & Crabtree, A. (eds), *Taking the Next Steps*. Ecotourism Association of Australia, Brisbane, pp. 93–6.

Wilson, R. M. S., Gilligan, C. & Pearson, D. J. (1994). *Strategic Marketing Management, Planning, Implementation and Control*. Butterworth-Heinemann, Oxford.

Wolff, C. (1996). Tapping into the travel bazaar, *Lodging Hospitality*, 52(3), p. 43.

World Commission on Environment and Development (1987). *Our Common Future*. WCED, Oxford University Press, Melbourne.

Yochum, G. R. (1985). The economics of travel advertising revisited, *Journal of Travel Research*, 24(2), pp. 9–12.

Yuan, M. S. (1990). Linking tourism and wilderness: The Federal role. In Lime, D. W. (ed.), *Managing America's Enduring Wilderness Resource*. University of Minnesota, St Paul, p. 661.

Index